Let's change
the world.

Joshua Davis

Positively 4th Street

A Baby Boomer's Guide to the Promised Land

Joshua Simon, MD, EdD

POSITIVELY 4TH STREET
A BABY BOOMER'S GUIDE TO THE PROMISED LAND

Copyright © 2018 Joshua Simon, MD, EdD.
Author Credits: Joshua Simon

All rights reserved. No part of this book may be used or reproduced by any means, graphic, electronic, or mechanical, including photocopying, recording, taping or by any information storage retrieval system without the written permission of the author except in the case of brief quotations embodied in critical articles and reviews.

Scripture quotations marked NIV are taken from the Holy Bible, New International Version®. NIV®. Copyright © 1973, 1978, 1984 by International Bible Society. Used by permission of Zondervan. All rights reserved. [Biblica]

iUniverse books may be ordered through booksellers or by contacting:

iUniverse
1663 Liberty Drive
Bloomington, IN 47403
www.iuniverse.com
1-800-Authors (1-800-288-4677)

Because of the dynamic nature of the Internet, any web addresses or links contained in this book may have changed since publication and may no longer be valid. The views expressed in this work are solely those of the author and do not necessarily reflect the views of the publisher, and the publisher hereby disclaims any responsibility for them.

ISBN: 978-1-5320-6186-8 (sc)
ISBN: 978-1-5320-6187-5 (hc)
ISBN: 978-1-5320-6188-2 (e)

Library of Congress Control Number: 2018913222

Print information available on the last page.

iUniverse rev. date: 11/12/2018

Contents

Introduction xi

Chapter 1   Keter—The Crown 1
Chapter 2   Hokhmah—Wisdom 30
Chapter 3   Binah—Contemplation 52
Chapter 4   Hesed—Love 87
Chapter 5   Gevurah—Fear 127
Chapter 6   Tif'eret—Beauty 162
Chapter 7   Netzach—Endurance 187
Chapter 8   Hod—Majesty 228
Chapter 9   Yesod—Foundation 256
Chapter 10 Shekhinah—Presence 281

Appendix 295

Note: In kabbalah (Jewish mysticism), ten emanations, or Sefirot, represent divine forces by which God reveals Himself and creates. These ten Sefirot form this book's ten chapter titles with their Hebrew-to-English translations in the context of kabbalah. They are also pictured as interconnected parts that together form a whole, spiritual primordial[1] man called Adam Kadmon, as shown in the following figure.

---

[1] *Primordial* refers to existing before the formation of the universe, before the big bang.

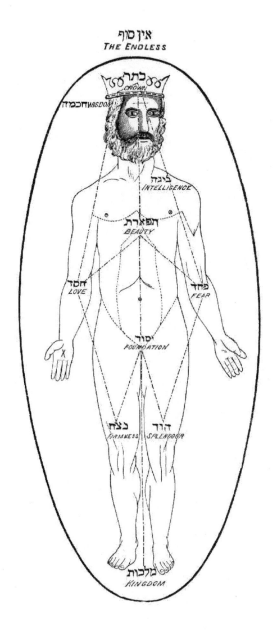

Figure 1
Qabbalah by Isaac Meyer, 1888.

Introduction

Here is my secret. It is very simple: it is only with the heart that one can see rightly. What is essential is invisible to the eye.

—Antoine de Saint-Exupery, *The Little Prince* (1943)

If I wanted a one-sentence definition of human beings, this would do: humans are the animals that believe the stories they tell about themselves.

—Mark Rowlands, *The Philosopher and the Wolf* (2008)

"Chances Are"[2] that two elephants are in the room right now, two glaring issues that most people rarely face up to. One is your tendency to procrastinate, and the other is thinking that you are not good enough. Overcoming either of these problems is not easy, but by the time you finish reading this book, you will be well on your way to overcoming both. And in doing so, you will find yourself on the road to the Promised Land. That is this book's promise.

On your way to the Promised Land, four avenues of exquisite design—math, music, emotions, and mind—will come together to create a powerful voice that can be heard across the universe. It's the

---

[2] "Chances Are," sung by Johnny Mathis, was released on August 12, 1957. Music by Robert Allen and lyrics by Al Stillman.

voice of change—a change that beckons you precisely because each and every moment of your life deserves your undivided attention.

Just take a look at your past. When something didn't work out the way you would've liked, your mind filed that memory away under the category "not good enough." If you were punished by your parents, interpretation—not good enough; parents arguing or other family turmoil, interpretation—not good enough; teased by others—not good enough; not the highest score, not the star of the football team, not invited to the party, not enjoying your after-school job, not dating the most desirable person, interpretation—not good enough; not following the rules—not good enough. By the time you finish high school, you carry that weight of thousands upon thousands of thoughts about not being good enough stored in your memory. It becomes easy to think that something is wrong and that that something is you.

In response to these memories, you set out to prove to the world that you are good enough and that you do have value. You attach your identity to the things and ideas valued by your family and culture. "What do you want to be when you grow up?" A ten-year-old boy might say a football player and a girl, a pediatrician. Most boys and girls will choose something identified with status, something that gets a lot of attention, or something people associate with being talented, brave, intelligent, or powerful. A smart-aleck kid might answer the question, "What do you want to be when you grow up?" with "Rich!" We want what others want and value because we think that if we have those things, we will be wanted and valued.

If your culture values wealth, then wealth validates you. If your culture values marriage and a family, then marriage and a family validate you. If your culture values education and expertise, then college degrees and people seeking your advice validate you. If your culture values Christianity, then attending a Christian church or just saying you are Christian validates you. If your family or culture honors serving in the military, then military service validates you. You are validated by winning and holding a position of power and authority—anything that brings you to the attention of others.

All this thinking about how to be valued and validated is all wrong because these things don't create a lasting sense of self-worth. The problem is not that you aren't good enough or that you don't have enough value. The real problem is that you're not asking the right questions.

Don't all human beings have value, an immeasurable value? Why don't I realize that just by being human I already possess all the value I will ever need? Why don't I realize that I deserve a wonderful life without having to prove anything to anybody? Furthermore, if I deserve a wonderful life, then why have I yet to experience it?

Let me repeat this most important realization: just because you're human, you already deserve a wonderful, fulfilling life in which you feel safe, confident, joyful, and focused. But as many of us know, it's one thing to deserve a wonderful, fulfilling life and quite another thing to experience it. The good news is that you need not wait any longer to experience the beautiful life that you so richly deserve. Just treat others the way you would like to be treated. "So in everything, do to others what you would have them do to you" (Matthew 7:12 NIV). That's the Golden Rule.

Just treat others the way you would like to be treated, and your life will work out better than you could ever "Imagine."[3] Unfortunately, it's not easy to follow this simple maxim. It has perplexed paupers, pirates, poets, pawns, and kings, Nobel laureates, and thinkers of

---

[3] "Imagine," by John Lennon, is third on *Rolling Stone*'s 500 Greatest Songs of All Time (2004). *Rolling Stone* is an American biweekly magazine that focuses on popular culture.

all kinds for centuries. "That's Life,"[4] and it raises many questions about humankind's ability to follow the Golden Rule.

"How many roads must a man walk down before you call him a man?" asked a 2016 Nobel laureate, Bob Dylan, back in 1962 as he raised questions about whether we are capable of following the Golden Rule. "How many roads," as many of you know, is the opening salvo to Dylan's iconic song "Blowin' in the Wind." You might not know, however, that *Rolling Stone* rated it fourteenth on its list of the 500 Greatest Songs of All Time. Though the answers to Dylan's questions about humankind's inhumanity to humankind are "blowin' in the wind," the wind has direction, and its direction points directly to the Golden Rule, first articulated thirty-five hundred years ago when Moses descended Mount Sinai with the Ten Commandments. A thousand years later, after walking down many roads, the Buddha found the answers in the 4 Noble Truths.

Ten Commandments, Four Noble Truths, fourteenth-greatest song... What's going on? According to a mystical branch of Judaism known as kabbalah, what's going on are numbers containing hidden truths. It might be more than coincidence that 10-4 is the code for "message received" and that there are compelling "messages" to be "received" in the Ten Commandments and Four Noble Truths. It also might not be just coincidence that "Blowin' in the Wind" would end up as the fourteenth-greatest song of the baby boomer generation. Furthermore, "My Generation"[5] raised a lot of questions, such as "What'd I Say?" by Ray Charles and "What's Going On?"

---

[4] Dean Kay and Kelly Gordon's song titled "That's Life," popularized by Frank Sinatra, reached number 4 on the *Billboard Top 100* on December 24, 1966. The lyrics include "I've been a puppet, a pauper, a pirate, a poet, a pawn and a king."

[5] "My Generation," by the Who, is eleventh on *Rolling Stone*'s 500 Greatest Songs of All Time (2004).

by Marvin Gaye, which, interestingly, are ranked tenth and fourth on *Rolling Stone's* list!

Are you familiar with these songs? If so, then you know that "What'd I Say?" raises questions about desire and rejection, "What's Going On?" about war and conflict, and "Blowin' in the Wind" about morality and the elusive Golden Rule.

To find answers to these questions, people have looked to Moses's Ten Commandments and the Buddha's Four Noble Truths. People have also looked to the life of Jesus Christ, as well as to Muhammad and his twenty-three years of revelations. What is fascinating is how these four spiritual giants—Moses, the Buddha, Jesus, and Muhammad—reveal themselves as well in a kabbalistic way. As you are about to see, their message crystallizes when we carefully examine another road that Dylan walked down, "Positively 4th Street," a song he recorded on my fourteenth birthday, July 29, 1965.

By delving deep inside the number 4, we'll discover the music, math, emotions, and mind upon which the Buddha, Moses, Muhammad, and Jesus wrote their powerful messages. Derived from truths, commandments, revelations, and life itself, the four bases of the Golden Rule create the road to the Promised Land.

Four Bases of the Golden Rule

First Base: Be aware of and sensitive to how your actions affect the feelings of others, for this is *something* to behold and the way of the Four Noble Truths. (Buddha)

Second Base: Don't do for others what others can do for themselves, for the Jews were not to *carry that weight*. The Egyptians were left to build their own pyramids

	and learn the Ten Commandments on their own. (Moses[6])
Third Base:	Say "no" and set limits with those who act selfishly; protect yourself *because* it is your birthright to be safe, and twenty-three years of revelation have shown that the powerful and the rich, who take advantage of the weak and poor, can be stopped by a force of faith. (Muhammad)
Home (4th):	Never judge others to be undeserving of your kindness or generosity, for if humankind is ever going to *come together*, then you must love others as I love you. (Jesus)

By following these four bases of the Golden Rule, no matter what your circumstances—wealthy or poor, talented or ordinary, free or imprisoned—a wonderful life awaits you. Filled with balance, joy, and meaning, that's a life in which getting to the gym, sticking to a healthy diet, and managing your money wisely are relatively easy. It's a life in which your senses become fully engaged—colors shimmer, sounds resonate, touch heals, water purifies, and sparks of divinity fill the air. Peace, contentment, and a "get 'er done" mentality thrive at the end of your journey, the Promised Land, when you follow the four bases of the Golden Rule.

As the music played in the summer of 1969 during the historic Woodstock Music and Art Fair, the ideals of peace, love, and understanding coalesced into a wave of "Good Vibrations"[7] that

---

[6] Charlton Heston, born on October 4 (10-4, message received) in 1923, portrayed Moses in *The Ten Commandments* (1956).

[7] "Good Vibrations," by the Beach Boys, is sixth on *Rolling Stone*'s 500 Greatest Songs of All Time (2004).

washed ashore at the Abbey Road Studios in London. As Woodstock was nearing its end, the Beatles were also nearing theirs.

John, Paul, George, and Ringo gathered on August 18, 1969, to record their final song, aptly titled "The End."[8] And that song's last fourteen words (10-4, message received), "In the end, the love you take is equal to the love you make," spread the word. The Beatles left us with the same message that emanated from Woodstock and the four heavy hitters of history (Moses, Buddha, Jesus, and Muhammad). If you want to be treated with love, you need to treat others with love. It's the Golden Rule. If you want to be treated with "R-E-S-P-E-C-T,"[9] you need to treat others with respect.

Note that four *Abbey Road*[10] songs—"Something," "Carry That Weight," "Because," and "Come Together"—are integrated into the four bases of the Golden Rule. Can you picture *Abbey Road's* iconic album cover? It's the Fab Four striding positively across the street, "Positively 4th Street." Unfortunately, by the time *Abbey Road* finished production, the Fab Four were no longer walking in stride. A rift had occurred, and the Beatles were disconnected.

Four years before the breakup of the Beatles, Dylan had recorded his own feelings of disconnection from some of his closest fellow musicians when he wrote "Positively 4th Street." The genius of Bob Dylan is that even though "Positively 4th Street" is filled with biting criticisms, it fosters the realization that in order to feel positive, you

---

[8] "The End," from *Abbey Road*, was the last song the Beatles recorded. Their first song was Buddy Holly's "That'll Be the Day" (July 12, 1958), recorded as the Quarrymen. The band changed their name to the Beatles to stay connected to Holly's band, the Crickets.

[9] "Respect," sung by Aretha Franklin, is fifth on *Rolling Stone*'s 500 Greatest Songs of All Time (2004).

[10] *Abbey Road* ranked fourteenth (10-4, message received) on *Rolling Stone*'s 500 Greatest Albums of All Time (2003).

must first confront your negative emotions and learn to accept them. Accepting life's hardships is not easy and requires much effort, but in the process of learning to accept your most painful emotions, you acquire skills that build empathy, compassion, and grace.

So how does "Positively 4th Street" guide us to the Promised Land? The answer, my friend, begins on a rather sad musical note in history, February 3, 1959. "That'll Be the Day"[11] that Buddy Holly was killed in a plane crash, along with Ritchie Valens and J. P. Richardson, the Big Bopper. Then in 1972, thirteen years later, Don McLean's tribute to Buddy Holly, "American Pie," hit number 1 on the *Billboard* charts. Also, most importantly, on February 3, 1972, I hit numero uno when I met Elizabeth, my first real love.

Just two days after we had come together, Elizabeth confessed that she had made plans to transfer to another college. I didn't think much of it at the time. After all, we barely knew each other. *That'll be the day when you say goodbye. It's no big deal*, so I thought. However, just seventy-four days later, when Elizabeth said "goodbye," my heart broke. That day turned out to be "the day that I died." Memories upon memories of not being good enough steamrollered back into my consciousness. My ego was flattened, and "Oh Boy,"[12] how I cried.

So on that solemn anniversary in musical history, February 3, 1972, I met Elizabeth. Then just seventy-four days later, it was "bye, bye Miss American Pie."[13] I was heartbroken, inconsolable over the end of a relationship that had lasted a mere ten weeks and four

---

[11] "That'll Be the Day," by Buddy Holly and the Crickets, is thirty-ninth on *Rolling Stone*'s 500 Greatest Songs of All Time (2004).
[12] "Oh Boy," by Buddy Holly (October 1957). On the B side was "Not Fade Away," number 107 on *Rolling Stone*'s 500 Greatest Songs of All Time (2004).
[13] "Bye, bye Miss American Pie" starts the refrain in Don McLean's "American Pie."

days. Aha,10-4, message received! So did I receive a message? You bet: "Love Hurts."[14] How I longed and pined for her. *Oh! Darling Elizabeth, I want you.* But to no avail. My self-esteem slumped. "What'd I say? What's going on?" A dark cloud of sadness loomed over me. Why was Elizabeth dating other guys? Was I not smart enough, strong enough, handsome enough, wealthy or talented enough? It was easy to think that in my life life was not working out well.

Dylan's "Positively 4th Street" describes a time when his life was not working out well. As I mentioned earlier, he recorded this song on my fourteenth birthday (10-4, message received). The message is right in the opening line when Dylan, looking for validation from his so-called friends, realizes that they couldn't care less about his heartfelt feelings: "You've got a lotta nerve to say you are my friend. When I was down, you just stood there grinning." The world turned unfriendly when Elizabeth ignored my heartfelt feelings. Like Dylan, it felt like I was without value, "Like a Rolling Stone."

Recorded several months before "Positively 4th Street," "Like a Rolling Stone" catapulted Dylan into the rock and roll stratosphere. It was named the number 1 greatest song of all time by *Rolling Stone* in 2004. Amazingly, the song recorded on my fourteenth birthday, "Positively 4th Street," came in at number 203—or February 3, the day I met Elizabeth, the day the music died, and then just ten weeks and four days later, the day my ego died.

Even with my skies blackened by the loss of Elizabeth, I never gave up hope. I thought that surely she would come back to

---

[14] Written by Boudleaux Bryant; recorded first by the Everly Brothers in 1960, then by Roy Orbison in 1961. The Scottish band Nazareth made "Love Hurts" twenty-third on *Billboard*'s Year-End Hot 100 Singles of 1976. They chose the name of their band from the opening line of "The Weight" by the Band: "I pulled into Nazareth, was feeling 'bout half past dead."

me—and indeed she did, but only occasionally. Eventually whatever commitment she had made to our relationship fell dormant. By 1977 all communication between us had stopped. My skies darkened again, and the torch I carried could hardly light up more than just a road of sorrows.

But behind every dark cloud there's a silver lining. Here comes the sun! I am happy to report that the silver lining is insight into why we think, feel, and act the way we do—insight to be found not only in Dylan's version of "Positively 4$^\text{th}$ Street" but in mine as well. Insight that begins with the quote from *The Little Prince* at the top of this introduction: "It is only with the [unbroken] heart that one can see rightly." With my heart broken by Elizabeth, I couldn't see rightly. I continued to distort reality by thinking that I wasn't good enough. Let it be known, however, that when your heart is whole, you will see the truth, which is that your heart can be broken only by your own thoughts.

As it turned out, my heart was already broken before I met Elizabeth, though I didn't know it at the time. It was broken by the genetic code. The twenty-three chromosomes of our DNA has us hardwired to think that we aren't good enough unless we can convince ourselves that we are one of the strongest bulls or most desirable cows in the valley and can attract one of the strongest bulls or most desirable cows. Because of this programming, our subconscious gives our disappointments the interpretation that we aren't among the strongest, greatest, or best of the best. But what if we don't actually need to be among the strongest, smartest, richest, or most attractive group to lead a beautiful, fulfilling, meaningful life? What if all we need is a beautiful attitude—a beatitude? "Blessed are the meek for they will inherit the earth" (Matthew 5:5 NIV).

Despite the complexity of human behavior and culture, our capacity to experience joy and to feel confident and hopeful ultimately rests on our ability to see through two common errors: (1) thinking that we aren't good enough unless we are among the best of the best[15] and (2) acting selfishly. That's it! These two mistakes underlie just about all the misery and suffering that we heap onto ourselves and dish out onto others. Furthermore, these two fundamental mistakes can disrupt our golden slumbers, our sleep.

The good news is that memories of past acts of selfishness and thoughts of not being good enough can be reversed. Go ahead and recall a memory of when you acted selfishly or angrily, or remember a time when you didn't think you were good enough. As I'm about to explain, you can alter this memory. By seeing it in a positive light, you'll take the sting out of it and understand it for what it really is.

Keep in mind that people act selfishly when fearful and that it's much easier to anticipate fearful situations when you think you aren't good enough. Furthermore, keep in mind that we often attempt to alleviate our fears by trying to get proof or validation that we are good enough. Well, what proof is there? What is your yardstick for measuring whether you are good enough?

People typically use various combinations of money, credentials, status, attention, sex, power, and influence as their yardsticks. We also measure the approval of peers and authority figures and our likes and dislikes in things such as music, sports, or cuisine. The deepest notches on our yardstick measure our values based on

---

[15] We want to think that any group, tribe, nation, or religious sect to which we attach our identity is better, superior, or, at a minimum, at least as good as any other group or tribe and that our own individual actions and efforts within our group will win the respect of our fellow group members. In this way, we will rise to the top and be among the best of the best. This paradigm is perhaps the most pronounced way in which organisms with large cerebral lobes and flexible neural networks express their instinctual drives.

religious, political, and philosophical beliefs as well as on customs and traditions.

We tend to think that people whose values aren't similar to our own aren't as good or as deserving as we are. At the same time, we often don't think we measure up even when we use our own yardsticks, but that's a distortion of reality. The truth is that we are already good enough to deserve a beautiful life without needing to prove anything. This goodness cannot be tarnished by our circumstances or what others might say about us. The true yardstick for joy, happiness, contentment, and a meaningful life is the compassion and understanding found in the four bases of the Golden Rule:

1. Be aware of and sensitive to how your actions affect the feelings of others.
2. Don't do for others what others can do for themselves.
3. Say no and set limits with those who act selfishly; protect yourself.
4. Never judge others to be undeserving of your kindness or generosity.

Furthermore, if others act in an uncaring way toward you, it's not because you aren't good enough. Instead, they're using their own free will guided by ignorance rather than insight, and they're blind to the fact that they are already good enough and deserving of a beautiful life without having to do anything to you, prove anything to you, or get anything from you.

When you look to others to validate you and relieve your doubts about whether you're good enough, but you don't get the response that you want, a painful memory forms. However, now you know that this pain is not reality. It is just a memory from a time when you used the wrong yardstick and distorted reality by thinking incorrectly that you weren't good enough. However, these painful memories do have a purpose: they help you create a yardstick that measures the four bases of the Golden Rule.

Are you ready to redeem your past? When you realize that you've been good enough all along, your memories will no longer carry "The Weight"[16] they once did. As Bob Marley sang so poignantly, "Emancipate yourselves from mental slavery."[17] Stop distorting reality, and start seeing the truth. "People Get Ready."[18] The truth is that you're already good enough.

What happens when you live in a world where people don't use the Golden Rule as their yardstick? You encounter all sorts of people carrying unnecessary baggage, people busy trying to prove things or get things that they never needed in the first place. I should know because I once led a status-driven life. I was busy "movin' on up" like *The Jeffersons*.[19]

I was going to show Elizabeth, the girl who broke my heart when I was twenty, that I was good enough, though I didn't quite know how. Upon graduating from college in 1973 with a degree in geography, and feeling uninspired by my college education, I lined up an executive trainee position with a textile company where I had worked during my summers. Unfortunately I continued to flounder,

---

[16] "The Weight," by the Band, is number 41 on *Rolling Stone*'s 500 Greatest Songs of All Time (2004). The Band lived, worked, and played with Dylan, the artist with number 14, "Blowin' in the Wind." "The Weight" and "Blowin' in the Wind" both delve into morality and their rankings are mirror images: 14 = 41. 10-4, message received: be moral.

[17] Bob Marley's "Redemption Song" (1980) is number 66 on *Rolling Stone*'s 500 Greatest Songs of All Time (2004). We use sixty-six books to redeem ourselves when using the King James Bible. Sixty-six also happened to be my age when I wrote this footnote.

[18] "People Get Ready," by Curtis Mayfield and the Impressions (1965), is twenty-fourth on *Rolling Stone*'s 500 Greatest Songs of All Time (2004).

[19] CBS sitcom, 1975–85.

just as in my undergraduate years, but then a break came my way. I was laid off during the oil crisis of 1973–74, which forced me to make a change. But what change?

Jane, my sister, suggested that I go back to school and study physical education. Really? School, again? Ugh! For me, college had been about staying out of Vietnam. But on January 27, 1973, four months before I was set to graduate and lose my student deferment, the military went to an all-volunteer army. I was no longer subject to the draft. By the way, guess what lottery number July 29 pulled in the military draft for those born in 1951? Positively, the number 4!

In graduate school, unlike during my undergrad years, I was actually motivated. I studied activities that brought me intrinsic joy, such as movement—dancing to rock and roll, playing basketball, playing catch with a baseball or Frisbee, or just running or jogging. I began to flourish, and my interest in sports and fitness, combined with strengths in math and science, quickly led to a master's degree in physical education from Sonoma State University, followed by a doctor of education degree from Columbia University in exercise physiology[20]. I taught for two years at the University of Maine and three years at Columbia University. Then I went to medical school where, to my surprise, psychiatry captured my imagination—a sound mind in a sound body.

As I progressed through graduate school and medicine, my "movin' on up" attitude, that instinctually driven need to stand out, began to give way. My professors and fellow students at Columbia, Michigan State's College of Human Medicine, and my psychiatry residency at the University of Florida were often role models of compassion and concern for the well-being of others, just as my own family had been

---

[20] Exercise physiology is the study of the physiological responses and adaptations to exercise with applications to sports, fitness, and the prevention and treatment of disease.

while I was growing up. And then, in a stroke of good luck, I met her majesty, Minerva, and we brought forth two beautiful children. As I matured, with a lot of help from Minerva, my sense of service to others deepened and status took a back seat.

Despite my extensive education and on-the-job training as a husband and father, there was a gap in my knowledge when it came to helping myself and others reach our full potential. As it turned out, a dose of religiosity, spirituality, and the mysticism of numbers filled in that gap. In the pages ahead, you will see how numbers in dates, rock and roll, the Bible, and even baseball have brought to light the four bases of the Golden Rule.

According to kabbalah, numbers are packed with meaning and might even reveal hidden messages about our creation at the moment of the big bang. As any scientist knows, when you want to understand reality and verify the truth, there is nothing you can count on more than numbers.

In kabbalah, the numbers 1 through 10 formed ten divine utterances, emanations, or Sefirot that our creator used to guide the stars, the planets, and everything in between to where they are today. After forty days on Mount Sinai, Moses decoded these ten emanations, which led to the Ten Commandments to guide our thoughts, speech, and actions. Each of the ten chapters of this book will conclude with a dialog on one of these Ten Commandments.

In the account ahead, you will find strength in numbers, both literally and figuratively. Chronologically, Moses comes first and uses the Ten Commandments to establish a covenant with God by codifying the Golden Rule. Then the Buddha arrives with his Four Noble Truths, to teach us how to increase our awareness and sensitivity. Shortly thereafter we hear a new commandment:

"You are to love others as Jesus loves you,"[21] which is embodied in the number 18 since the tenth and eighth letters of the Hebrew alphabet spell *chai*, the Hebrew word for "life." When we learn of the Hebrew or Jewish life of Christ, our chai shines eternal. Then finally Muhammad arrives and underscores, with twenty-three years of revelations, the importance of coming together by putting the Golden Rule into action because everyone deserves to feel safe.

The numbers 1 through 10 add up to 55, as do the numbers 10 + 4 + 18 + 23, thereby drawing additional attention to Matthew 5:5: "Blessed are the meek." According to kabbalah, coincidences with numbers, such as this example with 55, tie ideas together and add further meaning and depth. Let me add that the Bill of Rights, composed of the first ten amendments to the Constitution of the United States, had exactly fifty-five signatures. Thus the Ten Commandments, the beatitude in Matthew 5:5, the Bill of Rights, and the four bases of the Golden Rule all describe aspects of a covenant with God—a covenant whose composition draws upon empathy, prudence, forethought, and compassion. It's the ability to put yourself in the shoes of others and act accordingly.

Should you think that this book is some kind of esoteric, hyperreligious, mystical, new-age-fangled tribute with some kind of cockamamie number scheme thrown in—well, you're right, but only in part. It's really about using the Golden Rule to channel your passion and stay on track. It's about realizing that you often waste time trying to prove, get, or fantasize about things that you never needed in the first place.

No matter what your particular interests or desires, and regardless of your cultural or religious exposure, the wisdom of the Golden Rule will avail itself to all intellects, high and low. The accompanying

---

[21] "A new command I give you: Love one another. As I have loved you, so you must love one another" (John 13:34 NIV).

insights will complement pure reason, scientific inquiry, and religious values, as well as skeptical thought. Please challenge everything I say. Be a critical reader, so that you will know what I know. Then if someone asks, "Does this book really guide you to the Promised Land?" you can answer with an emphatic, "10-4, message received!"

Read this book if you would like to stop procrastinating. Read it if you would like to feel confident. Read it. Learn it. Teach it to your loved ones. "Be a miner for a heart of gold."[22] That's the message and it's the four bases of the Golden Rule. And when you "Listen to the Music,"[23] it's "Positively 4th Street."

---

[22] Neil Young's record "Heart of Gold" reached number 1 on April 8, 1972. Exactly two years later, Hank Aaron, my boyhood hero, reached number 1 with his own record. Roll over Babe Ruth and tell Willie Mays the news—Hank has just hit home run number 715. *Rolling Stone* rated "Heart of Gold" the 297th best song of all time.

[23] "Listen to the Music," by the Doobie Brothers, from their second studio album, *Toulouse Street* (1972).

1

Keter—The Crown

We are fortunate enough to live in a world that offers infinite possibilities for exploring not just the realm of "what is" but the realm of "what could be."

—Liane Gabora and Scott Barry Kaufman[24]

To arrive at knowledge slowly, by one's own experience, is better than to learn by rote, in a hurry, facts that other people know, and then, be glutted with words, to lose one's own free, observant and inquisitive ability to study.

—Johann Heinrich Pestalozzi (1746–1827)

Keter, the first Sephirah, is associated with the head, leadership, or a crown.[25] The crown of your head sits atop the thoughts and ideas that lead you into action. Keter is where you feel empowered, just as our creator felt empowered when "in the beginning, God created

---

[24] Liane Gabora and Scott Barry Kaufman, "Evolutionary Approaches to Creativity," in S. B. Kaufman and R. J. Sternberg (eds.), *The Cambridge Handbook of Creativity* (Cambridge University Press, 2010).
[25] See Figure 1.

the heavens and the earth" (Genesis 1:1 NIV). Keter is known by the divine name Ehyeh, which means "I shall be."[26]

"I shall be in Elizabeth's life," or so I believed. I maintained that belief despite the fact that she came by my dorm room on Monday, April 17, and said, "We need to talk. My feelings for you have changed." Over the next four years, Elizabeth and I stayed in touch with each other. Every now and then, she would respond to me romantically, but most of the time that was not the case. When my romantic gestures were not reciprocated, I felt deeply pained, but I never tried to distract myself from or desensitize myself to those painful feelings. I needed to understand why I felt the way I did, and I thought that those painful feelings would teach me what I needed to know. As it turned out, what I needed to know was how to change my way of thinking.

Making Changes to How We Think

Being rejected repeatedly by Elizabeth didn't feel good. According to Buddhist philosophy, my attachment to Elizabeth resulted in suffering. Fortunately, I don't suffer that way anymore. So how did things change?

Changing the way you think can make a big difference in how you feel. You don't ordinarily think about *how* you think—you just do it. You don't think about each breath either. You just breathe. But there's a lot going on behind every thought that reaches your consciousness.

For every conscious thought, neuroscientists have estimated that you have a million times more activity in those areas of the brain that

---

[26] Arthur Goldwag, *The Beliefnet Guide to Kabbalah* (Three Leaves Press, 2005).

are involved in subconscious thought—a million times![27] Sometimes with insight and effort you can figure out what's going on in your subconscious, thereby, some subconscious thoughts get transformed into conscious ones.

As an example of this kind of insight, imagine the subconscious activity that happens while you're getting dressed for work: What if I don't shave or wear matching shoes? What if I leave late for work or my car looks messy? What if my colleagues notice that I'm late or that my car needs to be washed? What if a colleague is critical of me because they noticed my shoes, my beard, my tardiness, my car, or what I said or didn't say when I greeted them? What if getting a promotion or being laid off depends on what I wear, how I smell, what I drive, and whether people relate to me in a positive way? Will others' view of me affect whether I get promoted or fired? Will it affect whether coworkers include me in their after-work activities? If I am fired, what if I can't find another job? If I don't have a job, how will I feed myself and my family? Who would want to hang around a loser like me?

As you decided which pair of shoes to wear to work, your subconscious mind used that minor decision to form all these seemingly logical connections. With a million times more activity going on in your subconscious than in your conscious thoughts, this example represents only the tip of the iceberg. Subconscious activity influences markedly why some people don't care much about their appearance, whereas others dress immaculately. Your subconscious remembers how you were cuddled as a child and a myriad of interactions with your peers, family members, romantic partners, and authority figures through the years. There is too much subconscious activity going on for you to be fully aware of all the factors that influence your conscious thoughts. But there are some

---

[27] Bruce H. Lipton, *The Biology of Belief: Unleashing the Power of Consciousness, Matter, and Miracles* (Hay House, 2008).

major themes to your thought patterns that will allow you to get a handle on how you think and—more importantly—perceive the world.

Albert Einstein

Albert Einstein, *Time* magazine's choice as the most important person of the twentieth century, changed how we perceive the world. Not an immaculate dresser, he preferred a casual, Bohemian appearance. However, he was meticulous when it came to evolving theories regarding physics, energy, and the origins of the universe.

Einstein's childhood and adolescent precociousness extended beyond the sciences to social matters as well. In 1895, at age sixteen, he had already had enough of Germany. Einstein found his first high school so highly regimented and German culture so militaristic that he renounced his German citizenship. He then transferred to a high school in Aarau, Switzerland, where the teaching methods of Johann Pestalozzi were practiced. (See quotation at the beginning of this chapter.) The Pestalozzi method incorporates the Buddha's approach to getting at the truth, which is to seek knowledge and insight through experience, the senses, and reason.[28] At Einstein's new school, teachers encouraged students to learn through active participation rather than rote learning.[29] Einstein's critical thinking was then able to soar even higher.

Pestalozzi's teaching methods were first championed in the United States by the educator Edward Austin Sheldon, who was born on 10/4/1823. It's fascinating how the numbers 10, 4, 18, and 23—all found in Sheldon's birthday—match the Ten Commandments from

---

[28] James A Santucci, "Educational Concepts and Practices in Early Southern Buddhism" (Hsi Lai Journal of Humanistic Buddhism, 2003).
[29] Walter Isaacson, *Einstein: His Life and Universe* (Simon and Schuster, 2007).

Moses, the Four Noble Truths from Buddha, the number 18 for the eternal chai found in Jesus, and the twenty-three years of revelations from Muhammad.

Numbers can reveal the connection of ideas and beliefs across multiple cultures. Furthermore, when those ideas and beliefs come together, as they do in the four bases of the Golden Rule, profound insights will follow and you'll start to understand that the forces of attraction (pleasure) and repulsion (pain) have been influencing your day-to-day living, often without your conscious awareness. You will also begin to appreciate that the forces of attraction and repulsion derive their initial energy, as do all forces, from the big bang that formed the universe.

Perhaps the most practical insight is not how the various forms of energy led to the formation of the universe, but how they can form a conscience that knows right from wrong and has compassion for all people. This compassion can free your mind from all the things you think you need to feel worthy and validated. You are freed because your conscience assures you that just by being human, you already have all the value you'll ever need.

When you stop worrying about what you think others are thinking about you, more of your conscious brain is available to focus on other things. With this enhanced focus and awareness, you increase dramatically your ability to acquire knowledge through your senses, experience, logic, and reason. The Golden Rule can change the way you view the world, just as it did for Einstein. With a social conscience so highly developed at an early age, Einstein's view of reality was closer to the truth than anything that had come before.

Einstein is most remembered for the equation $E = mc^2$, which translates as energy equals mass times the squared speed of light, but his most profound statement actually came in the form of a question.

When asked, "If you could come back five hundred years from now, what question would you like answered?" Einstein responded with four words: "Is the universe friendly?"[30] Applied to our personal lives, this question has great significance. After we receive information about other people, will we perceive them as being friendly? In chapter 6, I'll explain why your answer to this question might be the single most important factor in your health and well-being.

Bob Dylan's opening line to "Positively 4th Street" addresses the question raised by Einstein: "You got a lotta nerve to say you are my friend." Is Dylan singing about a specific person or the universe itself?

The Speed of Light Defined Mystically

According to physics, 3×10^8 meters/second is the speed of light in a vacuum. Let the number 3 represent the love found in Christianity's Holy Trinity: Father, Son, and Holy Ghost. From kabbalah, the numbers 10 and 8 form chai ("life" in Hebrew), as I explained in the introduction. When we reexamine the numerical expression for the speed of light, 3×10^8, does it mean that Christian love (3) combined with a Jewish Life (10^8) moves us at light speed? You do the math. Jesus did.

Reception and Perception of Divine Energy

Einstein's vision removed the blinders that just about everyone else wore when it came to the laws of physics. He realized that the three dimensions of space (height, length, and depth) are intertwined with time in a four-dimensional time-space continuum. He also realized

---

[30] Robert W. Fuller, http://www.psychologytoday.com/blog/somebodies-and-nobodies/201208/einstein-s-question-is-the-universe-friendly.

that our frame of reference affects our reality. According to Einstein's Special Theory of Relativity, as an object approaches movement at the speed of light, time slows down and the object's mass enlarges without limit, such that the object can never travel faster than the speed of light. If you moved at light speed, time would halt and the past, present, and future would be occurring simultaneously. Your mass would become infinite and be equal to the mass of the entire universe.

Jehovah (JHVH)

As outlined in Einstein's theory of special relativity, humans can travel at the speed of light only in our imaginations. We can also imagine surpassing the speed of light using "warp drive," as depicted in *Star Trek*, but obviously this is not reality. In a mystical sense, however, we can surpass the speed of light if we think of imagination as a form of enlightenment. Was not Einstein enlightened, and was not *Star Trek* a most imaginative TV series set in the twenty-third century? According to Einstein's principles of special relativity, when any mass—human or nonhuman—reaches the speed of light, time comes to a complete stop and that mass becomes equivalent to the mass of the entire universe. In this sense of enlightenment, we truly do become one with everything.

Most of us can't imagine this ultimate timeless reality. Even more difficult is trying to imagine its creator, which is precisely why God is thought of as all parts of time rolled into one—past, present, and future. As "the one who was, is, and will be," God is expressed by the Hebrew letters *Yod*, *He*, *Waw*, and *He*—or *YHWH* when transliterated into Latin letters. These four letters are not an actual word but rather the Tetragrammaton—four letters that represent

God's all-encompassing nature.[31] We hear it as *Yahweh* or more commonly *Jehovah* (JHVH), from the German in which *J* = *Y* and *V* = *W*, as in Jehovah's Witness.

One with Everything

Standing with his pushcart in front of the United Nations building, a hot-dog vendor asked the Dalai Lama what he would like. Handing the vendor a twenty-dollar bill, the Dalai Lama said, "Make me one with everything." When he got his hot dog with ketchup, mustard, relish, and sauerkraut, the Dalai Lama asked, "Where's my change?"

"Ah," said the vendor, "don't you know? Change comes from within."

Einstein's change came from within when his visionary thinking removed the blinders worn by other scientists and he saw the bigger picture. What about you? Can you go through life without blinders and see the bigger picture? Unfortunately most of us suffer from confirmation bias, which means that we see only what we want to see. We look for information that confirms what we already believe to be true, and discard or devalue other ideas or points of view. We often tell people what we think they want to hear, rather than feeling confident that the truth or our own ideas deserve to be heard. In some situations, we are downright afraid to express what we're truly thinking.

Politicians are famous for telling people what they want to hear while keeping their real intentions hidden. It's not uncommon to hear a politician declare that our nation's Founding Fathers knew best. The TV show *Father Knows Best* typified the period of the 1950s when the questioning of authority was not in the mainstream. In contrast,

---

[31] Rabbi David Aaron, *Seeing God: Ten Life-Changing Lessons of the Kabbalah* (Tarcher/Putnam, 2001).

the 1960s were far more turbulent owing in part to the widespread questioning of authority by a large segment of baby boomers. These baby boomers were critical of what they perceived to be the hidden intentions of people in positions of power and authority. Those who didn't agree with these baby boomers, similarly, were critical of what they saw as the hidden intentions of people challenging the status quo.

We tend to be critical of people who don't agree with us. Conservatives are uptight, liberals lack a backbone, and hippies are lazy. I like John's clean-cut looks but not George's biker tattoos. Real men don't eat quiche. We use criticism to raise the status of the group or "pack" with which we identify and to raise our own status within that group. We want others to love us and our values because that means that our status in the pecking order is rising. But if we aren't loved, then we want others to be afraid of us and of what we can do to them if we're displeased.

It is natural to use criticism to elevate your status, but if your criticisms are wrought with prejudice, then you're no longer following the Golden Rule. Prejudicial thoughts turn you into a spin doctor, much like the highly critical political pundits in the media. Unlike Sean Hannity or Rachel Maddow, however, your spinning is done below the radar in your subconscious.

Using values to elevate our standing is an example of one of the ways in which we compete. Competition is instinctual and puts the blinders on. It narrows your field of vision quicker than you can say "Jackie Robinson."

Much of the time people don't realize that they are competing. Competition, in a large way, underlies the formation of your identity based on family, community, religion, philosophy, profession, political persuasion, nation, race, marital status, sexual orientation, and gender. Schoolmates, coworkers, friends, sports teams, fashion, music, and almost any interest can become a part of your identity, which determines the group, pack, clique, or tribe within which you function.

Like a wolf within a pack of wolves, your subconscious mind thinks that your group or tribe is more deserving of valuable "hunting grounds" than other groups and that you should be prepared to do whatever it takes to maintain this position of superiority. Furthermore, you want to be sure that your position in your group's pecking order is high enough so that there will be enough meat left on the carcass when it is your turn to eat. However, all of this activity is happening primarily within your subconscious thoughts.

People choose values, often subconsciously, on the basis of what is acceptable to authorities who could raise or lower their position in the pecking order. Also, we often modify our values to appear attractive to those people to whom we are attracted.[32] We typically advocate for values that could enhance our holdings, generate positive attention, or increase our access to fun and pleasure. However, our values often contain prejudices, biases, and inequities. For example, the clothes worn by a defendant in the courtroom might subconsciously influence whether they are found innocent or guilty, even though we consciously know that clothing shouldn't have any bearing whatsoever. Show up in court dressed one way and you're innocent, but another way—guilty. Any four-year-old would know that this isn't right.

---

[32] Values also can be developed out of revulsion, such as taking a pledge of nonviolence because of the ravages of war or, in direct contrast, joining the military because of the horrors of 9/11. Counterculture values may develop in response to our perceived inability to meet the expectations of the mainstream. Why be low in the pecking order in the mainstream when we can be higher up in a counterculture?

So how can we go through life without being limited by our prejudices—without wearing the blinders that limit our view? The goal of kabbalah is to let the entire universe remain within our field of vision. *Kabbalah* is the Hebrew word for "to receive." Think of how much more information we receive when our blinders are removed. But how can we know in advance whether any particular way of looking at life will remove our blinders or have the opposite effect by further narrowing our field of vision? How can we know that by trying to answer the question "Is the universe friendly?" our vision will be broadened rather than narrowed? Some people might reasonably say, "Study the science of physics if you want answers to the most important questions." Others might say, "Study scriptures."

Four Ways to Perceive Scriptures

"It is said that there are four ways to perceive the scriptures. The first is literally, the second allegorically, the third philosophically, and the fourth mystically."[33] Each way of perceiving scripture adds a new dimension to our understanding of the world around us. A four-dimensional approach aligns itself with Einstein's theory that the universe is a four-dimensional time-space continuum.

According to kabbalah, there are ten dimensions or Sefirot, and Einstein's general theory of relativity is actually a combination of ten equations.[34] Also, one of the most current theories of physics, superstring theory, proposes a ten-dimensional model to provide "a single mathematical framework in which all fundamental forces and units of matter can be described together in a manner that is internally consistent and consistent with current and future

---

[33] Z'ev ben Shimon Halevi, *Kabbalah: The Divine Plan* (Harper San Francisco, 1996).

[34] Don Howard, *Albert Einstein: Physicist, Philosopher, Humanitarian*. The Great Courses (The Teaching Company, Chantilly, Virginia, 2008).

observation."[35] Is it possible that these ten dimensions are the ten Sefirot or emanations that burst forth when the universe was created?

According to the mystical approach to scripture, Moses was chosen to receive, perceive, and interpret these ten emanations, which led to his authorship of the first five books of the Bible—Genesis, Exodus, Leviticus, Numbers, and Deuteronomy—collectively known as the Torah. It is in the Torah that we find the Ten Commandments to guide our behavior. Moses was chosen, but what about you and me? If there are indeed divine forces at work, can ordinary people receive directly these divine emanations from our creator?

Let's say that kabbalists are truly on to something. They somehow sense the original forces that began to disperse from the moment the universe was created, commonly known as the big bang. Kabbalists also believe that what existed before the big bang, which couldn't be anything more than nothing, was *Ein Sof*, the highest and most absolute level of divinity. Without beginning or end, *Ein Sof* is nothing—no thing—and beyond anyone's ability to fully comprehend.[36]

Some of today's most advanced theoretical and particle physicists, who study the interactions of subatomic particles, theorize that the mass or matter that occupies the universe was formed from massless particles.[37] Are these massless particles sparks of *Ein Sof*, the "no thing," popularized in recent years as the God particle? According to $E = mc^2$, if mass is zero, then energy must be zero—zippo, zilch, nada. How did the mass that fills our universe form as the result of massless, energyless particles of nothingness?

---

[35] Patricia Schwarz, *The Official String Theory Website*, www.superstringtheory.com (2012).
[36] Arthur Goldwag, *TheBeliefnet Guide to Kabbalah* (Three Leaves Press, 2003).
[37] "Q & A: The Higgs Boson," *BBC News: Science and Environment Website*, www.bbc.uk/news/science-environment (July 4, 2012).

In 1964, physicist Peter Higgs proposed that such a force exists as a subatomic particle that has since become known as the Higgs boson. In 2013 Higgs and Francois Englert received a Nobel Prize for their work, although many other scientists also were involved—some developing the equipment, and others performing the experiments necessary to prove or disprove the existence of the Higgs boson.

On July 4, 2012, two separate teams of physicists using the CERN particle accelerator near Geneva, Switzerland, confirmed experimentally the existence of the Higgs boson.[38] Physicists and most of the news media agreed that this discovery was profound. Matter is formed because of the presence of massless subatomic particles. We now have scientific evidence to help explain how the universe formed from nothingness.

But how can particles possessing neither mass nor energy have an effect on anything? As difficult as that is to understand, it was numbers that showed the way. Computers read the information coming from the particle accelerators, turned that information into numbers, and crunched the numbers with statistical analysis. The numbers identified and described the Higgs boson, thus enlightening the physicists. Kabbalah is all about numbers revealing hidden truths.

I doubt that the scientists at the CERN laboratory realized that they were working on a theory—the mass of the universe formed from nothingness—that had already been hypothesized many centuries earlier by practitioners of kabbalah. These kabbalists attribute their awareness and knowledge of this theory to the presence of the ten Sefirot, distinct forces or emanations from God that formed the universe.

---

[38] Steven Weinberg, "Why the Higgs Boson Matters," *New York Times* (July 13, 2012).

The first Sefirah, Keter, is also known as Ayin, which means nothingness. This might be a clue to how kabbalists figured out that the universe formed from nothingness. Keter refers to the head or crown, which houses our brain and its thoughts—thoughts that are massless and occupy no discernible space. Maybe it was the mystics' pure brainpower and use of deductive reasoning that led them to ask the question: If God could not be created, then how did God come into existence? Their conclusion was that something had to come from nothingness, and that nothingness is nothing. So contemplating the formation of God and His creation is like contemplating the formation of nothing.

The practitioners of kabbalah were not alone in recognizing the importance of nothingness. Lao-tzu, a Chinese philosopher and mystic who lived at about the same time as the Buddha, knew that nothingness is everything. His magnum opus, the *Tao Te Ching*—or *Great Way*—touches upon this book's theme: the relationship of nothingness to self-esteem.

The *Tao* formulates the realization, as did the Rolling Stones in their 1965 hit song "Satisfaction,"[39] that when you "can't get no satisfaction," it's because you think that you aren't good enough. Furthermore, as a consequence of your low self-esteem, you'll feel compelled to acquire wealth and status, which will turn out to be things you never needed. To experience a beautiful life, the only thing you really need, according to the *Tao*, is no-thing. A beautiful life is your birthright.

Motivational speaker and author Wayne Dyer explained brilliantly the *Tao* to American audiences. According to Dyer, the *Tao*

---

[39] "(I Can't Get No) Satisfaction," by the Rolling Stones, ranked right behind Dylan's "Like a Rolling Stone" as the first- and second-greatest songs of all time according to *Rolling Stone* magazine. What a rock slide of rolling stones we have here!

emphasizes that we came from no-thing, will return to no-thing, and need no-thing.

> You don't need beautiful words, since there is no-thing for you to describe. There is no-thing to argue about, as there are no possessions to fight over. There's no faultfinding or blaming, for all that exists is the hidden virtue of the *Tao*. And finally, there is no-thing to collect, amass, or accumulate, which leaves you in a state of creative giving and supporting.[40]

This alignment of particle physics with Jewish mystical beliefs and Taoism signifies a most important concept. It's fine to doubt ideas about cause and effect that cannot be proven using statistical methods, or to doubt our ability to be free of bias when interpreting statistical data. If we can maintain an open mind and accept that it's reasonable to have such doubt, then our most cherished religious and philosophical beliefs can exist in harmony with science's most cherished building blocks. Science and religion are not at odds with each other. They both exist, as the Buddha tells us, to reduce unnecessary suffering.

Constructing New Sensors

Scientists needed to construct a laboratory containing a particle accelerator and equipment capable of sensing minute energy fields before they could confirm the existence of the Higgs boson. Similarly, if there are ten Sefirot or any other kind of signals from a divine guiding force, we must first develop a way to detect their existence.

---

[40] Wayne Dyer, *Change Your Thoughts—Change Your Life: Living the Wisdom of the Tao* (Hay House, 2007).

Without some kind of sensor, we will be unable to receive or detect these guiding forces, if such forces really exist.

We cannot receive or perceive light without the organ of sight, the eyes. We cannot receive or perceive music and other sounds without our ears. We need sensory organs that can receive energy in its various forms so that our brains can provide meaning to these perceptions. Moses, the Buddha, Jesus, and Muhammad make it clear that we need to expand our ability to perceive and anticipate more than just those things that reach our five senses. Being compassionate is vitally important, but compassion requires the ability to perceive more than just those things that we can see, hear, touch, taste, or smell.

Proverbs 4:23 Leads the Way

How can you perceive more than those things that reach your five senses? By letting your heart be your guide. Allow that four-chambered organ that reaches viability outside the womb at twenty-three weeks gestation[41] to be your sixth sense. Proverbs 4:23 says, "Above all else, guard your heart, for it is the wellspring of life" (NIV).[42]

The best way to protect or guard your heart is to strengthen it by using it. Literally, the heart provides the force for the delivery of nutrients needed for physical action. Figuratively, the heart is the force that delivers the ingredients that inspire us to act spiritually as well. If you don't use your heart, like any other muscle, it will weaken, atrophy, and fail to provide sufficient force.

---

[41] Adam Wishart, "Premature Babies Battle for Survival at 'Edge of Life,'" BBC News Health (March 7, 2011).
[42] New International Version (1984)

Four Spiritual Acts

How can you strengthen your heart? The answer is the four spiritual acts:

1. Altruism: acting on behalf of the needs of others without any thought of getting something tangible in return. Prayers are often altruistic and will help you focus on the needs of others.
2. Attention to creativity in nature, science, and the arts. Giving your undivided attention to creation in nature, such as watching a sunset or taking a walk in the woods. Trying to understand mathematical and historical relationships. Studying basic sciences. Paying attention to creative arts such as art, design, music, and dance. Being curious about the emotions that underlie our use of language, words, stories, poetry, drama, or comedy. Using any innovative tool, device, program, instrument, or puzzle. Engaging in creative ways of expressing or explaining the presence or nonpresence of a higher power.
3. Movement: getting in touch with your essence. You are energy, and energy is about movement, such as dancing, surfing a wave, feeling the wind, rolling down a hill, moving with speed, engaging in physical exercise, or participating in sports.
4. Meditation: connecting your heart with your mind, which provides a sense that there is something greater than yourself. While you're meditating, your worries, fears, or anxieties no longer attach themselves to your thoughts.

Movement can literally strengthen heart muscle, and the other three spiritual acts strengthen the heart metaphorically. Genesis 1:3, the "let there be light" passage from the Bible, aligns its ever-shining light on the 1:3 literal to metaphorical acts that strengthen the heart.

When you're practicing the four spiritual acts, your heart opens and lets in the light, making it easier to let the four bases of the Golden Rule guide your actions. Together, the four spiritual acts and the four bases of the Golden Rule form the four-by-four pursuit of happiness. This four-by-four pursuit provides better traction, less slippage, and less veering off course on your way to the Promised Land.

The benefits of the four-by-four pursuit of happiness include the following:

1. You reduce mental clutter. When you practice the Golden Rule, you don't have to worry about what others think about you. You don't have to think about pleasing others so that they'll like you, because you know that you already deserve to be liked. Should others dislike you as you practice the Golden Rule, you know that they're confused and guided by ignorance rather than insight. They mistakenly think they need to prove something or get things they never needed in the first place.
2. When your brain isn't cluttered with thoughts about trying to please others, your awareness and sensitivity to pleasurable activities becomes heightened. You become more alert to the selfish acts of others while it's still relatively easy to set limits, nip things in the bud by saying no, or remove yourself from the situation.
3. With the Golden Rule guiding your actions, you build good memories. With these good memories in place, it becomes easier to like wherever your train of thought takes you.
4. With pleasant memories circulating in your brain, it becomes easier to set aside time for the four spiritual acts, which rejuvenate your body and soul, reduce mental clutter, add a dose of friendliness to the universe, and make following the Golden Rule that much easier. It's an upward spiral.

When you shift into the four-by-four pursuit of happiness, your heart, rather than your five senses, provides greater direction and influence over your thoughts. These heart-directed thoughts, like Moses guiding us through the desert, will lead you to the Promised Land. Your other five senses will be delighted along the way. Furthermore, when you strengthen your heart both literally and metaphorically, you might be constructing an apparatus—a spiritual sensor—that can detect the divine forces or Sefirot that created the universe.

From a physiological standpoint, here's how heart-directed activities can influence your thoughts. The heart's neural activity interacts with the brain's cortex by way of the brain stem. The cortex is the large, highly evolved area of the brain where you consciously attend to your environment and plan your daily activities. During meditation, neural activity in some regions of the cortex intensifies, while in other regions it slows down.[43] It is likely that these changes during meditation interact with the neural activity of the heart. Perhaps similar changes in neural activity between the heart and brain also take place during the other three spiritual acts: altruistic behaviors, enjoyment of movement, and undivided attention given to creative works. Furthermore, these neural changes might be responsible for the phenomena known as the sixth sense, a spiritual sensor that is responsive to forms of energy undetected by the other five senses.

Maybe other religious activity, such as traditional religious rituals, church services, and prayer, also help to develop this spiritual sensor. In the same light, other spiritual practices—fasting, yoga, and treks away from civilization, for example—might also help. The systematic study of the sciences (such as physics, engineering, math, chemistry, biology, geology, astronomy, and anthropology) and creative arts (such as music, sculpture, painting, design, dance,

---

[43] Matthieu Ricard, Antoine Lutz, and Rich J. Davidson, "Mind of the Meditator," *Scientific American* (November 2014).

drama, comedy, and poetry) might prime us in a way that makes it easier to sense the existence of forces that ordinarily defy a scientific rational explanation.

If we possessed a spiritual sensor that could detect energy or a force of some kind that stimulates more than our five senses, an energy or a force that might be derived directly from our creator, how would it be perceived? How would we interpret it? Are these divine messages friendly? Furthermore, if such a force exists, must we have faith in a divine creator in order to be guided by this divine force?

Is it possible that some of us have already developed methods to receive and perceive this energy in a way that falls outside the scope of religious or spiritual belief? Is the discovery of the Higgs boson an example of nonreligious activity that reveals a part of our creator's message? Can an atheist or nonbeliever be tuned in to the divine energy of the universe without being aware of its existence or without interpreting it as divine? Yes, quite possibly. "Whoever has ears, let them hear" (Matthew 11:15 NIV).

The conscientious, mindful atheist or nonbeliever typically attributes their highest ideals (love, compassion, and altruism) simply to being human, without the necessity of some religious background or supernatural intervention. Similarly, we are able to use computers and the internet without needing a background in physics, engineering, or programming.

Supernatural Intervention

One day John, my friend and fellow college freshman, asked me if I was interested in hearing someone talk about God. "Okay," I said, even though I didn't believe in God. I thought that God was some kind of wishful thinking that helped people cope. But I was curious to hear what they had to say, and then I would share with them my viewpoint on the subject.

Later that day, John met me at my room (220) on the second floor and we walked down to his room (104) on the first floor. There I met two young, clean-cut, neatly dressed white men who looked about twenty-five years old. They were there to meet me, a hippie-looking eighteen-year-old raised by nonreligious Jewish parents. Jews will often identify themselves as Jews even if they don't believe in anything that has to do with the religion of Judaism. Even Jews who practice another religion will often call themselves Jews because their cultural identity is independent of their religious beliefs.

The two young men were representatives from Campus Crusade for Christ, and they began by simply asking me if I was interested in receiving Christ into my life. When I replied, "Yes," they asked me to repeat in earnest a sentence or two about Jesus being our lord and guiding light. Immediately after I said those words, I felt a warm sensation enter the area of my inner thighs, which is the bodily area associated with Foundation, the ninth Sefirah.[44] This sensation traveled up my body to my head, and it was remarkably different from anything that I had ever experienced. This took place in room 104 (10-4, message received).

Years later, I was told by someone familiar with Christian beliefs that what I had experienced was an anointing in which Christ's spirit or Holy Ghost had entered my body. But how do I know that I was given a biased or unbiased explanation of my experience with those two evangelists? How should I measure that so-called anointing? What should you, the reader, think of that experience? How can we evaluate it without shading it with our biases? The Buddha will help us answer these questions. He spent his life trying to figure out

---

[44] See Figure 1.

how to interpret experiences without distorting reality with biases, prejudices, anxieties, and insecurities.

If I told the Buddha of my experience with the phenomenon called the Holy Ghost, what would the Buddha think of this experience? To answer this question, I call on the expertise of Dr. Mark Meusse, W. J. Miller Professor of Religious Studies at Rhodes College.[45] According to the Buddha, my encounter with this phenomenon was an "awakening" as a result of "direct knowledge or understanding gained and confirmed by immediate personal experience." However, the Buddha urges us not to attribute more to this experience than what it was—a claim of a unique and unexpected sensation felt by one man when two men, calling themselves evangelists, asked that man to repeat words about Jesus being Lord, ostensibly to let Jesus come into his life. Dr. Meusse emphasizes the Buddha's warning about accepting evidence as the truth:

> [According to the Buddha] the usual grounds on which most people accept something as true were insufficient for living the spiritual life ... [We] should not accept anything simply because it was based on a claim of revelation, or it was rooted in tradition, or commonly repeated as fact, or because it came from scriptures, or because it conformed to logic and seemed rationale, or because the teacher was competent and possessed a fine reputation. These grounds were not enough he thought for a claim to pass muster as genuine knowledge.

The Buddha put forth his knowledge twenty-three centuries before the writing of our Declaration of Independence, which said that a government was to be formed specifically to address the "pursuit of

---

[45] Mark W. Meusse, *Confucius, Buddha, Jesus, and Muhammad*, The Great Courses, 2010 (The Teaching Company, Chantilly, Virginia) .

happiness." John Adams, Thomas Jefferson, and others from the Age of Enlightenment realized that "reason, not revelation, should have primacy in human affairs."[46] The Buddha warns, however, that just because something seems reasonable, it is not necessarily the truth. Furthermore, the Buddha says that the test for truth is that when it is fully understood, it will result in a sense of personal happiness without bringing suffering to others.

Perhaps the purpose of a revelation is to provide a rational explanation of how to pursue happiness without causing suffering. This explanation should then be able to stand on its own merit without the need to cite that a divine revelation led to its formation. For example, a claim of truth, such as "Thou shalt not kill," should make perfect sense to believers and nonbelievers alike. "Thou shalt not kill" is a truth, whether you believe it was written by God or an out-of-work musician.

When the evangelists approached me, I was quite naive about religious rituals and beliefs. I knew very little about Judaism, let alone Christianity. I was not aware that an anointing awaited me or had been experienced by others, and I didn't know whether my experience was of any significance. Afterward, I didn't pick up a Bible or attend church. I went about my life no differently from before except for one thing: I had experienced a phenomenon that defies logic and supports the belief that there is a God.

Based on my anointing, my best explanation is that the evangelists helped me create a spiritual sensor that detected an energy that I had not previously detected. Do I understand the significance of this force or energy? No, I don't. But as I reflect upon this experience over forty years later, I believe that I've been given an opportunity to

---

[46] Jon Meacham, "Free to Be Happy," *Time* (July 8–15, 2013).

understand the human condition in a way that makes it much easier to feel confident and much harder to procrastinate.

At first it seemed that my encounter with the Holy Spirit at age eighteen was not going to have much influence on my life. But everything changed two years later when I fell in love with Elizabeth and accepted her into my life unconditionally. My hypothesis is that Jesus's influence brought about that unconditional love. His influence allowed me to understand that the insecurities that I sensed in Elizabeth were essentially the same as the ones that I had been overlooking in myself. Up until this point, those insecurities had led me to think that I should break up with her. However, now with my new understanding, I wanted Elizabeth to know that she deserved to be loved and lead a beautiful life, whether or not we remained together. I chose to get closer to Elizabeth rather than breaking up. Then about two months later, she broke up with me, leaving me sad and lonely.

My self-esteem took a big hit when I lost Elizabeth, but with the help of the four heavy hitters of history, my happiness has been restored. Moses, the Buddha, Jesus, and Muhammad showed me that everyone deserves a beautiful life. But to actually experience the beautiful life you deserve, you need to treat others like they deserve a beautiful life by following the four bases of the Golden Rule. The more you incorporate these four bases into your daily life, the happier and more positive you will be.

You probably first became aware of the Golden Rule as a child, when a parent or teacher scolded you with these words: "How would you like someone to do that to you?" After this reminder to be considerate of others, you probably went back to whatever you were doing without giving it much more thought. Because of my behavior as a child, I heard the Golden Rule many times, but its wisdom didn't sink in. I was too focused on trying to stand out. I wanted to be a professional baseball player. I wanted to be among the best of the best. I didn't realize that just by being kind, I would experience more happiness than I could ever have possibly imagined.

The Best of the Best

It is understandable that I would want to be among the best of the best because I needed a defense against thinking the intolerable, "What if I'm not good enough?" While growing up, I naturally drew the conclusion that the group to which I attached my identity (I was an American opposed to the war in Vietnam) was better than those who supported the war in Vietnam and that my own words and actions would win the respect of my fellow group members. In this way I would rise to the top and be among "the best of the best."

Fortunately, at age eighteen, I began to learn that striving to be among "best of the best" was not necessarily the best way to find happiness. I was awakened with the help of my friend John and two evangelists to the existence of a phenomenon that we called God. That awakening strengthened my ability to understand the importance of the ideas and principles embodied in the four-by-four pursuit of happiness. The four bases of the Golden Rule and four spiritual acts can give us a glimpse of the eternal life or chai found in the life of Jesus and provide an answer to Einstein's question, "Is the universe friendly?"

My faith and intellect agree that it's beyond my ability to know for sure what an eternal life truly means, although I believe that it has something to do with love and light. Obviously an eternal life is not something that I can confirm by personal experience. I can easily imagine Mr. Spock saying to Captain Kirk,[47] "It is nòt logical to experience an eternal life. Only when a life is over can we know its length. When it's over, Jim, it's no longer eternal."

What I have experienced to be the truth, though, is the practice of the four bases of the Golden Rule: be aware of and sensitive to the feelings of others, don't do for others what they can to do for themselves, say no to people who act selfishly, and don't judge others as undeserving of my kindness or generosity. As I engage in this practice, I no longer suffer from low self-esteem and I feel more confident. I have freed myself from thinking that my value is determined by things, opinions, and people to whom I once attached my identity. I have freed myself from tying my self-worth to the circumstances of my genetic inheritance, which includes my height, looks, athletic abilities, and intellectual strengths and weaknesses. I have freed my self-worth from the circumstances of growing up in a society whose system of justice isn't guided by the Golden Rule. I have freed my self-worth from the history of mistakes I made while I was guided by ignorance rather than insight.

Though I have found the truth in the Golden Rule, what does the Buddha say about you finding it as well?

> The Buddha discouraged faith in matters of ultimate importance. He wanted everyone to see the truth of his teachings for themselves, and not to rely on his authority as a holy man, or as a famous teacher, or what his followers said, nor was it enough for someone to consider his teachings true just because it seemed to make sense ... When you know for yourselves that these teachings are wholesome, that

---

[47] Mr. Spock (Leonard Nimoy) and Captain James T. Kirk (William Shatner) are the two highest-ranking characters from *Star Trek*, the TV series created by Gene Roddenberry that ran on NBC from September 8, 1966, to June 3, 1969.

they are blameless, that they are to be praised by the wise, and that they, if undertaken and practiced, lead to benefit and happiness, then you should accept them and abide in them ... For a spiritual teaching ... to qualify as true, a doctrine or claim must be known by immediate experience. Mere belief was not enough when it comes to matters of ultimate significance ... Belief is inferior to seeing for oneself. Indeed beliefs without direct knowledge can actually be dangerous.[48]

If practicing the four bases of the Golden Rule results in happiness, better self-esteem, more confidence, or some other benefit, and if this practice causes no one else to suffer, then we can safely say that these four principles are indeed a true spiritual teaching.

Speaking of the truth, in 2004 I went to see Mel Gibson's movie *The Passion of the Christ.* My friend from work and fellow movie devotee, Todd, had gotten two tickets from a church, and we met at the theater on a Saturday afternoon. Like most of the audience, I cried repeatedly during the movie. It is deeply disturbing to watch torture, but it's even worse if you feel love for the person being tortured. When the movie was over, many people wept as they slowly left the theater. I commented to Todd that *The Passion of the Christ* reinforced two very important concepts: people in positions of power and authority often feel threatened by people who express love, and my burdens are infinitesimally small compared with those carried by Jesus.

On my way home from the movie theater, I decided to stop at a place with an open view of the Everglades and watch the sunset. As I pulled off the Sawgrass Expressway and into an unofficial parking

---

[48] Mark W. Meusse, *Confucius, Buddha, Jesus, and Muhammad*, The Great Courses, 2010 (The Teaching Company, Chantilly, Virginia).

area, I noticed what looked like a book lying on the shoulder of the road. I parked the car and walked back to find a leather-bound Bible folded open at chapter 18 of the book of Numbers. Furthermore, there was a ribbon bookmark at chapter 13 of the book of Job. At the top of the page was a quotation corresponding to Job 13:18: "This is my case: I know that I am righteous." Well, I'd like to think that this was more than just a coincidence. On the side of the road, I had found a Bible lying open to book four, Numbers, with a bookmark at book eighteen, Job, and a highlighted message that says, "I know that I am righteous." And that happened right after I saw *The Passion of the Christ*. Give me a break!

The Bible was open to chapter 13 of Job, and the number 13 is composed of two numbers, 1 and 3. Genesis 1:3 indicates enlightenment, the four spiritual acts include one literal and three metaphorical ways to strengthen our hearts, and our four guides to the Promised Land are the one Buddha and three prophets: Moses, Jesus, and Muhammad. Is this mysterious Bible showing us the way? Is it a sign that my job (Job) is to exercise the necessary perseverance (a major theme in the book of Job) to see that righteous ideas are communicated clearly, published in an easily accessible way, received by people of various faiths and backgrounds, and perceived in a way that makes the world a friendlier place?

If you fold open a book so that the front cover is touching the back cover, two pages will be revealed. This is how I found the Bible: Numbers 18 facing up and Numbers 19 facing down. Job 13:18 appears to give me a sign of encouragement with the case I've been making about the four bases of the Golden Rule and how the human psyche works: "This is my case. I know that I am righteous."

The following verse, Job 13:19, is for you, the reader of *Positively 4th Street*. It says, "Who could argue with me over this? If you could prove me wrong, I would stop defending myself and die." This is a sign that if you are to get the most out of this book, then your job (Job) is to question the truth, validity, and logic of my words. According to the Buddha, as mentioned earlier, my words are true only if you experience them as being true. Only if my words raise your self-esteem, make you more confident or friendly, make your life more meaningful, or in some other way bring you happiness without causing others to suffer—then, and only then, are my words to be considered true. Furthermore, if they are not true, then according to verse 19, I will stop defending these ideas and this book.

First commandment: "Thou shalt have no other gods before me." If there were more than one god, would not the gods compete with each other? Competition separates winners from losers. But a relationship with God is built on love. Love, in direct contrast to competition, connects us to each other. If our gods are about love, rather than competition, then all the gods would be connected to each other, forming one indivisible God. Therefore, there can be only one God, unless we are guided by self-serving goals and trying to distinguish ourselves from others.

2

Hokhmah—Wisdom

We are unconscious of many of our own motivations and patterns of thought and behavior until they are reflected back to us by others ... We are unconscious of our cultural background, knowledge and assumptions ... Each society tends to cultivate blind spots around the specific forms of social suffering that it produces.

—Laurence J. Kirmayer[49]

Listening to others who disagree with me and who are willing to criticize me is essential to piercing the seduction of certainty. Doubt, I've learned, is wisdom.

—James Comey, *A Higher Loyalty* (2018)

From Keter comes Hokhmah or Wisdom. This second Sephirah is an infinitesimal point that contains within it all that will ever be. Hokhmah is the universe before the big bang, except that it never explodes. Hokhmah contains the potential for all of the truth and

---

[49] Laurence J. Kirmayer et al., "The Cultural Context of Clinical Assessment," in A. Tasman et al. (eds.), *Psychiatry*, 3rd ed., (John Wiley and Sons, 2011).

wisdom that will be manifested by creation. Its letter is *yod*, the smallest in the Hebrew alphabet.[50]

The Golden Rule, which expresses much truth and wisdom, is perhaps the only concept universally accepted by all the great religions and humanistic philosophies. When you follow the Ten Commandments of Moses, learn how to truly love your neighbor as taught by Jesus, or raise your awareness and sensitivities to the feelings of others by practicing Buddha's Four Noble Truths, you will feel connected to those around you. In the sixth century, Muhammad knew of Jesus and Moses to his north and west and the Buddha to his south and east. Yet Muhammad did not readily witness any unifying principle guiding the peoples around him. I can easily imagine Muhammad saying, "I have had enough of religions and philosophies that try to distinguish themselves from each other. There is only one God, Allah. It is the first commandment."

Muhammad must have realized that, in order to abide by the first commandment, we needed a better way to make the Golden Rule a part of our everyday consciousness. Inspired to find this better way, and with the benefit of twenty-three years of divine revelation, Muhammad laid down the framework to bring humankind all together now with the Five Pillars of Islam:

1. Professing that there is only one God, Allah
2. Praying five times daily
3. Giving alms to the poor
4. Observing Ramadan by fasting from dawn to dusk during the ninth month of the Islamic calendar
5. Making a pilgrimage to Mecca, if possible

Two of these pillars relate to enhanced awareness: there is only one God, and we are obliged to help the less fortunate. The other

---

[50] Arthur Goldwag, *The Beliefnet Guide to Kabbalah* (Three Leaves Press, 2005).

three pillars relate to sensitivity: prayer, fasting, and a pilgrimage. By practicing the three pillars that raise our sensitivity, we become increasingly aware of God's presence in our lives and our need to be of service to others. These five pillars strengthen the Golden Rule as a guiding force.

When humankind practices the Golden Rule and acknowledges that there are enough resources on this earth for all 7.6 billion[51] of us to have what we need to raise healthy families, we can limit the unnecessary suffering caused by so much unnecessary competition. Competition undermines happiness and distorts reality by getting us to think that we need to be better than others to survive or that we need to be better than others to be valued. In reality, we just need to be better at following the four bases of the Golden Rule.

Where Does the Truth Lie?

If competition undermines happiness, then where does the truth lie? Rene Descartes (1596–1650) thought that the truth is to be found in our thoughts: "I think, therefore I am." We wouldn't be aware of our existence if we weren't aware of our thoughts. We could reverse Descartes's pronouncement and it would make just as much sense: "I am, therefore I think." We, as a species, are the great thinkers.

"To be or not to be, that is the question,"[52] argued Shakespeare, but I beg to differ. The real question is whether to think or not to think. Shakespeare's life began at his birth (or conception, if you prefer), as did yours and mine. Like us, he was endowed with four nucleic acids encoding twenty-three chromosomes, and his four-chambered heart reached viability at twenty-three weeks gestation. Unlike you

---

[51] World population as of May 2018: en.wikipedia.org/wiki/World_population
[52] William Shakespeare's *Hamlet* was written when Descartes was about four years old.

and me, however, not only was Shakespeare born on 4/23 (April 23, 1564) but he died on 4/23 (April 23, 1616) as well.

Recall Proverbs 4:23, "Above all else, guard your heart, for it is the wellspring of life" (NIV). Because he heeded these instructions, out of Shakespeare's heart there flowed a wellspring of literature—sonnets infused with virtues, delights, and beauty; and plays filled with characters beset by tragedy because they failed to guard their hearts. After being beset by tragedy, Johnny Cash began his path to redemption by guarding his heart: "I keep a close watch on this heart of mine." That's the opening line to his first number 1 hit record, "I Walk the Line," recorded on April 2, 1956, at Sun Studios in Memphis, Tennessee, which is where Elvis Presley got his start. *Rolling Stone* ranked "I Walk the Line" at number 30 on their list of the 500 Greatest Songs of All Time. In June 2014, *Rolling Stone* placed "I Walk the Line" at number 1 on its list of the 100 Greatest Country Songs of All Time.

Descartes and Shakespeare pondered deeply what it means to think or be, but most people don't give much thought to such things. Instead we think about what needs to be done, what we want to be doing, and how we are going to do it. We also think about what other people are thinking. We wonder, for example, what kind of impression we'll make at a job interview or on a date. Teenagers often worry incessantly about what their schoolmates think of them. Lawyers rely heavily on their ability to anticipate what people will be thinking. From the basic survival standpoint of a pack animal, a standpoint our subconscious mind maintains, we want to know what others are thinking so that we can better assess our position in the "pecking order." We want to know what raises our standing and what decreases it.

Considering the availability of tabloid newspapers, magazines, and entertainment news on TV, "Enquiring minds want to know"[53] where people in the public eye stand as well. We want to associate with people held in high esteem—"The 'In' Crowd,"[54] A-listers, the popular kids. When you like a person whom you don't know personally—Arnold Schwarzenegger, for example—you associate yourself psychologically with that person. If that person does something that violates your sense of right and wrong, you want to know so that you can let others know that you no longer like him. Furthermore, if you express *why* that person has fallen out of your favor, you create the impression that you're of a higher moral character and should be judged favorably. One of the main reasons why we gossip is to give the impression that we're of a higher moral character than the people about whom we gossip. Subconsciously, we believe that gossiping moves us up the pecking order.

We Think Subconsciously to Take Action

If I were an outspoken fan of a celebrity, such as the already mentioned Arnold Schwarzenegger, and then read or heard about that person's unfaithfulness to his wife, I would likely take the first opportunity to tell others what a jerk he is. Subconsciously, I would worry that not doing so would lead other people to think that I still admire the fallen celebrity, which, in turn, could lead to thoughts of disapproval about me. We don't like other people's disapproval or rejection because negative judgments move us down the pecking order and can affect our instinctual drives to procreate and survive. People don't mate with, protect, or offer jobs to people about whom they harbor negative judgments.

---

[53] *National Enquirer* advertising slogan.
[54] "The 'In' Crowd," 1965 hit record sung by Dobie Gray, written by Billy Page, instrumental version by the Ramsey Lewis Trio.

If you slow down and think about it, you might realize that you have subconsciously pondered the following: If I don't take action, if I stay in bed all day, then my situation (or the situation of someone I am expected to care about) could take a turn for the worse or I could feel bored or lonely. When you are experiencing—or anticipate experiencing—something unpleasant, your subconscious brain is stimulated to think. For example, if you think consciously about losing your job, you'll probably formulate a swarm of subconscious thoughts about how horrible your life would be like if you were evicted from your home. So you consciously think to set an alarm clock to ensure that you'll get to work on time.

Two Basic Instinctual Drives

Anticipating a turn for the worse usually relates directly to two basic instinctual drives: the instinct of survival, and the instinct of reproduction or procreation, which involves sexual attractiveness or prowess. We don't like it when either of these two basic drives is compromised. No money, no food, no water, no sex appeal—that's no good.

Sometimes we think back to a time when we missed an opportunity at a better paying job because we were discriminated against or someone else had a more impressive résumé. Maybe if we had put more effort into our education, a better paying or more interesting job could have been ours. We remember not buying a property or holding on to a stock whose value later skyrocketed. We remember missed opportunities for partnerships with talented friends or associates. We remember failing to please family members. Perhaps what stands out the most are memories of not being able to attract the attention of someone to whom we were attracted, or memories of disappointing a loved one.

Unless you change how you think, you will subconsciously categorize yourself as a failure for not being good enough, bold enough, or smart enough—but that's not reality. Moses, the Buddha, Jesus, and Muhammad can show you that you are good enough, no matter what you have experienced in the past. An important part of their message is to remember to treat other people like they, too, are good enough—good enough to be free of any negative judgments you may be harboring toward them or negative judgments about yourself that you may be projecting onto them.

In addition to failure, we also pay close attention to people or situations that create fear. Our media reports on crimes, accidents, fires, wars, epidemics, and natural disasters with great frequency. Our TV programs and movie theaters are filled with threatening situations and outright horror. Our subconscious wonders if we are smart enough, good enough, or prepared enough to avoid the troubles that beset others.

Competition

If fear and failure were not enough, our subconscious brain also sizes up almost every situation as a potential competition. Everyday events present opportunities to raise or lower our status and position in the pecking order. If I do my homework, hit a home run on a video game, or land a high-paying job, my status is improved. If I am greeted warmly at work, then my status is enhanced. Conversely, if I end up in a low-paying job or my coworkers ignore me, my status declines. For some people, just beating other cars through an intersection, when the traffic light changes from red to green, increases their self-perceived status.

Games and sporting events become symbolic. If my favorite athlete has a good game or my favorite team wins, my subconscious translates that as enhanced status. If my team loses consistently but I remain loyal, then my loyalty raises my status. If you say to me that my mother is fat and weighs too much, my status is lowered. However, if I retort, "I don't know how you'd know what my mother weighs since your mother broke the scale," and that gets bigger laughs, then I have won the competition and my status goes up. In politics, if I just get even one more vote than you, I have won the competition.

If I am discriminated against, then I'm put at a competitive disadvantage. Competition is going on all around us, even though we often aren't consciously aware of it. So much is going on in our subconscious thoughts. Favorable opinions raise our status, whereas unfavorable opinions lower it. Just the appearance of being more reasonable or logical than others is interpreted by our subconscious as winning the competition. Politicians, academicians, theologians, athletes, and artists are famous for their battles over whose work, performance, or ideas are better. We call this ego.

Ego

Our ego wonders what others are thinking about us. Our ego evaluates all experiences from early childhood right up to the present moment. Our ego is also analyzing every personal encounter as a possible challenge to our sexual prowess or a competition for limited resources. Are others working with me or against me?

Based on our subconscious thoughts, our ego evaluates how we're doing regarding our instinctual drives and where we stand in the pecking order. Our self-esteem is handled primarily by these subconscious thoughts that we call ego. With a million times more neural activity in our subconscious brain than in our conscious brain, we are rarely conscious of the reality that so much of our daily activity is directed by an instinctually driven ego.

Joshua Simon, MD, EdD

Our Conscience Resides in Our Conscious Thoughts

There is more to our conscious thinking than just being able to recall some of the subconscious thoughts attended to by our ego. There is more to our conscious thinking than making plans to minimize or distract ourselves from the fear of being without basic needs. There is more to our conscious thinking than improving our position in the pecking order. There is more, if we have a conscience.

Our conscience, which lets us know right from wrong in terms of our conduct or motives, resides in great part in our conscious thoughts but our conduct is too often guided by subconscious thoughts. Fortunately, we have the Ten Commandments to shift us out of our subconscious thinking by strengthening those areas of the brain that think consciously about what it means to be moral. Americans describe morals using these nine adjectives: kind, caring, compassionate, helpful, friendly, fair, hardworking, generous, and honest.[55]

By frequently contemplating the Ten Commandments, we exercise the conscience within our conscious thoughts, thus strengthening the involvement of these neural networks. Jesus asks us to strengthen our conscience through the power of love. Muhammad raises our sensitivity to right from wrong through prayer, pilgrimage, and fasting. The Buddha shows us that our conscious mind can rise to greater heights through meditation.

With less subconscious brain influence during meditation, our thoughts are less driven by fear and anxiety. Our conscious mind remains active during meditation, possibly more so than in other states. When we meditate, we're focused on spiritual thoughts

---

[55] Jen Sheng, assistant professor at the Center of Philanthropy at Indiana University, as quoted in David Wallis, "Getting Into a Benefactor's Head," *New York Times* (November 8, 2012).

or other thoughts not driven by subconscious fear, anxiety, or instinctual desires.

If we follow Moses's lead, our sense of love and our spiritual relationship with a higher power depends on a heightened awareness and sensitivity to the conscience that resides within our conscious thoughts. If the thoughts that reside in our conscience are not exercised sufficiently by practicing, for example, the four-by-four pursuit of happiness, then our conscience will weaken, just as a lack of physical exercise allows our muscles to atrophy. When our conscience is weakened, our instinctually based subconscious, with its "all's fair in love and war" mentality, will exert greater influence on our sense of justice, our philosophical approach to solving problems, and ultimately our behavior. With a weakened conscience, for example, we can even justify torture.

"But I tell you, love your enemies and pray for those who persecute you" (Matthew 5:44 NIV). Jesus tells us that we can protect ourselves without letting our conscience weaken, even when dealing with problems related to war and criminal behavior. By using the four bases of the Golden Rule as our guide and consciously practicing the Golden Rule, we can increase our sense of safety without sacrificing our conscience. We can set limits with others who act selfishly while continuing to care about them. We need not judge others as undeserving of our kindness in order to protect ourselves.

Importance of Prayer

Muhammad made prayer five times daily one of his Five Pillars of a spiritual life. At daybreak, noon, midday, evening, and before going to sleep at night, we are to limit our subconscious thoughts through prayer and use our conscious ability to focus on the highest ideals of humankind. Muhammad somehow recognized that to unite all of humankind, we need to work on our conscience by strengthening consciously those thought patterns involved with compassion.

Perhaps the creation of a spiritual sensor occurs when conscious thoughts, formed by our conscience, somehow override most of our subconscious fears. As I described earlier, after repeating the words that were said to me by the evangelists, I immediately felt warmth in my upper thighs and that warm sensation traveled up my body. Were these sensations the result of a newly formed spiritual sensor detecting the presence of the Holy Spirit entering my body? Alternatively, were these physical sensations caused simply by brain activation and deactivation in some synchronized way that had nothing to do with some kind of spiritual sensor?

Despite growing up in an atheist household, by the age of eighteen I had probably been exposed to enough teachings about Jesus, in everyday American culture, that I associated him with a higher consciousness. When I was asked to focus on "Jesus Our Lord," could it have altered neural circuits between my brain's subconscious structures and those forebrain structures that are involved in conscious thought? Could my conscience have been strengthened while other circuits involved in instinctual thoughts were diminished? Could such changes in neural activity have spread to other parts of my brain, thereby causing the unique bodily sensations that I experienced? Despite these hypothesized neural changes, I am still more inclined to believe that some kind of outside force entered my body at the moment I repeated those words from the evangelists.

At that infinitesimal point, or Hokhmah, when I invited Jesus into my life, something totally unexpected occurred. Since an interpretation of any particular event is influenced by everything that preceded it, fully appreciating what happened to me requires perspective. It is now clear to me that all of history, the universe in its entirety, exerts an effect on our every thought and bodily sensation.

As John Muir, the famed naturalist, said, "When one tugs on a single thing in nature, he finds it attached to the rest of the world." Everything is connected.

Before the big bang, the universe existed as a super-concentrated dot in which everything was infinitesimally close and connected. But what if after the big bang, as things separated, there were strings attached and these strings are the ten Sefirot or the ten variables of string theory or the ten equations in Einstein's general theory of relativity? That would mean that everything in the universe really is connected to everything else. Only about 5 percent of all the matter in the universe is visible. The other 95 percent, which is unresponsive to light, is known as dark matter and dark energy.[56] Could this dark matter and dark energy, though invisible, somehow connect visible matter together? Could dark matter and dark energy light up when we use our hearts to guide our thoughts and actions?

I Think, Therefore I Am Problem Solving

By raising your awareness and sensitivity, you can gain insight into the thought process that usually occurs without your conscious awareness. Then you can more easily realize that the overwhelming majority of your thoughts focus on solving problems. Like it or not, your subconscious is still analyzing previous mistakes, anticipating what could go wrong in the future, assessing where you stand in the pecking order, and determining the degree to which others value your most cherished social, political, and religious beliefs.

However, if the only reason you think is to solve problems, then what problem are you trying to solve when you think about a spiritual experience, music, getting a massage, or spending time with a friend? What problem are you trying to solve when you're thinking about

---

[56] https://www.sciencedaily.com/releases/2009/11/091102121644.htm.

going to the beach or a movie? What could possibly be the problem or unpleasant thought that precedes thinking about eating ice cream? The answer to these questions will be explained shortly. But first, let me get back to Rene Descartes, the "I think, therefore I am" man.

What was the unpleasant feeling or problem that stimulated Rene Descartes to think about why we think? I speculate that it was his feelings about living a life without meaning, which can be so unpleasant for some people that their lives become dominated by the search for meaning. "I need to do something that others will remember. No one is going to think I'm a loser!" Perhaps Stephen Paddock, the man who launched the deadly attack on concertgoers in Las Vegas on October 1, 2017, was possessed by a need to leave his mark on history.

Unlike Paddock, most people think of positive ways to have a meaningful life. People often look for meaning through validation—winning a contest, making the dean's list in college, or dating or marrying an attractive person, for example. We associate the positive attention that comes from success with an increase in status and moving up the pecking order. In American culture, and perhaps most cultures, the most obvious way to improve one's status is by accumulating wealth.

Competing successfully in sports, getting good grades, being popular, serving in the military, occupying a leadership position, making money, looking sexy, having children, having a lasting marriage, making charitable donations, and participating in community activities are some of the ways you can get positive feedback. But at some point, you realize that just having other people look up to you doesn't necessarily result in a meaningful, purposeful life.

How you find meaning affects the choices you make. For the baby boomer generation, one of the biggest decisions a young man faced was whether to willingly accept the military draft, which meant facing combat in Vietnam. Some young men rushed to join the marines or special operations forces to fight gallantly. Others chose to voluntarily join a branch of the service that was less likely to put them in harm's way, such as the National Guard or Coast Guard, or to join ROTC and subsequently enter military service as an officer. Other options included taking no action and being drafted, getting a deferment for medical training or college, going to jail, or moving to Canada or elsewhere. Some young men were determined to be psychologically or physically unfit for military duty, resulting in a 4F classification, and others filed as conscientious objectors. Baby boomers asked, "What does it mean to serve my country?" It was hard not to have an existential point of view when faced with a decision with such dire consequences.

Existentialism

Existentialism is about how decisions made in everyday life relate to how you find meaning. Would Rene Descartes have continued to ponder philosophical and mathematical issues if he had been sent into a war zone, forced to leave his home, or put in jail? Our lives are influenced not only by a search for meaning but also by basic issues of survival, which are often accompanied by a sense of urgency. Suddenly the meaning of life could simply be "Stayin' Alive."[57]

In general, you act to avoid pain or obtain pleasure. You consciously or subconsciously feel uneasy when denied an opportunity that could bring you sensual pleasures. You feel comfort when protected from anything that might harm you. You enjoy food and sex. Right now, your subconscious brain may be wondering if you have access to sensual pleasures such as ice cream. If so, you can take steps to

---

[57] "Stayin' Alive," by the Bee Gees, released December 13, 1977, is number 189 on *Rolling Stone*'s 500 Greatest Songs of All Time (2004).

put the ice cream into your mouth—or you can tell yourself that you should skip that pleasure because it's too fattening. Either way, the thought of being denied pleasure was the stimulus for thinking about ice cream in the first place.

If you see a group of friends on their way to the beach on a hot day, you might say to them, "Hey, me too!" You don't want to miss out on the pleasure of cooling off, not to mention the displeasure of thinking you aren't good enough to be included in the group. Your subconscious attends to where you stand in the pecking order, anticipates problems, and tries to prevent missing out on pleasure. If someone in the group replies, "I don't like you, so you can't come along," you might experience hurt feelings. That person's negative judgment could deny you access to the sensual pleasure of cooling off on a hot day.

You grow up realizing that what other people think and do can affect you. Judgments made by others can affect your ability to avoid pain and to find pleasure and comfort. Rejection hurts. Acceptance feels good.

Suppose a schoolmate arranges for her mother to drive a group of friends to the movies, but you aren't invited. You may have the unpleasant thought that you weren't invited because your schoolmate thinks you're not good enough. "Hey, I have a great idea," you tell yourself. "As soon as I'm sixteen, I'll get my driver's permit. Then I'll go to the movies whenever I want, and I'll be the one deciding whether or not to ask others to join me. With a driver's license, I'll have a lot more control." You don't ordinarily think that one of the reasons you get so excited about getting your driver's license is that with a car you can limit the degree to which others can interfere with your access to pleasurable activities.

People do think a lot about what they think others are thinking. Most people take the approach that if they can appear reasonable to others, then they can avoid the effects of negative judgments. Thus people conform.

When you cannot avoid negative judgments, such as those that typically accompany failing grades, you can redefine your values. Getting good grades is for losers who blindly accept the status quo and don't know how to have fun. Then you go out and find a group of friends who don't place much value on getting good grades. Within this group, you can think that you are accepted for who you are; you are not being judged negatively. Your status is not being lowered because of your poor grades. This group of friends will invite you to the beach on a hot day and defend you if someone tries to bully you. This group of friends is more likely to have someone who finds you attractive physically.

Whether we identify with the main culture or a subculture, we pay close attention to the norms of our family, peer group, and community. But people don't often consciously realize that all of this thinking, our conformity or nonconformity, is instinctual and meant to solve the following problem: "How can I avoid being excluded from pleasurable activities and feel safe?" Instead we think that the values we have formed, in the process of appearing reasonable, make us who we are, and that we are different from people who have different values.

The reality is that we all think and act instinctually, and even our values are instinctually driven. Our instincts stimulate belief systems in which we are more deserving than people with a different set of values. We rationalize that our values are supposed to give us advantages. "It's the hardworking men and women from the heartland of America who built this country, not those city folks on the coast. That's why the Electoral College should stay the way it is." Yet, looking at it another way, is it fair that, when using the Electoral College, a vote for president in Wyoming counts 3.6 times more than a vote in California (based on the 2010 census)?

What do people who favor or disfavor the Electoral College want? They want what we all want. We want to avoid being excluded from pleasure and to feel safe. Feeling safe and experiencing pleasure includes avoiding an unpleasant afterlife, for those of us who believe in an afterlife, so we form values that we think will affect our afterlife as well.

Risks and Rewards

We weigh the risks and rewards in the choices we make. Will the pleasure obtained today be worth the pain, discomfort, or punishments it might cause in the future? Will the pain or discomfort that we endure today be worth the pleasure, comfort, or rewards that should follow at some future time? Most of our daily thoughts deal with assessing each situation for potential pleasure or pain and maintaining a posture that will be pleasing to others to avoid the consequences of negative judgments. These thoughts are in direct response to our instinctual drives—instinctual drives which are no different from those of any other sentient animal, whether a dog, cat, elephant, orca, chimpanzee, or other animal capable of sensation and consciousness.[58]

Unifying Theory of Human Behavior

As previously mentioned, on July 4, 2012, nuclear physicists announced the discovery of the Higgs boson—also known as the

---

[58] www.psychologytoday.com/blog/animal-emotions/201208/scientists-conclude-nonhuman-animals-are-conscious-beings.

God particle since it explains how mass forms from nothingness, a feat of creation that only God could perform. Physicists have also identified four fundamental forces in our universe: gravity, electromagnetism, strong nuclear forces, and weak nuclear forces. These four forces can explain the actions of all matter, whether subatomic particles or the movements of an entire galaxy. But the search continues for a unified theory, such as superstring theory, that could explain how all four of these forces are interconnected. The Higgs boson will likely shed some additional light on this question.

Similar to the four fundamental forces of physics, there are four basic fears that can explain human behavior from all cultures and time periods. Like my counterparts in physics, however, I recognize exceptions that don't fit neatly into this unified theory. As you will read shortly, those exceptions have to do with our relationship to a higher power.

Four Basic Fears

As previously discussed, your instinctual drives get you to think about what's happening or might happen in terms of pleasure, pain, comfort, discomfort, rewards, punishments, and judgments. You also search for meaning or a purpose. I have organized these factors into the four basic fears:

1. The fear of death, physical pain, or unpleasant emotions in the present moment
2. The anticipation of death, physical pain, or unpleasant emotions in the future
3. Thinking that others do not understand why you think or feel the way you do, and that consequently they will not mate with you, work with you, protect you, or include you in

  their activities; you socialize, in part, to receive feedback on whether or not you are perceived by others to be reasonable
4. The fear of living a life without meaning, excitement, adventure, or pleasure; feeling bored or lonely

Regardless of culture or time period, almost every human behavior, including the formation of personal values, is motivated by one or more of these four basic fears. Whether you are aware of it or not, most of your thinking is devoted to finding ways to reduce the intensity of these four fears. The exceptions are the four spiritual acts referenced earlier: meditation,[59] altruism, attention to creativity, and the joy of movement.

Four Basic Loves

You are acutely aware of the four basic fears because you are programmed genetically to avoid pain, maximize protection, stand out, and seek things that bring you pleasure. Yet there is much more to your existence than just fear or anxiety and the pleasure associated with food, sex, power, wealth, fame, and glory. Relationships don't have to be about satisfying your drive for sensual pleasure, forming alliances for protection, or getting your ego stroked. Relationships can also be about love.

A wonderful, mind-expanding experience occurs when you're free of the four basic fears. Without fear, you can experience love and see the beauty in and around you. Love is the absence of fear, and fear

---

[59] The Meditation Society of America distinguishes prayer from meditation by noting that in prayer we ask God for something, but in meditation God speaks to us. However, if our prayers ask God to help reduce pain and suffering in others without any thought to our own needs and desires, then these altruistic prayers are likely meditative as well.

is the absence of love. When unafraid, you sense love and act with a spiritual purpose.

It's easy to sense a basic fear, but it's more difficult to cultivate a relationship with another person or a higher power in a way that extinguishes fear and allows love to guide your actions. In healthy relationships with other adults, you can experience each of the four basic loves, which correspond to the absence of each of the four basic fears. As such, relationships play an important role in your life. However, if you're afraid of not being good enough, you will place expectations on your friends and family that represent the presence of fear, which blocks your ability to sense the presence of love.

A typical expectation might be that during any given time period (such as spring break, for example), your best friend will spend more time with you than with anyone else, or that your friends and family will support your actions even if you violate one of the four bases of the Golden Rule. Your expectations, including the expectation of loyalty, function as blinders. You don't want to know if others disagree with you, because if they do, you might be forced to confront your subconscious thought that you aren't good enough. Thus some people surround themselves with sycophants and take great enjoyment in flattery.

You have a better chance of experiencing love if you believe that no matter what problems you face, you're confident that your life will work out just fine. In other words, you have taken to heart the ideas expressed in this book's introduction that your memories about not being good enough are distortions of reality—distortions created by living within a society that doesn't follow the four bases of the Golden Rule.

The reality is that just by following the Golden Rule, you are good enough to experience a beautiful life. Following the Golden Rule builds pleasant memories that facilitate the growth of confidence and optimism. As you become more confident and optimistic, you will place fewer and fewer expectations on others. Confidence and believing that you are good enough are critical to experiencing love and minimizing the fear behind our expectations.

Examples of the interplay between expectations, fear, and love are discussed in the next chapter. But first "may I introduce to you the act you've known all these years,"[60] the four basic loves —loves you will experience with your friends, family, and acquaintances when you feel confident that you are good enough:

1. Sibling love: feeling protected in the present moment, as a caring sibling protects their brother or sister from being judged harshly by parents or the cultural norms of society. (Counteracts the basic fear of pain in the present moment.)
2. Spousal love: two people putting their collective wisdom and resources together to reduce the severity of problems likely to arise in the future. (Counteracts the basic fear of pain in the future.)
3. Friendship love: friends letting each other know that their feelings and thoughts are reasonable and understandable. (Counteracts the basic fear of not feeling understood.)
4. Romantic love: thinking and feeling that one's life is exciting, meaningful, and pleasurable, including the thrill of a romantic relationship. (Counteracts the basic fear of boredom or loneliness.)

---

[60] "May I introduce to you the act you've known all these years." Credit the Beatles, the Fab Four, with letting all four basic loves guide their artistry when they introduced us to their groundbreaking album *Sgt. Pepper's Lonely Hearts Club Band*, named the Greatest Rock Album of All Time by *Rolling Stone* in 2003.

Most of us are also familiar with two other kinds of love, a parent's love for their child and a child's love for their parent. However, the love between parents and children involves maturational issues with dynamics that are unhealthy in most adult-to-adult relationships. Finally, there might perhaps be a seventh love that is beyond our full comprehension—the love that connects us with a higher spiritual power.

For love to shine, you need to free yourself of fears and associated judgmental attitudes. The four spiritual acts will greatly assist you in this endeavor. Of the four, the spiritual act of altruism probably requires the most effort because it involves consciously focusing on solving problems and sometimes setting limits. By definition, altruism doesn't include the hope or expectation of a reward, but actually the rewards for altruism are great because it allows you to experience the four basic loves in your relationships with others.

Second commandment: "Thou shalt not take the name of the Lord thy God in vain." Taking the Lord's name in vain literally represents anger, which desensitizes you to your own feelings and the feelings of others. Taking God's name in vain also represents symbolically a lack of focus or discipline. Without discipline, it is easy to get distracted or trapped by fantasies and the allure of materialistic fortune, and therefore it becomes easy to worship the manmade gods of wealth, fame, and privilege.

3

Binah—Contemplation

Feelings of pain or pleasure or some quality in between are the bedrock of our minds. We often fail to notice this simple reality because the mental images of the objects and events that surround us, along with the images of the words and sentences that describe them, use up so much of our overburdened attention.

—Antonio Demasio, *Looking for Spinoza* (2003)

Live in each season as it passes, breathe the air, drink the drink, taste the fruit, and resign yourself to the influences of each ... Some men think that they are not well in spring, or summer, or autumn, or winter; it is only because they are not *well in* them.

—Henry David Thoreau (1817–62)

The third Sefirah, Binah, meaning contemplation or understanding, is Hokhmah's (Wisdom's) mate. She is the womb that receives the divine seed of Hokhmah and gives birth to the lower seven Sefirot. Hokhmah lights up Binah's palace, making it visible and stimulating our intellect; Binah, in turn, reflects Hokhmah's light, which would otherwise be too concentrated to be seen. Binah's letter is *heh*.[61]

With contemplation, when trying to understand how one idea connects to another, a positively amazing story with the number 4 began to unfold. As I conceptualized how past actions and events affect our present state of mind, four main concepts emerged in the province of goodness (four bases of the Golden Rule) and spirituality (four spiritual acts). Then the four basic fears and corresponding four basic loves emerged.

As I look back, it's clear that the number 4 has been there all along with a message. At age ten I was handed the number 4 on my Little League uniform (10-4, message received). The message was right on my uniform: Dodgers. My team was the Dodgers. With that number 4 on my jersey and later the number 4 in the draft, I became a "dodger" of the Vietnam War. Then the evangelists who brought Jesus into my life found me in room 4 on the first floor (104), which led me to the life of Jesus (10-4, message received). Then on July 1, 1970, as I listened to 1010 WINS all-news radio on my way home from my summer job, the first ten lottery numbers in the military draft were announced. My birthday—July 29, 1951—was number 4 (10-4, messaged received): keep that student deferment and get an education. Then on Thursday, February 3, 1972, I met girlfriend number 4, Elizabeth, my first real love. On April 17, 1972—that fateful "Monday, Monday,"[62]—just ten weeks and four days later, she said, "My feelings for you have changed," and my heart broke (10-4, message received): "Above all else, guard your heart, for it is

---

[61] Arthur Goldwag, *The Beliefnet Guide to Kabbalah* (Three Leaves Press, 2005).
[62] "Monday, Monday," the only number 1 hit song by the Mamas and the Papas, was released in March 1966.

the wellspring of life" (Proverbs 4:23, NIV[63]). That's four messages received!

Then I discovered that multiples of 4 can create the date July 4, 1776. And with this date comes our Declaration of Independence, which stands as a beacon of hope for all humankind with its pronouncement that "All men are created equal."

$$4 \times 4 \times 44 = 0704 \text{ (July 4)}$$
$$4 \times 444 = 1776$$

It's a date that immigrants (including my four grandparents from Eastern Europe) would come to celebrate on a continent where the native inhabitants already revered the number 4. Even before Columbus's discovery of the New World, Native Americans had revealed mystical properties of the number 4 associated with the four seasons, the four winds or directions, the four sacred mountains,[64] the four phases of life (childhood, youth, adulthood, and old age), and other divisions of four that appear in Indian art, myth, and rituals.

The words "All men are created equal" require us to go beyond simply *thinking* of each other as equals and actually *treat* each other as equals. If you and I are equal, then you should be treated the same way that I would want to be treated. "All men are created equal" is a paraphrase of the Golden Rule, which has been passed down since biblical times and appears in each of the four gospels: "Do to others what you would have them do to you" (Matthew 7:12 and Luke 6:31

---

[63] New International Version (1984)

[64] Mount Blanca in Colorado to the east, Mount Taylor in New Mexico to the south, San Francisco Peak in Arizona to the west, Mount Hesperus in Colorado to the north. Interestingly, these four mountains appear in the vicinity of the Four Corners, the only spot on the map where four states (Arizona, Utah, Colorado, and New Mexico) intersect to form a single point.

NIV), "Love your neighbor as yourself" (Mark 12:31 NIV), and "A new command I give you: Love one another. As I have loved you, so you must love one another" (John 13:34 NIV).

Knowing the Golden Rule, however, does not necessarily mean that you're going to abide by it. Have you ever wondered why our world is still filled with war, crime, corruption, pollution, and the incessant spinning of the news? Rules and guidelines were delivered to us through the lives of Moses, the Buddha, Jesus, and Muhammad, but making the world a better place obviously isn't simple or easy. During four billion years of evolution, competing rules have arisen, most notably Darwin's theory of natural selection or "survival of the fittest." These instinctual drives, which are fed by a desire for selfish gain and rarely concern themselves with kindness and spirituality, corrupt the message delivered to us by the four heavy hitters of history.

In their wisdom, our forefathers (four fathers) knew that it was one thing to write down beautiful ideas in a declaration or to familiarize themselves with passages from the Bible, but that it was quite another thing to codify the principle of equality into our system of justice. So how did the Founding Fathers of the Constitution of the United States deal with the reality that people in positions of power and authority often take advantage of others with laws that favor the rich and by limiting freedoms (such as free speech, religion, unreasonable search and seizure, and the right to assembly) should the users of these freedoms not openly support the authority's plans and programs?

Enter the number 4 again. Our fourth president, James Madison, safeguarded freedom and equality by making sure that the Bill of Rights, the first ten amendments to United States Constitution, became the law of the land. The Bill of Rights, in its essence, stipulated that those in positions of power or authority are to treat others the way they would want to be treated should they no longer be the ones in positions of power or authority. Only when these safeguards were put in place would the fifty-five white men representing the thirteen colonies at the Constitutional Convention ratify the Constitution of the United States.

Sadly, not all men and women were treated equally by the newly formed government. Native Americans were forced onto reservations, women were shut out of the electoral process, and most egregious of all, black men and women were enslaved and held in chains. Without true equality, as exemplified in the Golden Rule, we remained mired in a system that condoned cruelty that is until the number 4 squared up (4 squared = 16) and said "No!" to slavery.

Abraham Lincoln, our sixteenth president, stepped up to the plate and knocked slavery out of the ballpark. As he asserted in an 1859 letter to Congressman Henry L. Pierce from Massachusetts, "He, who would be no slave, must consent to have no slave."[65] Lincoln did more than any other president to promote the Golden Rule and work to make it the law of the land. With his Emancipation Proclamation and the Thirteenth Amendment to the Constitution, slavery ended once and for all. In his Gettysburg Address in 1863, Lincoln said, "Four score and seven years ago our fathers brought forth on this continent, a new nation, conceived in liberty, and dedicated to the proposition that all men are created equal … and that government of the people, by the people, for the people, shall not perish from the earth."

At that time, however, "the people" excluded women. To address that disparity, Elizabeth Cady Stanton, at only thirty-two years

---

[65] www.abrahamlincolnonline.org/lincoln/speeches/pierce.htm

old, organized the Seneca Falls Conference in 1848[66] where she put forward the Declaration of Sentiments and Resolutions, modeled after the 1776 Declaration of Independence, to address women's rights and freedoms. Sadly, rather than enduring "four score and seven" years without the right to vote, women had to wait seven score and four. The Nineteenth Amendment, which granted women the right to vote, wasn't ratified until 1920, 144 years after the Declaration of Independence. It wasn't until 1924 that Calvin Coolidge, the only president born on July 4, signed the Indian Citizenship Act granting full citizenship to Native Americans.

After Lincoln's presidency and fourteen presidents later with Calvin Coolidge's term in office (1923–29), major disparities continued to exist with an ever-widening economic gap between the privileged few and the men and women laboring in the fields. After Coolidge, as Herbert Hoover's administration presided over the aftermath of the 1929 stock market crash, things looked really bleak that is until the number 4 showed up again and "doubled down" on Franklin Delano Roosevelt.

Lincoln was the sixteenth president, and sixteen doubled brings us to the thirty-second president, Franklin Delano Roosevelt, the only president elected four times. FDR realized that the struggle for civil rights and equality did not end with Lincoln's proclamations and subsequent legislation. With his New Deal, FDR possibly did more than any other president to broadly share the opportunities that America had to offer. Sharing opportunity is a basic requirement of equality. Furthermore, faced with the Great Depression and the threat of a world war, FDR inspired us with his State of the Union

---

[66] Little did the sixty-eight women and thirty-two men who signed the Declaration of Sentiments and Resolutions at the Seneca Falls Conference know that 1848 would represent only the halfway point in the struggle of American woman to obtain the right to vote, an event that occurred finally in 1920. 1776 + 72 = 1848 + 72 = 1920.

speech known as the Four Freedoms.[67] In Roosevelt's eyes, freedom of speech and expression, freedom of worship, freedom from want, and freedom from fear are the basis for defending Americans and all others who respect these four freedoms here, there, and everywhere.

During World War II, the military remained segregated, Americans of Japanese descent were forcibly relocated and incarcerated, and racism was alive and well. So FDR's New Deal hadn't achieved equality and civil rights for all Americans, but progress was definitely made. In 1947, on a field with four bases, Jackie Robinson, number 42, broke baseball's color barrier. (Lincoln's last breath and Robinson's first major-league at bat both occurred on April 15.[68]) The following year, President Truman began the process of desegregating the armed forces.

As we know, the struggle for civil rights didn't end with Jackie Robinson or desegregation of the armed forces. In the 1950s and '60s, civil rights were championed by perhaps the most significant American of the twentieth century, Martin Luther King Jr., who, like Lincoln, died tragically from an assassin's bullet, on April 4, 1968. Shortly before his death, King said, "But I want you to know tonight, that we, as a people, will get to the Promised Land." I cannot help but think that the Reverend King's dream was becoming a reality when we elected the forty-fourth president, Barack Obama. Coincidentally, the first president, George Washington, was forty-four years old when the signers of our Declaration of Independence

---

[67] State of the Union address (January 6, 1941).

[68] With a little imagination, Lincoln's 16 expressed as 4^2 looks like a three-dimensional 42, the number Jackie Robinson wore for the Brooklyn Dodgers. Robinson's number 42 was retired by the entire league. No major-league baseball player will wear the number 42 again except on Jackie Robinson Day, April 15, when all players from every team wear the number 42. Now, that's a statement about equality and April 15, for which Abraham Lincoln shall not have died in vain.

proclaimed, "We hold these truths to be self-evident, that all men are created equal." Can you hear Martin Luther King Jr.'s voice reciting those same words during his "I have a dream" speech?

King's assassination on April 4 (4/4), 1968, was a wake-up call to the horrors incited by prejudice. As baby boomers, many of us were already aware of the contradictions inherent in racism, McCarthyism, and the Vietnam War, for a country founded on the principles of freedom and equality. Every morning, we woke to social commentary playing in 4/4 time on our clock radios—Peter, Paul, and Mary's cover of "Blowin' in the Wind"; the Rolling Stones singing "I Can't Get No Satisfaction" and "Paint It Black"; Janis Ian's "Society's Child"; Barry McGuire's "Eve of Destruction"; Simon and Garfunkel's "Sounds of Silence"; as well as many others. Our music inspired us to contemplate and change our values.

Fear, Love, and Spirituality

When you "contemplate" why you value some things, including loved ones, more than other things, you gain "understanding" or *Binah*. With contemplation you begin to understand why you might dress differently, act differently, relate differently, and perhaps even think differently from others because you understand that people have different wants, tastes, desires, and values—"different strokes for different folks," according to Sly and the Family Stone's song "Everyday People"[69] (1968). This understanding can give you the wisdom, or *Hokhmah*, to contemplate even further why these differences are the way they are.

With further contemplation and understanding, you can gain the wisdom that you are not nearly as different as you once thought.

---

[69] *Rolling Stone* ranked "Everyday People" at number 145 on their list of the 500 Greatest Songs of All Time.

With each round of contemplation, differences between us become smaller and smaller. Eventually, you realize that the same four fears, four loves, and four spiritual acts operate in all of us and create the condition we call humanity, both individually and collectively.

Four Basic Fears	Four Basic Loves	Four Spiritual Acts
pain and death now	sibling love	meditation
pain and death in future	spousal love	altruism
lack of validation	friendship love	attention to creativity
lack of pleasure	romantic love	joy of movement

Expectations at the Workplace

Individually and collectively, we work to provide basic necessities for ourselves, our families, and our communities. We also accept the unpleasantness sometimes associated with work because the alternative—being without work—is worse. We all have certain expectations about our jobs, such as the expectation that we will be compensated, and our work responsibilities are often articulated as a list of expectations. Our respect for coworkers is often conditional, based on whether they are meeting our expectation that they make a good effort to keep the company up and running.

In the workplace, it's relatively easy to see the relationship between our expectations and the second basic fear, the anticipation of unpleasant feelings or painful conditions in the future. After all, if we don't work, we won't have money for food, rent, or medical care. But what about our expectations for our families, friends, and romantic partners? With some additional contemplation or introspection, it's easy to see that, just like in the workplace, those expectations are based on our efforts to minimize one or more basic fears. We anticipate that our lives won't turn out well unless our expectations are met.

Spousal Love, Earning Money, and Future-Oriented Fears

One of the paradoxes in life is that our most intense expectations often involve our spouses, the people to whom we have pledged unconditional love. The reason for this intensity is that our relationships with our spouses touch on all four basic fears and corresponding four basic loves. This sets up some interesting dynamics, particularly when our conscious or subconscious thoughts tend to gravitate toward one particular fear.

Suppose Jill is highly educated and has had good paying jobs. But let's say that Jill felt very anxious around her colleagues in the workplace. In short, Jill would prefer to stay at home because too often she found work anxiety provoking and that working with others often led to frustration.

Should we find work very unpleasant or have doubts about our ability to earn a living, wouldn't it be nice if we had a spouse who could be the breadwinner? If we preferred that our spouse be the sole breadwinner, wouldn't we want him or her to strive for as much job security as possible? If this was the situation, wouldn't Jill get quite upset should her spouse say that he or she is thinking of leaving their job and trying something new? Under these circumstances, Jill might even accuse her spouse of not loving her. Even if Jill's spouse loved her completely in all four ways, she would feel very little love when her expectations went unmet. The expectation that interferes with Jill's ability to sense the love from her spouse relates to the second basic fear: the anticipation of death, pain, or unpleasant feelings in the future when we think that we could lack the means to provide for basic needs.

Jill feels insecure about earning a living, and insecurity often prevents us from feeling or expressing love in our relationships with others. At any moment, Jill's spouse might have been directing the other three basic loves her way, but her insecurity about spousal love keeps her focused on the disappointment of her unmet expectation.

Wouldn't we prefer that our relationships with friends and family are based on love rather than suffer the fear that lies behind our expectations? Why would we maintain a relationship with a loved one, other than a child, that is based on expectations and the underlying fear? Because we lack confidence!

Expectations and Emotional Black Holes

When we experience low self-esteem and a lack of confidence, we need to be reassured that other people love and value us, so we set up tests to determine if our expectations are being met. If they are, we get the reassurance that we were looking for. For Jill, this test is whether her spouse strives for job security. Unfortunately, under these circumstances, our relationships are focused on the fear behind our expectations rather than on our love for each other. That fear can be so intense that it draws away all the love, creating an emotional black hole. All the life-giving, healing, soothing, and creative properties that emanate from a loving relationship get sucked into this black hole as long as we stubbornly hold on to our expectations.

When we love someone, thoughts like the following aren't helpful: if she truly loves me, she'll answer my letters quickly, or call me often while we're apart, or take me wherever she goes, or not be physically attracted[70] to other people, or take care of the kids while I work to support our family, or …

---

[70] Physical attraction is quite natural and at the whim of our subconscious mind. What is wrong is being untruthful or sneaky about explaining, planning, or having a sexual relationship.

We shouldn't be insensitive to other people's expectations, because everyone has neurotic tendencies that get transformed into expectations. If it's relatively easy to accommodate an expectation, such as practicing good table manners or calling home to check in, then do so. But expectations interfere with love when they carry intense emotions that correlate to memories filed under the category of "not good enough." The real issues arise when expectations aren't being met and couples aren't willing to get to the truth of matter, which usually is that one or both parties lack self-confidence.

Influence and Emotional Black Holes

One of the most subtle but common tests associated with emotional black holes is the test of whether we have influence over others. Offering advice is fine, but it's another thing to expect other people to follow our advice as a way of confirming that we are valued. Ideally, we already know that we have value simply by being human.

Sometimes people can wield their power and get us to succumb to their wishes because we fear what might happen if they became displeased. A mild example of this manipulative abuse of power might be, "If I don't do what my spouse expects of me, I'll be nagged to death." A more serious form of manipulation can occur when we link our self-esteem to our careers, as many people do. If we empower people who are in positions to advance our careers, then we'll feel pressure to please them. Unfortunately, people with influence and power are not necessarily practitioners of the Golden Rule. Harvey Weinstein, the movie producer accused of sexual misconduct by dozens of women,[71] is a prime example of a highly influential person who repeatedly violated the first base of the Golden Rule through his lack of sensitivity to how his actions affected the feelings of others.

---

[71] http://www.newsweek.com/harvey-weinstein-accusers-sexual-assault-harassment-696485. https://www.inaugural.senate.gov.

Powerful people also can influence us with their passion for good. For example, when John F. Kennedy was inaugurated as our thirty-fifth president in 1961, he spoke these inspiring words to the nation: "Ask not what your country can do for you; ask what you can do for your country."[72] Like the image of Kennedy often remembered, and unlike the one Harvey Weinstein most recently portrayed, people in positions of power and authority can inspire us just by modeling the four bases of the Golden Rule.

If we use fear, rather than compassion or kindness, to influence others, then we'll probably violate the first and fourth bases of the Golden Rule. In the 1950s, Senator Joseph McCarthy influenced other people to be judgmental (fourth base: don't judge others) by branding anyone who favored strong workers' unions and related causes as a communist and, as such, an enemy. He had people blacklisted from working in government, the movie and television industries, and at colleges and universities. McCarthy was insensitive (first base: be aware and sensitive) to how his actions affected the feelings of people who were blacklisted. As long as people would follow his directives, McCarthy could think that he was valued and his life had a purpose.

Unfortunately, the more judgmental, insensitive, and unkind we are, the more we worry subconsciously that what goes around comes around. "At whatever point you judge another, you are condemning yourself, because you who pass judgment do the same things" (Romans 2:1 NIV). Rather than becoming less judgmental, many of us will focus on proving to the world that we are worthier than those condemned by our judgments.

In McCarthy's case, he tried to prove—to himself and others—that he was also worthier than those who didn't despise the people

---

[72]. https://www.inaugural.senate.gov. Delivered on January 20th, 1961 at the 44th Presidential Inauguration, Kennedy's speech has become to be known as one the greatest inauguration speeches in U.S. history.

labeled as communists, and thus that he deserved to be spared the troubles that he thought should come to those whom he deemed to be un-American. When we violate the Golden Rule, we often try to project an unselfish image for others to see. I can easily imagine McCarthy trying to make the case that everything he was doing was for the good of the country, and how unselfish is that! It's like the organized crime boss who attends church and hands out free turkeys on Thanksgiving Day.

When we act selfishly, we also try to use whatever influence and power we have to prevent what goes around from coming around. Alternatively, a selfish person who lacks power or influence might try to seclude themselves in their own little fortress where they can believe they're in total control. But selfish, unkind people have no peace of mind or contentment, even in their private fortresses. There will always be one more fence or wall needing fortification.

For the rest of us who don't live in private fortresses, our selfish behaviors will lead to a whole slew of other demands. The more often we violate the Golden Rule, the greater the pressure we put on ourselves to acquire the things or status our culture values. The more selfish we are, the more difficult it becomes to think that other people will value us unless we are rich, smart, attractive, religious, influential, talented, or a member or supporter of an esteemed group such as the armed services.

The more selfish we are, the more our sense of self-worth depends on attaching ourselves to the things that we think other people value. It's difficult for selfish people to believe that simply because we are human, we are good enough and deserve a beautiful life, without having to prove anything to anyone. When we're selfish, it is hard to realize that to experience the beautiful life we already deserve, all we need to do is follow the Golden Rule.

Joshua Simon, MD, EdD

Expectations and Making Changes

How do you make changes if you've been acting selfishly? How do you stop focusing on trying to create an image that's pleasing to others? How do you stop expecting others to support your attempts at enhancing your image? How can you think outside the box, outside the pecking-order mentality that's ingrained in you from four billion years of evolution? Changes begin with insight. Selfishness and most of the expectations you have of others are based on the four basic fears, which foster doubts about your self-worth and whether the basic survival needs of your family will be met.

When we replace honesty in our relationships with tests, conditions, and expectations, it's because of our insecurities. When we're insecure and lack confidence, we doubt our ability to feel safe, earn enough money, be seen as attractive, be understood by others, and achieve purpose and meaning in our lives. This doubt and insecurity often translates into feelings of low self-esteem.

In addition to expecting honesty, we should expect cooperation and commitment in a relationship when children are involved or vows have been exchanged. It is reasonable to expect couples to cooperate with each other, share, and commit to making changes together—to feel safer, earn enough money, be attractive to each other, communicate better, and help bring a sense of purpose and meaning to each other's lives. If difficulties arise in the relationship and the available avenues for change bring no relief, then a separation is likely in order.

The one change that will do the most for improving any relationship is improving your self-esteem, which is predominantly an individual effort. Your partner can help, but only to a small extent. Your ability to improve your self-esteem depends on the degree to which you practice the four bases of the Golden Rule and participate in the four spiritual acts, which together make up the four-by-four pursuit of happiness.

By practicing the four-by-four pursuit of happiness, you strengthen your faith—or for people without faith, you strengthen your optimism. You become more hopeful as you see that your life has a way of working out despite your current circumstances. You also realize that whatever is keeping you from feeling perfectly wonderful right now will continue to do so, no matter what goals you achieve, wealth you obtain, or relationships you forge. By practicing the four-by-four pursuit of happiness, you learn that you already possess the greatest miracle of all, life itself. As you develop a deep appreciation of life, with all its beauty, fragility, and mysteries, you realize that you don't need to obtain or prove anything to enjoy the thoughts and feelings generated by this appreciation.

Difficult Times

It's helpful to think of difficult days as inclement weather. The sun will shine again, your emotions will rebound, and your physical pain will subside. As the title track to George Harrison's 1970 triple album says, "All Things Must Pass." With a little effort and insight, you already have everything you need to feel perfectly wonderful right now. You have the four-by-four pursuit of happiness, which strengthens nerve pathways that reduce physical and emotional pain. A bit of disappointment or frustration isn't the end of the world. However, if you aren't practicing kindness and spirituality, it's more likely that disappointment and frustration will linger and contribute not only to low self-esteem but also to muscle tension, headaches, bowel irritability, and other physical discomforts and dysfunctions.

Unless you practice the four-by-four pursuit of happiness, disappointment will have a lasting effect no matter how much influence you have, what you accomplish, or how much wealth and prestige you accumulate. Furthermore, you'll continue to place expectations on others and desperately need them to validate your self-worth. These needs and expectations are a direct consequence of not yet realizing that just by practicing the Golden Rule, you can acquire all the validation you need and enjoy a beautiful life.

These realizations about the key to happiness take time and maturity. It's perfectly normal for children to experience disappointments that negatively affect their self-esteem. A child's sense of safety depends on parental provisions and supervision, as well as on the approval of others. In a sense, we all start out with low self-esteem, but if your self-esteem remains stunted as you age, you'll continue to think and act like a child in your adult years. You will measure yourself with a distorted yardstick and grow up lacking confidence and continue to think that you aren't good enough.

Paradoxically, some people with low self-esteem communicate nothing but confidence, even though actually they're terrified. In psychology this is known as a reaction formation, a way of hiding your true feelings by acting in the exact opposite way. Treating someone you strongly dislike in an overly friendly manner is another example of a reaction formation.

So how can you transform from the prototypical needy, dependent child into an adult with confidence and with a slew of memories that feel good? To begin with, it's important to understand that confidence and pleasant memories relate only in a minor way to physical attributes, wealth, accomplishments or talents. Instead, they relate in a major way to your ability to recognize that you are capable right now of following the Golden Rule and that you were always able to create beautiful memories in this way despite the circumstances you were born into and despite the circumstances you helped create because of your previous lack of insight.

A Life in Memories

Everything in your life is a memory except for this instantaneous passing moment occurring right now. As such, a beautiful life means beautiful memories. As I explained earlier, only two things create memories that aren't beautiful: times when you doubt whether you are good enough, and times when you act selfishly. Procrastination extends and amplifies memories that aren't beautiful. When you spend time on activities that distract you from unpleasant thoughts or memories, you are reinforcing subconsciously your thoughts about not being good enough—good enough to take care of things you need to take care of. Procrastination is a serious problem, similar to using alcohol or other substances as an escape or distraction.

Procrastination Addiction

The American Society of Addiction Medicine, in its policy statement from April 12, 2011, says the following:

> Addiction is a primary, chronic disease of brain reward, motivation, memory and related circuitry. Dysfunction in these circuits leads to characteristic biological, psychological, social and spiritual manifestations. This is reflected in an individual pathologically pursuing reward and/or relief by substance use and other behaviors.[73]

It's easy to see how procrastination and substance use share similar motivations and have similar effects on how a person functions.

---

[73] www.asam.org/advocacy/find-a-policy-statement

Joshua Simon, MD, EdD

Procrastination addiction is a primary brain disease characterized by seeking distractions or practicing avoidance behavior despite harmful consequences, which include the following:

1. Accelerated decline of health caused by lack of exercise, poor posture and limited range of motion, poor nutritional habits, immoderate substance use, and avoidance of needed medical or psychological attention
2. Misplaced documents; missed deadlines; poor planning and time management leading to insufficient time for work, travel, education, recreation, and spiritual activities; cluttered home and yard; and missing routine maintenance or early repairs for home, car, and other equipment
3. Avoidance of social interactions, resulting in limited social support networks
4. Poor care given to dependents and pets
5. Uninformed political decisions at election time, which could contribute to public policies that procrastinate on issues affecting the climate, survival of plant and animal species, clean water, clean air, fertile soil, infrastructure, overpopulation, and social fairness and equality

When you procrastinate, it is likely that your subconscious is dwelling on memories about disappointments, not being good enough, and your own selfish acts at a time when you thought you knew better. Guess what? You're human. You didn't get to choose your life-form. We're all stuck in a condition known as Homo sapiens, and for most of us, we have a subspecies classification as well—Homo sapiens procrastiens.

To overcome the condition of Homo sapiens procrastiens, it's best to maintain your awareness of all the frailties you possess in this life-form. Then when unhappy memories surface, rather than escaping them by procrastinating, you can remind yourself that they are memories from a time when you incorrectly thought that you weren't good enough. Furthermore, because you thought that you weren't good enough, you distorted reality. If you had had a more accurate picture of reality and known that you were already good enough, then your memories of past disappointments would not feel nearly so unpleasant.

The good news is that you can break the old pattern of how you interpret your past. You can reshape your memories with the knowledge that you were good enough all along and that your unhappy memories aren't really unhappy at all. They were simply learning experiences from a time when you felt insecure and thought that you needed to obtain or demonstrate something of value. You may also have acted selfishly (or encountered someone who acted selfishly) because you (or they) hadn't yet incorporated the wisdom of the Golden Rule into your (or their) daily life. Can you forgive yourself and others for not knowing everything you or they needed to know when you were younger?

You don't need to start your day by thinking about all the ways you find pleasure and the activities in which you typically engage because they distract you from unpleasant memories. You don't need to turn on the TV, shop for more flattering clothing, or prepare for the barbecue, beer, and football game. You developed the habit of procrastination innocently enough, but it resulted from thinking incorrectly that you weren't good enough.

You are not stuck in your old ways. You can transform yourself from the very needy state of childhood to a state of healthy self-esteem—a place where you no longer need to rely on the approval of others to feel good about yourself. In this transformed state you will also know, as previously stated, that your life will work out perfectly fine regardless of the circumstances you were born into and regardless of the circumstances you helped create out of your previous lack of maturity and ignorance.

My contention is that it is difficult to make this transformation unless you find a meaningful life by tapping into the spiritual side of the human condition. Without involvement in one or more of the four spiritual acts and without practicing the four bases of the Golden Rule, you'll continue to seek external validation, set up expectations and tests in your relationships, and procrastinate.

Elizabeth

When Elizabeth married in 1979, communication between us had already stopped. Fourteen years later, I found out that we lived in the same state, more than a thousand miles from Long Island where our two families lived. I was then forty-two, and she was forty-one. We arranged to meet for dinner, where we reminisced about the people we had known and the things we had done together. When I returned alone to my hotel room, my feelings of rejection were just as intense as they had been when I was twenty years old. It was as if my self-esteem was zero. Yet I held two doctoral degrees, had recently won highly competitive awards from the American Psychiatric Association and the American College of Psychiatrists, and had just been appointed to the board of governors of my state's medical association. I was well on my way to financial stability and was married to an attractive, intelligent, and soulful woman with whom I had two beautiful kids. So why was I so distraught? Incidentally, from the time I scheduled the dinner with Elizabeth to the time we met five weeks later, I exercised and dieted furiously to get into shape. I wanted Elizabeth to desire me as much as I remembered desiring her.

As I discovered, the transformation from needy child to confident adult whose self-esteem is free of doubt has little to do with accomplishments, formal education, IQ, wealth, or physical attractiveness. Instead, it's about realizing that there's a loving force in the universe and that just by being human, you—and everyone else—are already good enough. Unfortunately, we are exposed to many judgments that purport just the opposite and imply that some people are better or more deserving than others.

Self-Discipline

It takes insight and self-discipline to override the natural inclination to think that you aren't worthy unless you accomplish something or possess attributes (skin color, physical attractiveness, creative talent, athletic prowess, ability to influence others, wealth, and so on) that your culture values. The development of this self-discipline might require training that used to be under the guidance of formal religion. Examples include meditation as practiced by Buddhist and Christian monks; yoga as practiced by Hindus, Buddhists, and Jains; the Native American and Gregorian practice of chanting; Jews studying the Mishnah, Talmud, and Torah to learn the 613 *mitzvahs* or good deeds; Muslims praying five times daily to delight in Allah's compassion for all of humanity; and Christians through Bible studies realizing that no one is undeserving of your kindness. These kinds of training allow us to override strong impulses to think in instinctual ways and instead allow us to think in spiritual ways.

Your spirituality will be enhanced by the self-discipline it takes to act with moderation and to follow appropriate nutritional and physical exercise guidelines to improve your general well-being and health. A sound mind and sound body reduce the burden of everyday emotional and physical aches and pains. With a lighter burden, your mind can more readily focus on being of service to others. You can also more easily focus on the existence of a loving force that favors no one and everyone. Furthermore, when you sense the existence of a loving force, your burdens will seem smaller and easier to live with.

It takes self-discipline to avoid the traps set by the seven deadly sins: pride, covetousness, lust, anger, gluttony, envy, and sloth. Perhaps my number 4 Dodgers Little League uniform symbolizes the need to be dodgers of the multitude of temptations by which we can distract ourselves as listed below. Distractions have little to do with the four-by-four pursuit of happiness and a lot to do with procrastination.

Sixteen Common Distractions

1. Drugs
2. Alcohol
3. Food
4. Promiscuity
5. Attention-seeking behavior
6. Gossip
7. Idle chitchat
8. Hanging out with the crowd
9. Changing jobs or settings frequently
10. Risk-taking adventures
11. Mindless entertainment
12. Fantasy
13. Shopping
14. Games and gambling
15. Sporting events
16. Fashion

It is easy to find distractions and procrastinate. It is easy to expect others to do for you what, with a little effort and resolve, you could do for yourself. Having others stroke your ego, hiring servants, and acquiring access to luxuries are not the best ways to create meaning in your life. Through self-discipline, by avoiding the distractions listed above, you can find meaning in your life in a way that isn't dependent on what other people are thinking or doing. Through self-discipline you find meaning and value in all of God's creations.

A simple way to assess your self-discipline is to evaluate your tendency to procrastinate. As self-discipline increases, procrastination decreases, and vice versa. Minimizing your tendency to procrastinate is difficult because the things you do while procrastinating bring you comfort. However, if you can be mindful and remind yourself of the things that really matter, then the things that really need to get done will bring you joy from the moment you decide to "get 'er done." Remind yourself over and over again "I am already good enough to get done whatever it is that needs to get done!"

Four Techniques to Minimize Your Tendency to Procrastinate

1. Remind yourself that there's no need to distract yourself from thinking that you aren't good enough; you are and always have been good enough to create beautiful memories. Then write down the habits, such as watching TV or playing video games, that you once used to distract yourself, and rehearse mentally how you'll avoid those habits from now on.

2. Muhammad asks us to pray five times a day. Have a picture or image of the things and ideals that you truly value, and think about this picture several times a day. At the same time, remind yourself that you are good enough right now to get done whatever it is that needs to get done.

3. Make a list of the tasks that you tend to put off. Pick just one task to focus on today. Integrate the results of completing this task into your picture or image of the things and ideals that you value. Remind yourself why this task is important. Some tasks might be ongoing activities of daily life that are never completed, such as paperwork, housework, or exercise and diet.

4. Using a small pad or your cell phone, keep a rough log of how you spend your time, what you eat, and your physical exercise. Make note of things that interrupt your focus on primary tasks or keep you from spending time with loved ones. Remind yourself that you don't have to be perfect and that it's okay to have gaps in the log, perhaps for several days or even months. Just don't stop keeping the log, because keeping track of these things helps build your self-awareness.

When you maintain awareness of how things that are meaningful to you relate to how you actually spend your time, it becomes easier to stay on task. In our formative years, many of us spent our time doing what we thought others expected of us, without giving much thought to what was truly meaningful to us. Without a meaningful life (fourth basic fear) activities that are exciting and pleasurable take on added importance and can easily become excessive.

Repetitive activities, such as daily chores at home and work, are typically unexciting and not pleasurable. Most of us would rather be socializing, playing games, watching TV, or doing something to garner the attention of others. We'd rather spend our time mastering skills that might set us apart from others in a desirable way. We want to be validated, so we like activities, such as social media, that bring us in contact with others who can let us know whether we come across as reasonable or worthy. Such activities seem far more meaningful to us than chores. However, almost everything we do has meaning, even the chores of everyday life.

The more often you participate in the four spiritual acts, the easier it becomes to find meaning in everyday activities at work and home. The more you practice the four bases of the Golden Rule, the easier it becomes to know that you are worthy and need little attention from others to validate your self-worth. By practicing the four-by-four pursuit of happiness, you'll procrastinate less. You'll also spend less time on activities designed to attract attention, whether real (such as newspaper accounts or hits on social media) or fantasized (such as watching your favorite team win).

Whenever you see your favorite team or yourself as a winner at some activity, you can fantasize that you're better than the losers. This fantasy takes you back to the "movin' on up" pecking-order mentality. The fantasy attached to winning is an example of how instinctual drives can derail you from a more spiritual path. It's easy to fantasize.

It's also easy to procrastinate, especially when you associate unpleasant childhood memories, albeit primarily subconscious memories, with current tasks. Maybe you had a mother who, when she checked your schoolwork, focused on your errors rather than on your ideas. Perhaps your father liked to point out your shortfalls on the baseball diamond or basketball court, but showed little interest in your relationships with teammates and other peers.

We try to avoid unpleasant childhood memories by avoiding any activity that might dredge up childhood feelings filed under the category of "not good enough." But with the awareness and knowledge you now possess about how to create a meaningful, joyful life, you can forgive yourself and others for having put too much emphasis on competition, winning, and perfection.

Forgive yourself for not knowing when you were younger that it wasn't a big deal if you lost a competition or made a mistake. Except when you're responsible for your own safety or the safety of other people, it's no big deal if you make a mistake. In Navajo culture, master weavers and pottery makers leave at least one imperfection in their work so that their spirit doesn't get trapped. The imperfection allows the spirit to be free. Feel free to undertake an activity in which making a mistake is more likely than not.

Joshua Simon, MD, EdD

Shallow Relationships: A Necessary Step in Our Transformation

In our formative years, it's easy to harbor doubts about our self-worth. In our attempts to distract ourselves from these unpleasant thoughts, friendships and dating behavior often focus on adventure, fantasy, and romance (fourth basic love and basic fear). I was never in a gang, but I imagine that gang activity also focuses on adventure, fantasy, and romance, which is how it was portrayed in the 1961 movie *West Side Story*. But romance—and its close associates, adventure and fantasy—is only one of the four components of love and probably the most difficult to maintain. The excitement and arousal that come with a new relationship wear off relatively quickly,[74] and new adventures are rare in everyday life. Teenyboppers are typically in and out of love in less than a month, and yet those relatively shallow relationships are important. They help us develop social skills, such as using tact, and we learn that relationships are not just about having fun.

I specifically mention tact because being tactful is another example of the Golden Rule. When you tactfully engage other people, you let them know that their feelings matter to you. You can convey this important message with the words you choose, your facial expression, your tone of voice, and/or your body language. When you're tactful, you spread the word that you are already good enough to deserve and experience a beautiful life without the need to prove anything, as is everyone else. Every time you let someone know that their feelings matter to you, assuming that you're being truthful, you create one more good memory.

Every encounter gives you a chance to improve your social skills and specifically your tactfulness. Similarly, you learn from each of your romantic relationships. Ideally you learn to expect less from others and learn more about how your actions affect the feelings of others. Then,

---

[74] *Habituation* is the psychological term for anything that becomes less arousing with repeated exposure.

if you're lucky, you obtain the wisdom to understand that the only two expectations needed in any relationship are honesty and tactfulness. It is easier to be open, honest, and tactful when you know deep in your heart that you're already good enough and have nothing to prove.

Sadly, many of us have doubts about our self-worth. We look for ways to keep our minds occupied to avoid confronting these doubts. As a consequence, we often find ourselves on the prowl for fun, adventure, or anything that can distract us from our doubts about feeling worthy or good enough. For these reasons, a young person might find joining a gang or religious cult appealing.

When filled with doubt about your self-worth, you seek validation by participating in activities that you see other people doing, such as romantic relationships or social groups. You expect others to validate the importance of your relationships, and you like it when your group achieves special recognition. You look for validation in personal relationships, a church, the military, a political party, a club, or a civic organization. You might even build a relationship with your own vanity when you fish for compliments. When your relationships and activities fail to provide you with the validation you're seeking, you will likely feel lonely or bored. However, if you act with kindness, you'll participate with fewer expectations and needs for validation, and then more intrinsic rewards will arise. Intrinsic rewards combat loneliness and boredom.

By using the four-by-four pursuit of happiness, which is the way to develop your sense of kindness, life becomes more meaningful and purposeful, and less anxiety provoking. You become part of something bigger than yourself, and it's easy to feel connected to the energy that formed the universe. No matter what you do, you don't feel alone. Pick up a book, and you're connected to the mind of the author. A walk in the woods or on a desert trail puts you in touch with the boundless beauty of nature. Learning a new language lets you see the world in more insightful ways. When you free yourself of the need to have others validate you, then your heart can see rightly, everything is connected, and you're never alone.

Fantasy

Yet when you don't see rightly, when you don't know that what is essential is invisible to the eye, it becomes easy to fantasize about a relationship or a time and place, where you are good enough, where you are validated. We heard it in 1962 with Marcie Blaine singing, "I want to be Bobby's girl."[75] How many love songs are built around the theme that, because of the way I feel about you, only I am good enough to deserve your affection and my life is nothing without you?

Fantasy is a quick fix for low self-esteem because it requires no action—just imagination. A timid man imagines a beautiful woman who adores him. A fast-food worker imagines herself performing brain surgery. A shy woman imagines herself as the life of the party. Army recruits imagine themselves and their fellow platoon members as heroes in combat, and so on.

Fantasies typically portrayed in the movies involve lives of excitement, including sexual excitement, or adventures in a land where the hero or heroine occupies an exalted position. (Thank you, Walt Disney.) When these fantasies maintain an adult's attention, it's because the adult doesn't know how to find meaning in everyday life. For children, fantasies serve a different purpose. They allow a child to transition from childhood, a state of dependency, to the reality of having adultlike responsibilities. The prince shows fortitude in his effort to find Cinderella. Simba gains perspective from Nala and Rafiki and matures before challenging his murderous uncle to regain his rightful place in the kingdom.

---

[75] "Bobby's Girl" was written by Gary Klein and Henry Hoffman.

A large part of why we might find a particular person, group of people, or occupation attractive is that they stimulate some kind of fantasy in us. We go to great lengths to attract people whom we find attractive. When this attraction also involves a fantasy, the overwhelming driving force behind the attraction is—drumroll, please—a lack of confidence combined with a lack of meaning in everyday life. These psychological concerns—meaning and self-confidence, or their absence—form the core issues addressed by existential philosophy. How does a person find meaning and feel truly confident? Not through fantasy which often is yet another form of procrastination.

The real work of developing self-confidence and a meaningful life actually materializes from nothingness. It arises from realizations that occupy no space and possess no known physical force, like a psychological Higgs boson. What are the realizations that form self-confidence and a meaningful life? (1) Just by being human, you're already good enough, and there is no-thing to amass and no-thing to prove to know this; and (2) you need to let others know that there is no-thing they need to prove or amass to benefit from your practice of the four bases of the Golden Rule.

If you make a commitment to honesty, and you're willing to get to the bottom of why you think about whatever you think about and why you avoid thinking about whatever you avoid thinking about, then no-thing will materialize from your massless thoughts. You'll find the *Tao*, *Ayin*, and your primordial self. You'll find the four basic loves and corresponding four basic fears.

Jack and Jill Do the Two-Step

Without self-confidence, Jill doubts that her life will work out well. However, if she can attract Jack, whom she finds attractive, then she can believe that "Maybe I'm not as bad off as I think." This attraction stimulates a fantasy about what life would be like if Jack becomes her boyfriend. Ironically, if Jack *does* become and stays attracted to Jill, she could eventually devalue him for being attracted to someone like herself—a flawed individual filled with doubt about her own self-worth. We often interpret doubts about our self-worth in terms of specific flaws—we're not smart or sexy enough, we're too pushy or shy, our breasts are too big or small, and so on.

If Jack has similar self-esteem issues, then a fascinating shift in the relationship is likely to take place. In a new relationship, there's typically one person pursuing (Jill) and a second person being pursued (Jack). The two-step dance of courtship has begun. If Jack begins to show interest in Jill, she'll lose interest in him. After all, he can't be that big of a catch if he's interested in a girl with as many flaws as Jill thinks she possesses. Similarly, Jack thinks that Jill can't be that big of a catch if she's interested in him, a boy with self-esteem issues who wishes that he had the qualities that he sees in other boys. This explains why Jack is somewhat indifferent as Jill pursues him at the start of the relationship.

But when Jill begins to lose interest in him, Jack no longer sees her as a girl flawed by an interest in a flawed boy like himself. This raises Jill's status, and she becomes more desirable to Jack. Their roles are reversed—Jack becomes the pursuer, and Jill is the person being pursued. All during this time, Jack and Jill each have had plenty of thoughts, mostly subconscious thoughts, about how their relationship could affect their status within their family, circle of friends, and community at large. This dynamic between Jack and Jill is illustrated marvelously in *The Two-Step: The Dance Toward Intimacy*, by Eileen McCann.[76]

The relationship of Jack and Jill is fairly typical of teens and even those of us in our twenties and early thirties. But we can reach a point when

---

[76] Grove Press, 1985.

we've had enough of life's hard knocks regarding dating. We think that there must be a better way to achieve validation than by fulfilling a romantic fantasy, and we shift to alternate fantasies involving, for example, power, wealth, and skills that set us apart from others.

What about Rob and Laura, a teenage couple who are relatively well adjusted? They know what it means to love in several different ways. They grew up in families with good parenting and witnessed spousal love, and they've experienced sibling love with their brothers and sisters. Thanks to the good relationships in their homes, they've also built well-grounded peer relationships and experienced friendship love. Just the same, their spiritual lives, as is the case with most teenagers, are still in their infancy. Therefore, Rob and Laura's expectations related to excitement, romance, and finding meaning (fourth basic fear) will stoke the flames of a romantic relationship.

Rob and Laura's expectation of a passionately romantic relationship will be the main attraction. It can be so dominant that it could easily interfere with their ability to sense the other three loves that they each possess. Some teens, such as Rob and Laura, however, will have enough maturity, and a temperament to match, such that they are able to broaden their horizons beyond just a romantic relationship. Under these conditions they are able to sense the other types of love that they each share, but this level of maturity for teenagers is by far the exception. When a greater level of maturity is present, a relationship begun in romance (fourth basic love) will last. Should Rob and Laura sense enough of the other three loves to fill the void created when the newness of the relationship wears off, then they will also likely realize that there is much more to a relationship than the fulfillment of fantasies including the fantasy of "movin' on up" the pecking order.

Feelings of Rejection

Jack keeps pursuing Jill, but she shows less and less interest in him. He finally comes to the conclusion, using his conscious reasoning, that he has been rejected. Another emotional black hole is created when we feel rejected. Fear is the culprit when we experience rejection, much like when our expectations aren't met. If you have ever felt hurt by rejection, it is because at some level you perceived or fantasized that the "rejecting person" had been providing you with basic necessities and/or protection, letting you believe that you are reasonable, and/or creating an atmosphere of excitement or meaning in your life. When rejected we often feel inadequate. If we lose a relationship associated with our fantasies, then we will likely feel, as the Rolling Stones sang out, "Shattered."[77]

Relationship between the Four Basic Fears and Rejection

Basic Fear 1: Fear of pain, discomfort, or death in the present moment. If rejected by someone who is in a position to protect you, you fear being punished, physically hurt, or even banned from your home. You will be more exposed to danger in the present moment if rejected.

Basic Fear 2: Fear of pain, discomfort, or death in the future. If rejected, you might be excluded from ways to earn money or you might lose access to money, basic necessities, or health care. You will be more exposed to danger in the future if rejected.

---

[77] "Shattered," recorded between October and December 1977, appears on the Rolling Stones album *Some Girls* (1978).

Basic Fear 3: Fear that others do not understand how or why you feel and think the way you do. If rejected, you might think that others don't understand you and that your feelings have not been validated. You might feel shame and worthlessness, and that you should be punished.

Basic Fear 4: Fear of boredom and loneliness, or fear of a life without meaning, excitement, pleasure, or adventure. If rejected, you might be excluded from fun, interesting, and exciting activities, including sexual relationships or a relationship that gives you a purpose for your life.

Exercise: Think of a time when you felt rejected. Can you explain how your feelings of rejection were related to doubts about your ability to handle at least one of the four basic fears? Can you see the connection between feelings of rejection and a lack of confidence, feelings of inadequacy, or a fear of not measuring up to other people?

Rejection is often associated with intense, negative, painful emotions. We'll all experience rejection, some of us more often than others. However, you are capable of greatly reducing the pain of rejection if you realize the following: (1) it's perfectly normal to experience intense emotions that don't feel good, and (2) a relationship with a specific person is not necessary for a life of enjoyment and contentment. What is necessary is to feel confident that your life will work out, no matter who enters or leaves it.

It is a lack of confidence or low self-esteem that causes the painful emotions associated with rejection, but we often blame the rejecting person for causing those emotions. Some people get angry after being dumped, whereas others think that if they could only get that person back, they'd feel good again. We don't realize that low self-esteem is the reason we feel bad after a rejection. When our self-esteem is healthy, the end of a relationship between two people isn't seen as rejection. But when we are rejected, it's our lack of confidence or low self-esteem that caused our pain—not the person who has rejected us.

Third commandment: "Remember the Sabbath Day, to keep it holy." Anything that strengthens our ability to follow the Golden Rule is holy or sacred. Anything is holy or sacred if it connects us to a loving force, our Creator, Allah, Jesus, Elohim, and even secular humanism—a loving force that extinguishes our tendency to think and act in instinctual ways. The Sabbath day represents time. Since we are not saints, we will stray from the path of love. We need to take time to reconnect to our noncompetitive, spiritual selves, which makes it easier to have a faith based in the belief that if we treat others with kindness, our basic needs will be met. By remembering the Sabbath, we recognize that spending time reconnecting to our spiritual side will actually make life more enjoyable, and we'll be less distracted by temptations that could interfere with our ability to meet basic day-to-day needs during the rest of the week.

4

Hesed—Love

Do not worry about what others are doing! Each of us should turn the searchlight inward and purify his or her own heart as much as possible.

—Mohandas K. Gandhi (1869–1948)

Oh, God said to Abraham, "Kill me a son." Well, Abe says, "Where do you want this killin' done?" God says, "Out on Highway 61."

—Bob Dylan, "Highway 61 Revisited"

The fourth Sefirah, Hesed, is love, compassion, or grace. It is God's overflowing benevolence and generosity, His mercy and kindness. As the right hand of the primal Adam, Hesed is associated with the south and the biblical patriarch Abraham.[78]

Hesed, the energy of love, compassion, grace, and kindness, is the fourth of ten emanations or energies that, according to kabbalah, were formed and released at the moment of the big bang. How fortunate to this story that the number 4, the number for love, is

---

[78] Arthur Goldwag, *The Beliefnet Guide to Kabbalah* (Three Leaves Press, 2005).

found in the four bases of the Golden Rule, the four spiritual acts, and the four basic loves.

Hesed, whose direction is south, points to April 4, 1968, the day we lost Martin Luther King Jr., a man from the South who led a crusade based in love with the principled doctrine that all men are created equal, a doctrine right out of our Fourth of July Declaration of Independence. Even before 1776, the number 4 played a central role to Native American beliefs whose spirituality cared for America well before the arrival of Columbus. How do we stay in touch with this energy we call *Hesed* or the love and kindness that encourages acts of empathy, compassion, grace, and generosity and guides us to the Promised Land?

Moses brought his people out of slavery to the Promised Land. For slaves and their descendants in America, the Promised Land was and is the land of opportunity, a land where all men and women are created equal and deserve to be treated with love, compassion, grace, and kindness. The understanding that we are all equal opens up God's umbrella of love. Trying to prove that we are superior, on the other hand, closes that umbrella and lets the seven deadly sins beat down upon our minds, bodies, and souls.

My parents, both devout atheists, lived by the belief that all men and women are created equal, so it's reasonable to think that they lived under God's grace without even being aware that such grace existed. I sensed my dad's zeal for equality while he and I were watching the 1958 World Series on our black-and-white TV. When Hank Aaron stepped into the batter's box, my father said, "Now, that's a good ballplayer." It was an "aha" moment for me, and Henry Louis Aaron, a black athlete wearing the number 44, became my boyhood hero. It's also interesting that Aaron tied Babe Ruth's career home run record on April 4, 1974—4/4/74—and then broke that record four days later in the fourth inning of the fourth game of the season.

At the age of ten, I was deeply moved while watching *Pride of the Yankees: The Life of Lou Gehrig*. Lou Gehrig, who wore the number 4, was the first baseball player to have his uniform number retired. Even as a teenager, Gehrig could hit a baseball so far that it earned him a scholarship to Columbia University. After batting .444 during his sophomore year, he was drafted by the Yankees and developed into the greatest first baseman of all time, with a .340 career batting average, fourteen consecutive years played without missing a game, and twenty-three grand-slam home runs.

Gehrig reminds me of Job from the Bible—persevering through hardship, maintaining faith, and never giving up hope. He suffered from amyotrophic lateral sclerosis, a debilitating neurological disease, and died at age thirty-seven. Near the end of *Pride of the Yankees*, Gary Cooper, who played Gehrig, delivers his July 4th farewell address: "People all say that I've had a bad break. But today—today, I consider myself the luckiest man on the face of the earth."[79] During this speech I began crying, which I distinctly remember because it was the first time that anything other than physical pain or discomfort caused me to cry.

Gehrig's story made me acutely aware that life can seem unfair. My dream as a boy was to be a professional baseball player, a dream that was meant to protect me—not expose me to disease and a premature death. What did Lou Gehrig, "the luckiest man on the face of the earth," know that kept him feeling positive despite his tragic circumstances? How did he maintain his empathy, compassion, grace, and generosity in the face of his impending doom?

---

[79] The 1942 movie modified Lou Gehrig's farewell speech. He actually said, "I might have been given a bad break, but I've got an awful lot to live for."

Joshua Simon, MD, EdD

The Binding of Isaac or Ishmael

Moses certainly wanted us to know how to act with empathy, compassion, grace, and generosity. In Genesis 22, we read about God asking Abraham to sacrifice his son Isaac. Because he loved God, Abraham fought through his fears and took steps to comply with God's request. In Muhammad's Quran, Abraham is asked to sacrifice his firstborn son, Ishmael.[80] In both accounts, a literal interpretation is that Abraham's faith was tested by God and that our faith will be tested too. Can we handle the tests we face in life with the love, faith, and kindness that Abraham exemplified?

Abraham's test of faith emphasizes how love and fear are contradictory forces. It's hard to feel love when fearful, but equally hard to be afraid when we sense the presence of love. A philosophical interpretation of the binding of Abraham's son is that love is the absence of fear and, conversely, fear is the absence of love. "There is no fear in love" (1 John 4:18 NIV). By not letting Abraham sacrifice his son, God demonstrates that He guides us with love. God is not indifferent or insensitive to Abraham's feelings toward his son. In fact, God cares very much, and in doing so, he demonstrates how to love. Indifference, on the other hand, is the absence of love, and in today's world, indifference is everywhere.

We show our indifference by clinging to our wealth and withholding needed resources from people who are suffering from a lack of food, shelter, or health care. We're indifferent to the suffering caused when misguided people use force to control others. We show our indifference by letting destructive activities go unabated, such as pollution of our land, air, and water, or by failing to let others know that their feelings matter to us. Indifference stems from a lack of

---

[80] In the Quran where Abraham's first son is cited, no name is given, but he is known from the Bible to be Ishmael.

awareness and sensitivity, an unwillingness to share, and a reluctance to identify with people who appear vulnerable.

Sharing: A Most Difficult Task

Why is it so hard to share? We instinctually think that sharing resources puts us at risk of not having enough for ourselves. Sharing could also take time or resources away from activities that could be used for the achievement of other, more interesting goals or accomplishments. Furthermore, we subconsciously fear that if we share our resources, either voluntarily or through a system of taxation and redistribution, the difference between the "haves" and the "have-nots" will shrink and we will no longer hold competitive advantages; our position in society will no longer be as exclusive. Why would the wealthy, who can afford to send their children to the best private schools and universities, want more tax money allocated to these schools such that tuition costs would be lowered, thereby making these schools affordable to a much larger segment of society? If this happened, the wealthy children of the world would have to compete against almost all children, not just the other wealthy ones.

As a species guided by instinctual drives, we like exclusivity. We like advantages. We do not like to think that we could lose an advantage or be put at a disadvantage. Consequently, we try to create advantages by elevating the values we identify with and by devaluing differing values. We are inclined to believe that our "superior" values should be rewarded and make life better for us. Based on nationalistic or ethnic pride, even if we're poor and therefore a member of the "have-nots," we can still identify ourselves as having advantages over nations or ethnic groups who are believed to hold inferior values.

Even though we may be poor, we may even identify psychologically with the wealthy and privileged and the values we believe the wealthy and privileged hold. In doing so we get to think that we are more desirable than those who are not considered, albeit because of prejudices, full-fledged members of the privileged class. Under these circumstances, we might join forces politically with the "have" class and oppose methods that could reduce the advantages the wealthy class maintains. Thus a poor individual might not support a higher tax bracket for the wealthy for the purpose of "redistributing the wealth" that could provide, for example, a safety net for those living in poverty. This poor person might think that he or she holds superior values to the values held by the people who live in poverty even though he or she may be living in poverty as well.

There is a strong case to be made, however, against any system of "taxation and redistribution." Such a system could allow some people, perhaps many people, to ride on the backs of others, which wouldn't be in anyone's best interest. This would violate the second base of the Golden Rule, which says, "Don't do for others what others can to do for themselves."

The bottom line is that resource sharing is never simple. So how do we raise the optimism of people who feel disheartened or marginalized because of poverty? How do we reduce the unnecessary suffering of people living in poverty, which is so often caused by circumstances beyond their control? The answer to this question involves the role that self-esteem plays in our ability to empathize.

Self-Esteem

Empathy, the degree to which we sense the feelings, needs, and problems of others, is affected by self-esteem. With low self-esteem, it is more difficult to be empathic. With low self-esteem, we worry a lot more about what we think others think about us. It is much harder to put yourself in someone else's shoes when you're busy trying to figure out what others are thinking about you, because this process usually turns into a situation in which you take your own thoughts about yourself and your judgments of others and then believe that these thoughts are what others are thinking about you. This psychological process is called projection, and projection is not empathy.

With low self-esteem, caring about other people's feelings poses additional risks. For example, you put yourself at risk of believing, or having others tell you, that you are no better than the people you care about. A classic example of this is when Jack, a racist white man, tries to form a lynch mob. When Steve tells the gathering men why lynching is wrong, Jack calls Steve a "nigger lover." The other men, who also have self-esteem issues, have a psychological need to believe that they are better than the "Negroes." Under these circumstances, it's reasonable to wonder, *If I'm not better than the Negroes, what's to prevent me from being enslaved or lynched?* The answer—*I must be better!*—is obviously a rationalization.

Jack's bigoted complaint about Steve stimulates our subconscious to raise the question "Aren't we better than others?" When we are in denial about our low self-esteem, which is the case for the lynch mob members, the answer to this question is "Of course we are." The lynch mob is now ready to prove their self-perceived superiority over others.

Because our subconscious minds make it easy to connect unpleasant feelings such as envy, boredom, loneliness, and pessimism to thoughts of being flawed or not good enough, it makes sense, from a competitive standpoint, to seek out people whom we perceive to be even more flawed than ourselves. Bullies think that if they can bully you, then you must be more flawed than them. No one wants to be at the bottom of the totem pole or last in line in the pecking order.

If there's a shortage of basic needs, won't those of us at the bottom of the pecking order be in grave danger? Our survival instincts incite us to think, *No, not me. I'm not going to be at the bottom.* If I'm a bully, I can push my way up the pecking order. If my belief system or religious practice is better than yours, then I don't deserve to be at the bottom—and I won't, because my superior beliefs and practices will earn the favor of God. I suppose you could call this "religious bullying."

We live among people who struggle to meet basic needs, which suggests that there is a shortage of resources. But that's not true. For example, when it comes to food, the problem is not a shortage of food, but a food distribution problem created in large part by a lack of sharing and cooperation. There's enough food right now to feed all 7.6 billion of us, even though one in eight people are undernourished.[81]

Any system or circumstance that limits access to basic needs and resources arouses fears. These fears stimulate people to form groups for the purpose of gaining advantages over other groups for what appears to be limited resources, ultimately leading to the formation of a class system. People in the upper classes know that the system is unfair, but they're not willing, understandably, to relinquish privileges that could help their gene pool survive for generations to come. Consequently, rationalizations are used to justify the inequities. The upper classes often purport that the lower classes have flaws. If the lower classes believe this misinformation about a flawed condition, their self-esteem will be lowered. As cited in the introduction, Bob Marley addresses this system of misinformation in his "Redemption Song" (1980): "Emancipate yourself from mental slavery. None but ourselves can free our minds."

---

[81] *2013 World Hunger and Poverty Facts and Statistics*, World Hunger Education Service, Washington, DC.

A class system creates the false impression that justice has been served. People in the lower classes are generally believed to be flawed and thus deserving of their lower station. These marginalized members of our society often have little choice but to "slave away" in low-wage jobs or unhealthy, dangerous environments to obtain food, shelter, and clothing.

Regardless of how we view our own class, seeing flaws in other people tends to lower our self-esteem as well. When we judge others to have flaws, we will wonder, consciously and subconsciously, how we stack up. There will always be people who appear stronger, better looking, more talented, better liked, richer, happier, more pious, and more self-confident than ourselves. Our subconscious files away such comparisons under the category "not good enough."

People don't really have flaws that can prevent them from finding meaning or contentment. What we do have is fear—fear that gets us to think and behave selfishly, fear that makes it easy to lose sight of the Golden Rule. Perhaps as a species, we do have one big flaw, the capacity to anticipate fear. But when our capacity for compassion is strengthened, we recognize that the flaws we see in others are the same flaws that we possess—the four basic fears.

People in highly competitive environments, such as politics and academia, try to demonstrate openly that other people's ideas and character are more flawed than their own. Even for gamblers, winning money can be secondary to the primary enjoyment of demonstrating that their card playing or handicapping strategies are superior. History is replete with people trying to prove that their method to achieve any specific goal is superior. If I can amass more wealth, power, or prestige than you, then I'll have proof that I am superior to you.

Joshua Simon, MD, EdD

Conquerors claim superiority over the conquered. The conqueror's culture finds fault with the sexual mores, body adornments, diet, justice system, religious beliefs, and other customs of those conquered. Our everyday existence is filled with examples of this kind of thinking on an individual scale within any given culture. We're quick to find fault with other people at work, at home, and in just about any setting. That's why the clothes that an accused person wears into a courtroom will be a factor in whether they're found innocent or guilty.

We are constantly competing to raise our positions within the pecking order, though usually more subtly than the politicians and political pundits. Competition among people in everyday life is evident in "probably" all cultures. I say *probably*, for who knows, maybe there is a Shangri-la out there somewhere. Just watch an episode of a soap opera made in the USA, Argentina, India, or anywhere else. Soap operas are typically about people trying to demonstrate that they're better than others. Characters in the soaps stay busy trying to distinguish themselves by their physical and mental attributes, by acquiring wealth and other forms of status, and by gaining exclusive access to their love object. Oh, the drama that ensues should they think they might not have exclusive access! An "all is fair in love and war" attitude drives the plot in most of these soaps. Power plays, intimidation, manipulations, loyalty to uncouth characters, betrayal, and especially the willingness to be deceitful can all pay big dividends.

The Bible has its share of soap operas, and the theme of many of them is deceit. Perhaps the most notable is found in Genesis 27, where Jacob tricks his father, Isaac, into thinking that he's Esau, Isaac's firstborn son. By means of deceit, Jacob is able to get his father's blessing and inheritance, which by tradition should have gone to Esau, the oldest son. Middle school—or "drama school," as it is sometimes called—resembles a soap opera too, precisely because kids twelve to fourteen years old are quite needy for attention and approval, and oh how they compete for it!

The Motive for Helping Others

Why share resources, especially if you think those resources are limited? Why empathize with people who don't possess any copies of your genes? Why care, especially if that obligates you to share limited resources? Wouldn't it be better not to care? The logic is that when it comes to the survival of your own gene pool, it is better not to care and share—unless caring and sharing will help get your genes copied into the next generation.

We often justify not caring and not sharing by finding flaws, real or imagined, in others. We often think that others are flawed if they don't share our religious beliefs or other values—or, as described in the introductory chapter, if they appear to be measuring life with a different yardstick. Ironically, our religious beliefs might actually direct us to help all people in need of basic necessities, regardless of whether they share our religious beliefs or gene pool.

The question of motive for helping others remains difficult to answer. Do observant religious people, for example, help others because they really care or because they're seeking God's blessing? Do they fear that if they don't appear to be contributing enough, they'll be rebuked by their neighbors or community's authority figures? Helping others could also be a way to demonstrate superior traits for the purpose of getting into heaven as opposed to a heartfelt measure without any ulterior motive. These same questions could be asked of nonreligious people who feel compelled to espouse their care for the less fortunate. Do they really care about others, or do they pretend to care about others so that they can think of themselves as being better than people who are perceived as uncaring and selfish?

The bottom line is that helping others in need is a good deed, a *mitzvah* in Hebrew. In Judaism, it's the action that counts because that's what demonstrates God's guidance. Any intellectual reasons, beliefs, or guilt that may underlie the action are simply not important. It's fine to think that your beliefs will open the gates to heaven because they're pleasing to God, but in Judaism the emphasis is on action—not beliefs. It's your *mitzvahs* that count. God is not just an idea. God resides in your actions. The universe was created by an action—not from a belief, and in kabbalah, it's the action of the ten divine Sefirot.

Judging the motives for somebody else's good deeds might be pointless, but understanding your own motives is not. How can you distinguish acts inspired by Hesed—love, empathy, compassion, grace, or altruism—from acts with ulterior motives such as self-gratification, self-preservation, or the raising of your standing or position in the pecking order? Do ulterior motives compromise or even corrupt your feelings of love for your fellow man? How do you know when love for others is based on an unyielding truth that is applicable at all times, as opposed to a love that is applicable only when the circumstances are favorable?

Back in 1776, the fifty-six signers of our Declaration of Independence (fifty-five after one signer recanted) probably believed that they were inspired by unyielding truths and compassion for all of humanity (though their description of Native Americans as "merciless Indian savages" would suggest otherwise). Thomas Jefferson, the document's principal author, likely held a strong conviction that love and kindness should not only guide us individually but also form the foundation of our government, as suggested by the second sentence: "We hold these truths to be self-evident, that all men are created equal, that they are endowed by their Creator with certain unalienable Rights, that among these are Life, Liberty and the pursuit of Happiness."

Have You Heard the Word Is "Hesed" and the Number Is 4?

Hesed, the fourth Sefirah, spreads love and kindness across the universe. Hesed and the number 4 also seem to align with our Declaration of Independence, which we celebrate every Fourth of July. Maybe there is some kind of mystical force that connects the following biblical, historical, and musical events:

1. The birth of Jesus reset our calendar such that our Declaration of Independence on July 4, 1776, would be "endowed by our Creator" with multiples of the number 4 ($4 \times 4 \times 44 = 704$, $4 \times 444 = 1776$). The Declaration of Independence speaks of self-evident truths of freedom and equality.
2. We have a Judeo-Christian foursome of the 1:3 kind, the relationship of the one God of Moses with the three forms of Jesus (Father, Son, and Holy Ghost), that spreads love and kindness across the universe.
3. Genesis 1:3 ($1 + 3 = 4$) says, "And God said let there be light. And there was light," the very light that spreads love, sunshine, and freedom across the universe.
4. A foursome (John, Paul, George, and Ringo) spread "The Word" in their 1965 album *Rubber Soul*. The Beatles also sing "Across the Universe," which could easily symbolize Jesus (a cross) and his love (the universe). "All Together Now," from the *Yellow Submarine* album, begins with "One, two, three, four, Can I have a little more?" followed by "Five, six, seven, eight, nine, ten, I love you." Do the Beatles love those ten numbers, those ten utterances, those ten Sefirot or emanations from God from which all creation begins—from which, before the big bang, everything was "all together now"?

How coincidental, perhaps prophetic, that the Beatles began recording "Across the Universe" on February 3, 1968, exactly nine years after "the day the music died" and four years before I met the girl who would break my heart. After Elizabeth left me, I felt like I was on a cross and the universe had forsaken me. Fortunately, though nothing was done to relieve my pain, in reality nothing went undone and my pain vanished. Such is the Tao, faith, acts of kindness, the Holy Spirit, secular humanism, the meaning of numbers, and the word:

LO

VE

How prophetic that in 1965 Dylan sang of "Highway 61 Revisited" nearly three years before history revisited that highway. On April 4, 1968—sixty-one days after the Beatles began recording "Across the Universe"—Martin Luther King Jr. was shot and killed nearby Highway 61 in Memphis, Tennessee. That's the highway in Dylan's song about sacrificing a son to God, which, in hindsight, foreshadowed the sacrificing of Martin Luther King's son, a man who truly bore a cross across the universe.

Our attention had already been drawn to Highway 61 in Memphis by the king of rock and roll, Elvis Aaron Presley. At age thirteen, "the King" and his family moved into the public housing projects along Highway 61 in north Memphis, where Elvis began his singing career with Sun Records. Highway 61, known as the "Blues Highway," runs from New Orleans through Bob Dylan's birthplace of Duluth, Minnesota, on its way to the Canadian border. Artists such as B. B. King, Muddy Waters, Howlin' Wolf, and Sam Cooke lived near Highway 61's path through the South. And in 1937, Bessie Smith, considered by many to be the greatest blues singer of all time, died in a car crash between Memphis and Clarksdale, Mississippi, on Highway 61.

In 2003, *Rolling Stone* put together a list of the 500 Greatest Albums of All Time. Bob Dylan's album *Highway 61 Revisited* was rated (would you like to venture a guess?) number 4. What topped the list? *Sgt. Pepper's Lonely Hearts Club Band* by the Beatles.

What tops the list as the most important event of all time? That has got to be the big bang. According to kabbalah, before the big bang, before our universe formed tangible matter from intangible nothingness, there were no conditions or situations like the ones we face today that could compromise or corrupt love, the fourth Sefirah. Before the big bang, the primordial Adam's (Adam Kadmon) love existed in pure form. However, at the moment of the big bang, at the moment of our universe's creation, *Ein Sof* (the totality of everything before and after the big bang, and the totality of what we perceive and don't perceive) used the ten Sefirot to spread nothing across nothingness, thus creating everything. According to kabbalah, however, the big bang's massive explosion damaged some bits of these ten Sefirot.

The perfect primordial concept of man before the big bang, Adam Kadmon, was transformed out of nothingness by the ten Sefirot into Adam Ha-Rishon, the Adam who comes to life in the Garden of Eden. But Adam, and later Eve, though both perfect at the moment of their materialization, were then living in a universe with some imperfect bits of energy that led them astray. Our job, according to kabbalah, is to repair the damage caused by the big bang and restore Adam and Eve, as well as ourselves, to perfection. Every time we perform an altruistic act, a *mitzvah*, we have repaired a damaged piece of our universe.

One of the most damaging bits of energy is involved with the art of deception. The world of politics, organized crime dramas, and the blending of the two in movies such as *American Hustle* (2013) make it clear that we, as a species, are also very deceptive, very good at pretending to care. The art of deception for the survival of other animal species is most obvious with the use of camouflage. For the human species, this "art," this pretense of caring, is our camouflage.

When perceived as a caring individual, our position in the pecking order rises and we gain the trust of others, which enhances our influence. With greater influence and trust, more opportunities will arise where we can take advantage of other people in several ways: (1) getting them to do the riskier, more dangerous jobs; (2) convincing them that our business model is a good investment for their time and money; (3) because of this trust and higher position, others could be eager to do us favors, and (4) others might let us use them for sexual gratification or might let their guard down and unwillingly become the victim of a sexual predator.

Deceitfulness is one example of how our instinctual drives lead us away from the Golden Rule. We can also be led astray by thought patterns. In fact, the positive thought patterns of a caring person can be twisted by a string of negative rationalizations and lead to grave results, as demonstrated here:

1. It's easy to believe that people who end up in trouble or lack basic needs are somehow flawed.
2. If we care about people in need, we could be equated with them and seen by others as similarly flawed. In fact, if our self-esteem is low, we could see ourselves that way.
3. Conversely, if we demonstrate that we don't care about people who are in need or perceived to be flawed, then we can falsely convince ourselves that we are free of the flaws we believe those people to possess.
4. How do we demonstrate that we don't care about people in need? By devaluation, stigmatization, and other forms of prejudice that enable us to (a) separate people from one another based on the concept that some people are better than others, (b) act with indifference toward those people

we have stigmatized, (c) form a lynch mob, and finally (d) participate in genocide. As Friedrich Nietzsche (1844–1900), the distinguished German philosopher, said, "In individuals, insanity is rare; but in groups, parties, nations, and epochs, it is the rule."

In contrast to thought patterns that separate people or take advantage of them, there are thought patterns that indicate that we do indeed care. These thought patterns arise from a heightened awareness of and sensitivity to how our actions or inactions affect the feelings of others. Caring thought patterns engender a sense of closeness or identification with those who suffer. Unfortunately, however, it follows logically that if we care less and less, then we will identify less with the feelings of vulnerability that arise within others and ourselves. In effect, we will be in denial of our own feelings of vulnerability. Furthermore, the less we care, the more easily we can convince ourselves that we are not as flawed and vulnerable as others. "Hey, why don't I show up at school, work, a concert, or nightclub with my submachine gun and kill as many people as possible? Won't that show everybody how little I care? Won't that show everybody that I'm not full of the flaws I see in everyone else, and won't that prove that I am not at the bottom of the pecking order? Won't that show everybody that I don't feel vulnerable?"

The less we care, the less we will associate ourselves with people whom we perceive, based on our own prejudices, to be flawed and highly vulnerable. On the other hand, caring and empathy are seen as favorable traits and engender trust, which moves us up the pecking order. How do we reconcile the fact that caring and empathy can be perceived both negatively and positively?

It should come as no surprise that our minds can desensitize us to feelings of vulnerability that arise in others while concurrently maintaining the self-perception that we are caring individuals. We use rationalizations. Rather than thinking that we don't care, when we withhold resources from other people, we tell ourselves that they are flawed and should "lie in the bed they made." Furthermore, we tell ourselves that because of their flaws, sharing resources with needy people isn't going to help much anyway. Wouldn't we all be better off if flawed people never existed in the first place, Adolf?

We subconsciously devalue other people as a way of preparing for the possibility that there might not be enough resources for everybody. Our instinctual brain insists, like a puppy pushing another puppy off its mother's teat, that we are more deserving of these limited resources than other people. To justify thinking of ourselves as more deserving, we pressure our brains to think in ways that will raise our value and lower the value of others, and we form thought patterns that lower the value of others while raising our own value.

People have an instinctual competitive drive to devalue other people, and what better way to do that than by causing them to suffer? Bullying, McCarthyism, racism, war, and genocide reek of psychological competition, devaluation, and suffering. Roman leaders had no difficulty filling the Colosseum with spectators when Christians were being thrown to the lions, and countless politicians have risen to power by tapping into people's subconscious need to devalue others.

The Psyche of Mass Murderers

The teenage gunmen who killed so many students at Columbine High School in Colorado and Marjory Stoneman Douglas High School in Parkland, Florida, must surely have suffered from low self-esteem. As a consequence, they didn't think that they measured up in some important way. Maybe they thought that they had little chance of attracting an attractive girl or that they'd have difficulty supporting a family. In other words, their genes had little chance of being passed down to the next generation—and no self-respecting gene is going to stand for that!

Those murderers were determined to prove that they were worthy, so their brains generated a series of rationalizations that led to grave results. Every time we take action, our brains have computed that our lives will be worse off if we don't do so. Those high school murderers rationalized that if they didn't walk into their high school and mow down students, their lives would be worse off in some way. They were determined to prove that they were worthy, despite the obvious tragic and counterproductive results. Their minds, through a series of rationalizations, elevated their value by the degree to which they devalued others and made certain that the world knew about it.

The Golden Rule is in stark contrast to the concept that some people deserve to be valued more than others. If all people are created equal, then they also deserve to be valued equally, which includes having equal opportunities, as FDR tried to achieve with his New Deal. What we make of those opportunities, equal or not, is a different story.

Because we already possess the gift of life, we already have all the value we'll ever need. Each of us is already good enough and deserves to be respected and treated in a dignified manner simply because we are human. Moses delivers this message in Genesis 1:27 (NIV): "God created mankind in His own image." If God is good, then so is each and every human being. How can we avoid letting our subconscious, competitive thought patterns lead us down the path that values some people more than others, a path that leads us to becoming "man-unkind"? The answer is that we need to partake in the four spiritual acts, with particular attention to acts of altruism.

We need to practice the Golden Rule by putting the four bases into effect.

These spiritual acts and golden bases (the four-by-four pursuit of happiness) connect us to a divine, loving, creative force, regardless of what name we give that force or even whether we believe that it exists. Furthermore, it is by our own acts of kindness that each of us individually can build our self-esteem and counteract the self-inflicted suffering caused by fear. When we extinguish our fears by using the four spiritual acts and four bases of the Golden Rule, we eliminate our indifference to the needs of others

Through our connection to a loving, divine, creative force (or for nonbelievers, a loving sublime force that fosters optimism), we gain the insight that our suffering isn't a result of not being good enough. We have always been good enough. Instead, we suffer because we think that we need to prove that we're better than others, perhaps by attaching ourselves to desirable things or people. We suffer when we think and act in ways meant to prove that we are one of the strongest bulls in the valley or one of the most attractive cows.

How can we avoid acting in ways that are meant to give our DNA advantages? Our DNA is here because it passed every test of survival through billions of years of evolution. It might seem absolutely natural to let your DNA call the shots, but you need to fight that tendency. As a human being, you aren't just an animal—you're also a spiritual being. Once again, let's turn to the relationship between God and Abraham.

When God orders Abraham to sacrifice his son, does this represent a prefiguration of the coming of Jesus Christ? Does Abraham need to know that there is more to a relationship with God than just trying to protect your progeny or working to get your genes replicated in future generations? Is there more to life than just evolutionary forces encoded in our DNA—evolutionary forces that instruct us to make choices based solely on how any given choice will affect the probability that our twenty-three pairs of chromosomes (or at least segments of our chromosomes or genes that are shared by other family members) will survive and be copied over and over again in future generations?

Abraham's test of faith also symbolizes the reality that life on this earth includes situations in which we and our loved ones could feel threatened. Yet many of us, who don't possess a faith as strong as Abraham's, will find it difficult to accept the reality that we are never fully protected from harm. History is filled with bad things happening to good people, and all people are vulnerable. Every day we move one day closer to death, and we can feel pain at any time along the way. Any day and anywhere, we could have an encounter with a disturbed person who devalues and dehumanizes others, as did those unfortunate students in Columbine, Sandy Hook, and Parkland.

In a mystical interpretation, it isn't by chance that the first name of Bob Dylan's father was Abraham, or that the album *Highway 61 Revisited*, which contains the lyrics "Oh, God said to Abraham, 'Kill me a son,'" was ranked as the fourth best album of all time by *Rolling Stone*. The biblical Abraham has two sons, Ishmael and Isaac, who play central roles in the Bible that has a great influence on three major religions: Judaism, Christianity, and Islam. Abraham Zimmerman, along Highway 61, fathers Robert Zimmerman (Bob Dylan), who has a major influence on three major musical genres: folk music, folk rock, and rock and roll. And a few years after Dylan's album is released, Martin Luther King's son is killed on the fourth day of the fourth month nearby Highway 61.

If we believe that God sacrifices his only son in Jesus, then the account of the binding of Isaac in Genesis 22 takes on even further meaning. God is not asking Abraham to do something that He is not willing to do Himself. A symbolic interpretation is that we shouldn't ask anyone to do something that we aren't willing to do ourselves, yet another nuance of the Golden Rule. Then when we consider that God loves Abraham's son and would not let him die injudiciously, a mystical interpretation is that God loves His son, Jesus, and would not let him die injudiciously. Thus Jesus lives, even though his body died on a cross. Jesus lives in our hearts, figuratively, and based on the neural connections between our heart and brain, possibly literally as well.

Evolution and Low Self-Esteem

The dilemma faced by Abraham, with the binding of his son, underscores the importance of preventing our evolutionary, competitive, survival-of-the-fittest mentality from overwhelming our thought patterns. Jesus warns us about the dangers of competition in Matthew 5:5 when he says, "The meek shall inherit the Earth." Earth represents the Promised Land, a place of peace and contentment. The meek are people who see themselves as ordinary and are comfortable being that way, yet at the same time appreciate that each individual in their own way is extraordinary. The meek are people who sense that they have nothing to prove, that the same forces of fear operate in all of us, and that how you see others is a reflection of how you see yourself. The meek get to experience the beauty that our Creator has placed in our hearts and all around us, in nature, in the energy of movement, and in the stillness of meditation.

If you define success as enjoying your life, which ultimately means enjoying your patterns of thought, then meekness is the way to go. However, from an evolutionary perspective, success is having your genes copied by the next generation and each succeeding "gene-ration." From this perspective, low self-esteem is thinking that you'll be unsuccessful at obtaining needed resources and attracting a healthy, attractive mate with good parenting skills who will give your children the competitive advantages necessary for having grandchildren, and so on. We pay particular attention to the differences between people with respect to health, intelligence, access to resources, and commitment to family, since these qualities are likely to affect the survival of future copies of our genes. However, we are anything but meek when we stress the differences rather than the similarities between people.

"I'd gladly lay down my life for two brothers or eight cousins."[82]

Differences matter from an evolutionary standpoint. Since siblings share half of their genes and cousins one eighth, sacrificing one's life for two siblings or eight cousins is an equal tradeoff from a genetic standpoint. We teach our children at a young age who their relatives are, and children are quite possessive when it comes to family. "This is my family, not your family." Children will typically be disturbed by words that are meant to insult their families.

In addition to kinship relations, we pay attention to the ways in which people can gain competitive advantages and status. We take note of the classifications that reinforce differences within our particular culture or subculture. Thus there are top-tier colleges, A-listers, and upper, middle, and lower classes.

We also imbue with importance the differences found in just about any category that holds any kind of attraction to us, from what sports or music we like to what religion we practice and how devout we are. We are much more willing to help, protect, share resources, make sacrifices, do favors, and root for family or people who feel like family.

---

[82] Robert Sapolsky, *Biology and Human Behavior: The Neurological Origins of Individuality*, 2nd ed. (Chantilly, VA: The Teaching Co., 2005).

We trust family because our family cares about us, and it's in our genetic self-interest to care about our relatives. With people who feel like family, we form pseudo-kinships that begin with similarities and shared interests and grow into trust and care. It's wise for a politician to show up at the most popular sporting events and invite popular entertainers to do benefits on their behalf. In the United States, where a large segment of the voting population is religious, it's also wise to demonstrate devoutness to religion, since that equates with caring and a shared interest.

Sports teams foster pseudo-kinships with their fans when their players support caring activities such as the Special Olympics and the United Way. Once again, we root for family or people who feel like family, and people who care about the things that we care about feel like family. For this same reason, and because they want our trust, many companies demonstrate that they care about the sacrifices made by the men and women in our armed services, perhaps by donating a portion of their profit to a charity.

Conversely, the less we see ourselves like others or the less we trust them, the less often we will form pseudo-kinships and the less we will think we are obliged to share with or help others. Mitt Romney's "47 percent speech"[83] in the 2012 presidential election campaign contained this kind of reasoning. Speaking to his base constituents, he made the case that 47 percent of the population are not like "us" and that therefore, "we" have little chance of getting their support. He put down 47 percent of the population by saying, in essence, that "they" don't have what it takes or just don't care to be self-sufficient. However, the bigger problem with his speech was the implication that since "they" are not like "us," we do not need to care about them when we are in power. The perception that Romney does not really care may have turned off quite a few people to his candidacy.

---

[83] *Mother Jones* (September 19, 2012).

However, Mitt Romney may care very much. He may realize that "doing for others what they can to do for themselves" is not caring.

Romney's 47 percent speech emphasized that "they" are different from "us," but we are hardly different from each other. We all have twenty-three chromosomes and experience the same four basic fears. No one claims that the Ten Commandments hold truths only for certain people. We are all connected to one infinite and finite universe.

When people focus on differences without empathy, fear is the culprit. This fear stems in large part from our ability to anticipate shortages. There could be a future catastrophic climatic or environmental event, as well as a war or stock market crash, that could greatly limit the availability of resources. One can never have enough wealth or resources for an unforeseen emergency. Furthermore, drawing upon a biopsychosocial view of humankind, Buddhism points out that our cravings and desires are insatiable; we never have enough resources or sensual pleasures to satisfy our subconscious thoughts—thus a billionaire strives to make even more money and have even more influence than he or she already possesses.

When we're worried about not having enough resources, it's easy to believe that others perceive us to be different in some negative way and that their negative attitude is holding us down. Hitler claimed that the attitudes and practices of the Jews held down the rest of Germany.

The political phenomenon known as populism arises when leaders are able to emphasize that they are different from the people in power and that the people in power hold negative views of them. On November 28, 2017, this strategy was demonstrated by Steve Bannon, executive chairman of Breitbart News and so-called populist leader, when he told CNN, "I look forward to standing with Judge Moore and all of the Alabama 'deplorables' in the fight to elect him to the United States Senate and send shockwaves to the political and media elites."

Populist leaders raise wedge issues (abortion foes versus those who believe in abortion rights, for the wall versus against the wall, raising taxes versus lowering taxes) that can create the appearance of us versus them. The complexity of these issues—and they are complex—is purposely ignored. Populist leaders are quick to espouse the opinion that we are suffering because the people in the opposition, who see themselves as different from us, don't care about us or respect us. Thus we hear people categorized as "those snobbish college-educated Washington elites" or "those self-righteous evangelicals." It's the negative, narrow-minded attitudes of others—but not our own negative, narrow-minded attitudes—that hold us down. Populist leaders are skillful at getting their constituent's negativity projected onto others.

Rationalizations of My Childhood

Because I grew up in metropolitan New York, where more people lived than anywhere else in the United States, I thought that I was more fortunate than others and that my fortunate circumstances gave me an advantage. After all, if there weren't advantages to being a New Yorker, why did so many people choose to live there? Furthermore, I thought that it was unwise for people to think of New Yorkers in a negative way, since we outnumbered everyone else. If I had been in a position to hire an employee when I was only ten, I probably would've favored someone who grew up in metropolitan New York.

As a child I harbored prejudices about why being a farmer or living out in the sticks seemed so undesirable. I knew that China was the world's most populous country, but I didn't think that meant that Chinese people were more fortunate than Americans. The point is that I rationalized why my own set of differences should bring me advantages. Since we are programmed genetically to find and obtain competitive advantages, we often cling to seeing ourselves as being different from others because we perceive our own differences to be advantageous.

We expect that favorable differences in terms of wealth, achievements, or membership in a specific religious or political group should demonstrate to others that we are worthy of respect. Without respect, it is easier to believe that authority figures would find us unworthy of their protection, other people would limit our opportunities for employment and exclude us from pleasurable activities, and we would appear less attractive to the people who attract us. The takeaway lesson for people in positions of power and authority, such as parents, teachers, and military leaders, is that when we discipline our children or troops, for example, it's wise to also remind them that we aren't withholding our interest in them or our protection from them.

All children need to know, and all adults should expect, that they are deserving of respect at all times. When a teacher tells a student to stay after school for detention, the teacher has an opportunity to let that student know that she cares about him and wants to see him do well. Then the teacher can explain how the student's unruly behavior, which led to the detention, will interfere with his progress both academically and socially.

For some of us, particularly those of us who are members of an organization with a history noted for its use of force and other violent acts, just about every interaction with others becomes an issue of respect defined by some arbitrary code of conduct that has been passed down from generation to generation. When in the presence of royalty, you kneel this way. When in the presence of the pope, you kneel that way. When in the presence of a superior military officer, you stand and salute this way. When in the presence of the godfather, you genuflect another way. All rise for the judge. The problem with these codes of conduct is that (1) the show of respect might just be a pretense to disguise our fear or our outright disapproval, and (2) they often value some people more than others.

A democracy thrives when people are not fearful of expressing their disapproval of selfish behaviors, especially selfish behaviors that have been passed down through the ages. Perhaps that's why Michelle Obama, knowing that women aren't treated equally in Saudi Arabia, chose not to cover her head, as prescribed by Saudi custom, when she met with King Salman in January 2015. However, though you might not think that some of our customs are the best or that the person occupying a position of power and authority is the best choice, it is reasonable to show respect for that person as you would for any other person and show respect for the responsibilities that person holds. So, let's all rise for the judge? Or should we?

Common Sense

Thomas Paine once said, "A long habit of not thinking a thing wrong gives it the superficial appearance of being right."[84] Those codes of conduct that show preferential respect fly in the face of the concept that everybody deserves to be respected in a way that does not violate the first commandment, "Thou shall have no other gods before me." It is God's power of love and creation that deserves deference, not man-made powers that have a long history of giving some people preferential status and advantages.

---

[84] Thomas Paine, *Common Sense* (1776).

We often think that we deserve to be respected because of our achievements or the position we occupy, or even because we have found the true path by which to worship God. As a consequence of thinking that respect needs to be earned, our minds become narrowly focused, consciously and subconsciously, on whether we are being respected properly. Under these circumstances, it's easy to miss the big issue. Why haven't we learned how to respect the feelings of vulnerability that arise in all people, not just in ourselves? Why haven't we learned that we have always deserved respect simply because we're human? Why haven't we learned, as the Beatles sang, that "the love you take is equal to the love you make," and the degree to which you are respected by others matches the degree to which you respect others? It is understandable that many people haven't learned this most important truth, since evolutionary, competitive forces, our survival-of-the-fittest mentality, can dominate our thought patterns.

Trust

Though respect does not need to be earned, trust does. Respect and trust are not the same. You can and should respect everyone, even though you don't necessarily trust everyone. Trust comes only to those of us who consistently act with kindness. Can you trust, based in your faith in God or the collective consciousness of humanity, that if you consistently act with kindness by using the four bases of the Golden Rule, your life will work out better than if you let basic evolutionary forces guide your behavior?

Cooperation, sharing of resources, honesty, and sensitivity to the feelings of others will allow you to enjoy the beauty that your Creator has placed all around you and in your heart. If your goal is to enjoy your life on this earth, there is no more effective way than by being kind and friendly. Do you really think that you need to be different from others in some desirable way[85] to be treated with dignity and respect? Your DNA answers this last question with a loud yes and uses a wide gate, but your spiritual side answers with a soft no and uses a narrow gate. "Enter through the narrow gate. For wide is the gate and broad is the road that leads to destruction, and many enter through it. But small is the gate and narrow the road that leads to life, and only a few find it" (Matthew 7:13–14 NIV). Ralph Waldo Emerson (1803–82) has been attributed for saying it this way: "Do not go where the path may lead, go instead where there is no path and leave a trail." [86]

Dr. Robert Sapolsky[87] has written a fascinating account of neurobehavioral research that supports the hypothesis that the smaller gate of empathy and cooperation generates more pleasant thoughts than the wider gate of wanting to outperform others. In games that require calculated strategies, the winners receive more extrinsic rewards than the losers. However, the pleasure areas of the brain are stimulated more, and the areas of the brain associated with the stress response are stimulated less, when people cooperate and act in a friendly way, even though these behaviors do not lead to more victories or more extrinsic rewards. The implication is that behaviors that result in increased goal achievement at the expense of empathy may undermine our health and well-being.

Vince Lombardi, legendary coach of the Green Bay Packers, once said, "Winning isn't everything. It's the only thing!" Perhaps the time has come to replace winning with empathy. Empathy isn't everything. It's the only thing! Vince Lombardi later admitted that

---

[85] Is the most desirable trait a belief that we somehow know the one true way to worship God?
[86] www.goodreads.com/quotes/16878
[87] Robert Sapolsky, *Biology and Human Behavior: The Neurological Origins of Individuality*, 2nd ed., The Great Courses (Chantilly, VA: The Teaching Co., 2005).

he wasn't fond of being associated with this "winning is the only thing" quote. If a player gave his best effort, Lombardi applauded him regardless of the outcome of the game.[88]

By participating in the four spiritual acts (meditation, altruism, creativity, and the joy of movement), with particular attention to the altruistic act of following the Golden Rule, you will already know that you are respected because of your karma. What goes around comes around. By participating in the four spiritual acts, you will already know that you are respected by the most powerful force of all—the massless force of nothingness that somehow created this universe.

Image

Every culture has rites of passage, status symbols, forms of address, titles, and exclusive groups associated with acceptance and respect, and fitting into these categories often serves a psychological purpose by creating an image that others will find acceptable. Our image serves as a shield to protect us from our fear that without our accomplishments, style, status, or image, other people will consider us unacceptable or not good enough.

Can people feel safe when they remove their shields? Can we be confident that we're good enough not because of our accomplishments, style, or status, but because of our own history of treating other people as though they are good enough? In other words, are you comfortable with the person behind your image? You've spent years cultivating your image to (1) gain a competitive advantage; (2) achieve recognition and acceptance from family members, schoolmates, a romantic interest, and coworkers; and (3) be accepted by people whom you admire or, in some cases, fear.

---

[88] *Lombardi*, HBO Films (2010).

Just by getting better at using the four bases of the Golden Rule every day, people will enjoy their lives far more than if they achieve every competitive goal on their bucket list—goals such as winning a championship, accomplishing something that most people are unable to accomplish, or gaining entry to exclusive clubs or organizations. Ideally, the goals on your bucket list have little to do with competition, but a lot to do with exploring creativity or being of greater service to others.

When the Golden Rule is not part of your everyday life, you'll put far more pressure on yourself and others to help you create or maintain an image that you find pleasing. Typically what pleases us is an image that is acceptable to the people whom we find attractive or powerful, or an image that strikes fear in the people whom we want to control. We also tend to believe that our image is enhanced by associating with people who are admired by others. "*Moi*? You've asked little old me to attend the Academy Awards ceremony? I can't believe it!" Our egos get stroked when others give us attention or recognize our achievements. Quite often, our values, religious beliefs, and political views are especially important to the image we expect others to support.

We become so focused on our image because we are still heading toward the wide gate of instinctual drives. We have yet to find the narrow gate by which the meek inherit the earth and the ordinary is beautiful. We find the narrow gate when we learn to value the person behind the image—a person who is essentially no different from anybody else. We all use the same four nucleic acids that encode twenty-three chromosomes, which give rise to the same four basic fears and corresponding four basic loves.

When our image is not working to our satisfaction, we often blame others for our unhappiness. We even blame others for the unfortunate circumstances that we created from our own lack of insight and poor decisions. We also criticize people who interfere with the attainment of our goals, particularly if they prevent us from acquiring more money. We criticize the government for taxes, the doctor or repair person for charging so much, and the airlines for attaching ridiculous fees when we need to change our flights. They're all crooks! We criticize the boss who fails to give us a raise.

We also criticize those who prevent us from standing out because we don't like thinking that we or our children are ordinary. The coach who doesn't start our child is a likely target, along with the teacher whom we accuse of playing favorites when our child doesn't get a good grade. We want more money, more children who star on the high school sports teams, and more bumper stickers that say, "My child is an honor roll student." Our DNA, with four billion years of history behind us, drives us to create an image that shouts out, "I am not ordinary!"

When I show up at school today, my hair will be dyed green and I'll be wearing a prominent nose ring. No one will think I'm ordinary ... But wait a minute. That won't work. I finished high school years ago. Aha, I've got a better idea, a more sophisticated idea, an idea more befitting of my age and standing. I am going to create a book extolling the virtues of the Golden Rule and citing Jesus, Muhammad, Moses, and the Buddha. And if anyone voices criticism of my book, finds it dull, or doesn't support its objectives, I can dismiss them for not being very bright or insightful.

It's easy to think that people who don't support your objectives, values, religious beliefs, or political views are being critical of you. It's easy to get angry and criticize people who don't admire the image you try to project. Also, if you're displeased with your image and you think your displeasure is justified, then you might be inclined to criticize people who don't admire the image to which you aspire. This partially explains why people with low-paying jobs, who dream of being rich and famous, favor lowering taxes on the wealthy. "Why are you punishing the people who have reached the status to which I aspire? Why are you punishing success?"

Alternatively, when our image is not working, we can direct our criticism and anger inward, causing depression and severe anxiety. But whether or not our self-image is valued in various social settings, the person behind the image—our authentic self—is loved by the meek, humble, and compassionate, and for believers, by a loving God. The 7.6 billion of us are, perhaps with a few exceptions, compassionate spiritual beings. Unfortunately, people are often so caught up in their image that they do not sense the love that exists for the person behind the image.

Simply because you are alive and part of God's universe, you deserve to be respected. You do not need to prove anything to anybody to deserve this respect. It's your birthright. However, your instinctual side wants you to believe that you do need to prove something or stand out. Your instinctual side wants your ego to get stroked.

It's a difficult task to mature out of this egocentric, instinctual viewpoint, which engenders feelings of dissatisfaction when our image is not applauded. Perhaps it is even more difficult for those who grew up in difficult circumstances—abusive homes, crime-ridden neighborhoods, abject poverty, war zones. Many of us grow up with self-absorbed parents who typically have trouble relating to their children's feelings. They often see their children as extensions of their own ego and teach them that anything less than perfection is unacceptable. The feelings of children of self-absorbed parents won't be validated if they do anything that detracts from, or fails to conform to, the image their parents are trying to project.

As children, we don't realize that we have always been deserving of respect without having to prove anything. Because we lack this realization, we look to others to bolster our self-esteem, and interactions often become tests of whether they're with me or against me. It seems like others are in control of how we feel and that little can be done to prevent the daily emotional bumps, knocks, and bruises.

As children we are dependent on other people to validate us. Far too often, this dependence continues into adulthood and it can feel like we are reliving our emotions from middle school over and over again. The alternative is to travel down "Positively 4th Street" with a healthy sense of self-esteem and confidence, which comes from understanding the feelings of vulnerability that arise in all human beings and the thought patterns that these feelings create. In doing so, you'll know that the person behind the image is good enough, no matter who includes or excludes you.

As you transform from a position of low self-esteem and thoughts of inadequacy to a position of confidence, your needing of ways to get your ego stroked will dissipate, including the need to get your image validated. Your image just won't interest you as it once did. Instead, you will have found your authentic self.

With a healthy sense of self-esteem, you can truly live in the present moment without worrying about what other adults expect of you, how to please them, or what you need to accomplish to feel worthy. (However, you do need to pay attention to what you and your children expect of one another.[89]) With a healthy sense of self-esteem, you need not expect much more of yourself, your friends, or romantic partner than what you'd expect, for example, from an encounter with a passing shopper at a store. A person with a healthy

---

[89] Because children lack more mature defenses and their spiritual life is often not yet well developed, they will rely more heavily on images that bring them comfort; these images carry expected roles for adults to play.

self-esteem expects and demonstrates truthfulness, tact, cooperation, and consideration.

Emotion Pollution

Tact is a form of respect. Tact can be defined as "sensitivity in dealing with others." Without tact, you create emotion pollution. Without tact, you subject others to your emotional issues, which can distract them from focusing on what really needs to get done. It's like noise pollution from a loud truck or a neighbor using a chain saw.

When you're being tactful, your words, tone of voice, facial expression, and body posture convey to the other person the fact that you value their feelings. By doing so, you also send them (and yourself) the message that they (and you) are already good enough to deserve a beautiful life. What you think of others, more often than not, reflects what you think of yourself. Every tactful interaction becomes a positive moment, even if it's just smiling at the person whose car pulls alongside yours at a red light. When your friends and family give you more of their time than a passing acquaintance at the checkout counter or a smile from a motorist, enjoy the love.

Moving Forward Guilt-Free

You plan your life around your friends and family, making accommodations for the people who bring meaning to your life. So what should you do when your living situation, your job, or your relationships aren't working out to your satisfaction? What if the people with whom you associate on a daily basis are not following the four bases of the Golden Rule, and their lack of sensitivity and the resulting emotion pollution are just too much for you? You might need to make some changes, both from within and from without.

When Making Changes

In a free society,[90] you need not worry that others are dependent on you for their basic emotional and physical needs. (Exceptions include children, aging or infirm relatives, or financially dependent spouses.) Other healthy adults need to depend on themselves, according to the second base of the Golden Rule: Don't do for others what they can do for themselves. However, this is not a license to be insensitive, because no one is perfect. We all have some insecurities or neurotic ways of seeing things that aren't easily changed and that attach us to the lives of others, so you might need to compromise when making changes.

Just the same, you aren't being insensitive when you say no to friends or family who cling to you. It is unhealthy for an adult to rely almost exclusively on just a few people for meaning or sustenance, perhaps with the exception of some traditional marriages. There are many different ways to find meaning and useful work, and we all need to develop confidence that our life will work out, no matter how personal or professional relationships change.

When you choose to make a major change—such as moving, changing jobs, marriage, or divorce—you can move forward guilt-free, but the people affected by your change deserve your kindness. Be honest with people, give them timely notice, and reassure them that their feelings still matter. Be sensitive to others' insecurities, and let them feel your friendship love. However, if someone around you suffers from low self-esteem or lacks confidence, they're likely to create rigid expectations. You'll sense their disappointment, and your friendship love might be overlooked.

---

[90] If we don't live in a free society, then some of us may feel responsible for the health and well-being of mature adults. An example of this situation was portrayed by Mr. Schindler in the Steven Spielberg movie *Schindler's List*.

Adjustments and changes will raise the anxiety levels of people affected. You should understand and be sensitive to the anxiety, insecurity, and emotions aroused when change takes place. Ultimately, however, it's up to each person to develop their own independent sense of confidence that things will work out, regardless of who enters or leaves their life. If you maintain a genuine spirit of friendship during periods of change, you will be helping others develop their own inner sense of confidence. However, if you've had dealings with them in which you were dishonest, then guilt feelings will arise.

Guilt can complicate matters because it can make you feel more responsible than necessary for someone else's happiness. However, guilt is a good thing because it indicates the presence of a conscience. For example, your guilt might convince you that a heartfelt apology to somebody is in order. Just remember that you're not perfect. We all make mistakes, which includes being untruthful at times, but you should learn from your mistakes, not repeat old mistakes, and problem solve in a spirit of friendship.

"Positively 4th Street": The Way to Problem Solve

There is a pathway that fosters a spirit of genuine friendship and reduces feelings of rejection and fear. There's a pathway that raises self-esteem without lowering the status of others. There's a pathway that removes expectations and allows us to work through our guilt. There's a pathway that allows us to lower our shields and rid ourselves of the images behind which we've been hiding. When we stop hiding behind an image and remove the blinders created by biases and

prejudice, all of life can reach our senses. "There's a Place for Us,"[91] and it can be found in our thoughts.

"I think, therefore I am." How we think—or more specifically, how we problem solve—determines whether the universe appears friendly and whether we like ourselves. It's how you problem solve, not what others think of you, that will fill your life with love, joy, and happiness. Each of us, regardless of our circumstances, has access to a way of thinking and feeling that brings warmth and contentment to our conscious awareness. We all have access to a loving force or spirit, and we can maintain a heightened sensitivity to the vulnerable feelings that arise within all living people and sentient animals. Everyone can follow the four bases of the Golden Rule and participate in the four spiritual acts. Let the four-by-four pursuit of happiness teach you how to find solutions to problems without causing harm or making others feel threatened.

Fourth commandment: "Honor thy father and thy mother." Honor relates to the realization that some people have sacrificed their own personal comfort for the benefit of others. When parents guide us with love through our formative years and teach us that we're no longer the center of the universe, they do a most important act for the benefit of all others. In teaching us this most important lesson, fathers, mothers, and other relatives and teachers in our lives will have sacrificed countless moments of their own personal comfort to tend to our needs. This is worthy of honor.

What about children who feel that their parents were unloving? We can still honor the gift of life that they gave us, regardless of the circumstances. Honor those times when they followed the Golden Rule, and understand that when they didn't, they had been led

---

[91] "There's a Place for Us" also called "Somewhere (There's a Place for Us)" from the 1957 Broadway musical *West Side Story*, music composed by Leonard Bernstein with lyrics by Stephen Sondheim.

astray by the fear that they weren't good enough. Consequently, they probably felt a need to do something to hide their feelings of inadequacy, such as spending time away from home while looking to get their ego stroked. They might have expressed dissatisfaction with you when you failed to fulfill their fantasies, which probably included the fantasy of having a child who stood out. Just the same, since we all have the gift of life, we all are already good enough. We all have access to the four-by-four pursuit of happiness, which gives everyone, regardless of who raised us, the opportunity to find peace and contentment.

— 5 —

Gevurah—Fear

Ever since Homo sapiens first coalesced into tribes, war has been part of the human condition. Inevitably, warring societies portray their campaigns as virtuous struggles and present their fallen warriors as heroes who made the ultimate sacrifice for a noble cause.

—Jon Krakauer, *Where Men Win Glory: The Odyssey of Pat Tillman* (2009)

Ants are so much like human beings as to be an embarrassment. They farm fungi, raise aphids as livestock, launch armies into war, use chemical sprays to alarm and confuse enemies, capture slaves, engage in child labor, exchange information ceaselessly. They do everything but watch television.

—Lewis Thomas, *Lives of a Cell: Notes of a Biology Watcher* (1974)

Gevurah means "judgment," "might," or "power" or the "fear" engendered by judgments of the mighty and powerful. Gevurah is Hesed's opposite and, at the same time, its complement. Love alone will not suffice unless we set boundaries and say no to people who act selfishly. Gevurah is the left hand of the primal Adam; the biblical figure it is most associated with is Isaac, and its direction is north.[92]

Gevurah, the power to judge, interfered dramatically with my sensing the love I felt with Elizabeth. After Elizabeth and I had dated for two or three weeks, Hesed (love) and Gevurah (power) were not yet in balance. My subconscious concerns, especially my anxiety over my own self-worth, made it easy for me to judge others. These judgments formed a shield that protected my ego from thinking, *What if I'm not good enough?* My judgments of others included Elizabeth. Based on the dynamics of the "two-step" described in chapter 3, my judgments lowered Elizabeth's value. I wanted people to see me with value, but I wasn't sure that I wanted them to see me with Elizabeth.

But then a significant event changed our relationship. As we stood in the food line in a crowded college cafeteria, Elizabeth was hugging and kissing me. I wasn't uptight about public displays of affection in general, but I wasn't comfortable letting everyone know that Elizabeth was my girlfriend. So I turned to her and said, "This is not the time or the place." She got upset, and I realized that I needed to reassess our relationship.

Up to this point, the idea that the two of us should split up was not an unpleasant one. I was filled with all sorts of doubts about our relationship. My number one doubt was about whether she was intelligent enough for me (in retrospect I realize I was projecting my doubts about my own intelligence onto Elizabeth). Other typical cultural issues, such as sexual mores, religion, and family background and wealth didn't occupy my mind much. It was several days after we met before I even asked about her last name, which turned out to be Hispanic, and found out that three of her grandparents grew

---

[92] Arthur Goldwag, *The Beliefnet Guide to Kabbalah* (Three Leaves Press, 2005).

up in Cuba and one in Puerto Rico. Her religion came up only after she shared with me that she had attended Catholic schools and had wanted to be a nun when she was younger. A Jew dating or even marrying a Catholic posed no issue in my household. However, with intelligence still a concern, I worried how others would judge me for having Elizabeth by my side.

On that eventful day in the cafeteria, I realized that Elizabeth was upset about my comment about "not the time or the place." *Won't she continue to be upset when she learns of my doubts about whether she is good enough for me?* I thought. I realized that if I was going to break up, then it would be better done sooner rather than later. So at that moment while standing in the cafeteria line, I began to think more deeply about my relationship with Elizabeth. Then for some reason I thought that I should block out all my thoughts about what others might think about her and about me for being her boyfriend. Instead I thought that my thoughts about Elizabeth should be entirely up to me. Then I focused my thoughts on Elizabeth's feelings and my feelings. Once I did this, I realized without any doubt that I cared very much about her and wanted Elizabeth to be happy. Somehow during the process of focusing intently on these feelings, my "shield" dissolved, love (Hesed) and fear (Gevurah) came into balance, and I found my authentic self.

During this reassessment, I didn't think about what Elizabeth could do for me. Instead, I focused on what I wanted the world to do for Elizabeth. During the weeks after this reassessment, I paid considerably more attention to her feelings, and with this newfound interest in Elizabeth's feelings, she transformed from an attractive nineteen-year-old to the most beautiful woman I had ever seen, more beautiful than Annette Funicello from the *Mickey Mouse Club* or Sophia Loren or Raquel Welch from the movies. Elizabeth even outshined the prettiest girl I knew, a girl who had caught my eye when we played together in kindergarten and whom I had continued to admire throughout high school.

As we learned from Sigmund Freud, my attraction at age five to the physical appearance of a kindergartner was biological. From birth to death, we are filled with psychosexual thoughts, including how we view our own parents in childhood. Elizabeth's beauty and physical affection not only rekindled how I had felt in my parents' arms as an infant but might also have provided some needed nurturance. My mother was more intellectual than affectionate and she was depressed during my first year of life, so she might have left a void that was later filled by Elizabeth's affection. In my deep subconscious, perhaps I bonded with Elizabeth in a way similar to an infant bonding with her mother.

Could it be that when I opened my heart to Elizabeth, I lost my identity? Did I let go of the cultural biases and blind spots that we use to judge the worthiness of others and form our own identity? Most of the world saw me as an upper-middle-class, Jewish, twenty-year-old man raised by nonreligious Jewish parents, attending college, majoring in geography, with white skin, long, wavy brown hair, and liberal American values. (And if the world could have looked at my transcript, it would have seen that this man, who was so focused on intelligence, had a grade point average just barely above a 2.0.) But when I cared deeply about my girlfriend's feelings, all the rationalizations that go into why we have identities went out the window. What is an identity, and why do people insist on categorizing themselves and others?

Origins of Identity

Picture a time and place when water was scarce and a man named Mark found a hidden source of spring water in a cave that he'd stumbled across by accident. With that water, Mark grew a wonderful garden, and people from far and wide came to him to trade and barter for his fruits and vegetables. Now picture a man named Josh, who was feeling the pangs of thirst. Josh stole some water that Mark had been collecting for his garden, rather than just asking for it. Josh didn't think that Mark would share because Josh wouldn't share with Mark if the situation were reversed.

It was hard work for Mark to haul the water back to his home and a bit dangerous to climb down into the cave. After Josh repeatedly stole water from Mark, Mark finally got angry. He fenced in his place and got guard dogs to scare Josh away. Mark could have shown Josh the well in the cave so that Josh could fetch his own water, but he didn't. However, Josh followed him to the source, so Mark vowed to go after Josh if he tried to get water from the cave.

Mark liked having what other people wanted and valued. If Josh had access to the water, people might have valued Josh more than him—and what if Josh had started his own garden? The more that Mark could restrict access to this water, the more other people would need his fruits and vegetables. Basic economics came into play—the greater the need, the greater the value.

Josh wanted to keep all the water that he had collected for himself, but he was afraid that Mark would catch him, take the water back, and try to hurt him. So Josh reluctantly offered water to other thirsty people, who gladly accepted. But Josh told them that this other guy, Mark, was going to try to take the water away from them. So then Josh had a group, the Joshovites, to protect him and the water in his possession. That group of people had a common goal and identity. They were the protectors of the water that Josh brought to them. Weren't they lucky to have a great man like Josh to share his water with them in such needy times?

Mark had water that he hadn't planned to share with anyone else, but Josh was a problem. Mark had worked hard to store the water near his garden, but Josh had stolen quite a bit of it—and then Josh had begun raiding the water source in the cave. So Mark explained to others how Josh had been stealing his water, and he told them that if they helped him protect his water, he would share it with them. Now Mark had his group, the Markovites, who supported Mark's claim of ownership of the spring in the cave and would help Mark protect the water and teach Josh, and anyone else who tried to steal, a lesson: "If you steal from us, we'll hurt you so bad that you'll never steal from us again."

Mark's group was formed to meet his needs. "We are the protectors of the water that Mark has brought us. What a great man Mark is for offering to share his water during such needy times! God must have chosen Mark to find the water and deliver it to his people." His people, of course, were those who would help him stop Josh and the Joshovites.

Over the years, two great nations developed: the Land of Josh and the Land of Mark. Both nations had great warriors to honor for their heroic and self-sacrificing work to bring needed water to their people. At first, the two nations competed with each other over water, but eventually they learned to compete with each other over almost anything.

Competing for Resources

We compete for water, land, wealth, and attractive men and women. We compete for resources that can improve the odds that our genetic material will be copied for generations to come. But what if an idea—not a physical thing or person but just an idea—was considered to be a resource even more important than basic needs? Wouldn't we compete for that idea as well? What if that idea was one all-knowing, all-powerful God?

A person's identity is a competition. We are either a Joshovite or a Markovite. We are either Navajo or not Navajo, American or un-American, Jewish or Gentile, male or female, educated or uneducated, old money or new money. Competition is not about sharing. It's about seeing ourselves as different from one another, when in reality we are essentially the same: four nucleic acids encoding twenty-three chromosomes. Galatians 3:28 (NIV) puts it this way: "There is neither Jew nor Greek, there is neither slave nor free man, there is neither male nor female; for you are all one in Christ Jesus." We all share the same feelings of vulnerability. We all have the same four basic fears. If skin color, land of birth, genitalia from birth, or anything else matters, then people are identifying with issues that have their roots in selfish acts or reactions to selfish acts.

Four Basic Competitive Drives

Underlying this selfishness are four basic fields in which we compete—our four competitive drives:

1. Access to land with food (sensual pleasure), water, mineral wealth, and other natural resources
2. Survival and protection from harm (pain avoidance)
3. Sexual partners (sensual pleasure) to make copies of our genes
4. The speed to be faster at any task (which would then leave more time for pleasure)

In their respective lands, Josh and Mark had preferential access to land, food, clothing, shelter, bodyguards, the fastest chariots, and plenty of wives to bear children. Despite being treated like kings, however, Mark and Josh did not lead happy lives. They rarely felt satisfied or content. They were takers, not givers. They didn't problem solve while remaining sensitive to feelings of vulnerability that arose within themselves and others. They never learned to like themselves, and their self-esteem was low because they acted selfishly and didn't follow the four bases of the Golden Rule. As a consequence, King Mark and King Josh constantly felt a need for others to show them that they were valued with gifts and monuments, cheering crowds, kowtowing before the king, and having their images placed on statues and paintings throughout their respective kingdoms.

Despite all their successes in building up their kingdoms and providing millions of people with food and water, Josh and Mark were filled with doubts about their self-worth. They needed admiration and external validation, which is typical of wealthy or powerful people with a strong history of achieving goals and a weak history of acting with kindness. Josh and Mark liked to be honored.

Mark and Josh liked it when people admired their material possessions, such as their palaces, collections of artwork, and harems. They liked it when people honored the symbols that were associated with their group identities, such as their countries' flags and national anthems and the symbols of their religions. Soon it became clear that people could win favor from Mark and Josh by setting up ways to honor them. Conversely, people in their respective countries could lose favor if they failed to honor Mark, Josh, or their symbols when an opportunity to do so arose. The irony was that the most powerful and protected person in each kingdom felt insecure.

Mark and Josh were more alike than they could ever have imagined. Had their situations been reversed so that Josh had first discovered the cave with water, the world would be no different. Josh and Mark weren't different from each other; only their circumstances were different. Markites and Joshovites were no different from one

another either; only their circumstances were different. Nevertheless, in order for Mark and Josh to maintain their exalted positions in their respective communities, they had to make people believe that there were differences—and that those differences mattered.

If people would share basic necessities, even during times of hardship, then these identities would not exist. Because we have a history of not sharing, we have separate identities. But these identities are not reality. We aren't different from one another. We just have a history of being selfish. Why do people continue to identify with being selfish?

The 4-23 Club

My identity is with the 4-23 Club. Anyone with four nucleic acids encoding a set of twenty-three chromosomes, anyone who lives on a planet tilted twenty-three degrees with four seasons, anyone with a four-chamber heart that reaches viability outside the womb at twenty-three weeks, is "In My Life"[93] and a member of the 4-23 Club. Joseph Campbell put it this way in his PBS telecast (1988) titled "The Power of Myth: Hero's Adventure":

> The only myth that is going to be worth thinking about in the immediate future is one that talks about the planet, not this city, not these people, but the planet and everybody on it. What it will have to deal with will be exactly what all myths have dealt with: the maturation of the individual, the pedagogical way to follow from dependency to adulthood, to maturity, and then to the exit, and how to do it. Then this myth will have to deal

---

[93] "In My Life," by the Beatles, the Fab Four, is number 23 on the *Rolling Stone*'s 500 Greatest Songs of All Time (2004).

with how to relate to this society and how to relate this society to the world of nature and the cosmos. That is what the myths [of all religions] have talked about and that is what this one has to talk about. But the society it has to talk about is the society of the planet and until that gets going, you don't have anything.

To share water during drought or food during famine with unrelated people requires an ability to override our basic instinct of survival. To share limited water is to think that maybe there'll be enough water to get us all through this drought but that if not we will die together. This shared experience requires us to override our fear of death in the near future, which allows us to live in happiness. I realize that sharing under these circumstances can sound idealistic. It's easy to imagine people saying, "I'm sorry, but if I have to drink all the water to save my life, I'm going to do it."

Unfortunately, the person who drinks all the water without sensitivity to or awareness of the feelings of others will have an unhappy life. Furthermore, if there is enough water for everyone but we choose to hoard it for fear of death in the future or just to enhance our status, we'll also have unhappy lives.

Perhaps we need to believe in miracles or just have faith that if we share the water, things will work out. And it does! People who die of thirst while sharing have been happy and free of fear. I even speculate that the frame of mind that allows us to override our survival instinct also frees us of the physical and emotional pain that accompanies dehydration. Furthermore, many people believe that dying, as we know it, is just a transition to another form of life.

Love after Death

How many of us still sense the presence of a dear friend or relative who has died? This is a common phenomenon, but there's no way to prove that it really occurs, just as there is no way to prove the existence of God. We have faith.

When we are able to override our basic fears and instincts with sensitivity to and awareness of the feelings of others, we are expressing love. I think of it this way: "If others die from thirst, then a part of me dies from thirst. Since I love all of me and won't let parts of me die, I'll share what little water I have left. Who knows when it will rain again?"

The poet John Donne (1572–1631) expressed it this way in "Meditation XVII":

> No man is an island, entire of itself; every man
> is a piece of the continent, a part of the main;
> … any man's death diminishes me,
> because I am involved in mankind.
> And therefore never send to know for whom
> the bell tolls; it tolls for thee.

What happens to love after we die? When someone dies, their body can no longer move, but body movement is not necessary for the experience of love. A body is necessary only for movements that satisfy conditions, but there are no conditions in real love. Love is not a quid pro quo arrangement. Real love is unconditional and doesn't require proof. Bodily movements aren't necessary in unconditional love, which means that our departed loved one's presence can still be perceived after death. This phenomenon also explains why we can feel love from people who are still alive, even when they're far away or can't communicate with us.

Joshua Simon, MD, EdD

Self-Esteem and the Need to Stand Out

We do not need to prove anything to feel and know love, and feeling loved is the surest way to know that we are valued. Isn't it ironic that, because of competitive factors, our egos are genetically programmed to let us believe that we're worthwhile only when we have proof that others see us as desirable?

Love and desire are not the same, but when our self-esteem is low, we often confuse the two. We make judgments that some people are more worthwhile than others and those that are judged more worthy are the loved ones. As a consequence, many of us set out to prove to the world that we are better than others in all sorts of competitive ways. In our history books and on television, we learn about people who have distinguished themselves. We try to be of worth by accumulating the status symbols of our culture and associating with others whom we think are desirable. In other words, feeling desirable, feeling worthy, and standing out in a crowd are all basically the same thing.

What would this world be like if the people whom we entrust to govern focused on love rather than on desire? What if our government leaders recognized people in other political parties as collaborators rather than competitors? What if government buildings weren't so physically imposing? What would this world be like if the people we entrust to govern focused on ideas and strategies that could reduce suffering, without the need for massive multi-pillared capitol buildings, courthouses, and monuments? What if we realized that no material object can house or contain love? What if we realized that the more we focus on acquiring material things, the greater the chance that the message of love will be overshadowed by the message that it's important to stand out? The beauty that God has placed all around us is simple, unobtrusive, and ordinary. Zen Buddhism makes it a point to recognize the beauty in the ordinary. A leaf, a ripple on a pond, and a thought of simplicity are all infused with beauty.

Tom Shadyac's 2011 documentary movie, *I Am*, does an extraordinary job of revealing how material success and acclaim does little for our sense of contentment. As the director of hit movies including *Ace Ventura*, *Patch Adams*, *Liar Liar*, and *Bruce Almighty*, Shadyac amassed wealth, prime real estate, and much positive recognition by his peers and the public, but he still felt empty inside. Despite standing out in culturally desirable ways, he realized, after much introspection, that contentment and a meaningful life have little to do with achievements—and much to do with showing concern for the well-being of others.

I Am makes reference to *The Last Hours of Ancient Sunlight*,[94] in which author Thom Hartman cites cultures of first contact such as the Spanish Empire and the Arawak in 1492 and the Europeans and Aboriginal Australians in 1788. In the exchange of ideas, cultures of first contact often agreed that the accumulation of private property beyond one's needs was a form of mental illness; it's a sign of psychological imbalance to take more than you need.

The Biggest Rationalization of All

The thought that we have worth and are a valued member of society only if we are desired by others is just not true. Therefore, this thought is a rationalization. I call it the biggest rationalization because our DNA and instinctual drives have programmed us to think that we are not worthy if we don't stand out or if we are not desired by the people who attract us.

---

[94] Thom Hartman, *The Last Hours of Ancient Sunlight* (Three Rivers Press, 1997).

Joshua Simon, MD, EdD

Isn't it sad that the great competitors in politics, religion, business, and the military monopolize our history? How often are people who have little interest in competition but much interest in reducing suffering mentioned in our history books? When have you seen a park or monument dedicated to someone who opposed a war? Martin Luther King Jr. is the rare exception.

On April 4, 1967, at Riverside Church in Manhattan (which coincidentally was the site of my graduation convocation from Columbia University), Dr. King spoke out against the Vietnam War in a speech titled "Beyond Vietnam: A Time to Break Silence." In his speech, he called on our government "to set a date that we will remove all foreign troops from Vietnam in accordance with the 1954 Geneva Agreement." King, a servant of Jesus Christ, recognized the wisdom in Buddhism:

> This is the message of the great Buddhist leaders of Vietnam. Recently one of them wrote these words, and I quote: "Each day the war goes on the hatred increased in the hearts of the Vietnamese and in the hearts of those of humanitarian instinct. The Americans are forcing even their friends into becoming their enemies. It is curious that the Americans, who calculate so carefully on the possibilities of military victory, do not realize that in the process they are incurring deep psychological and political defeat. The image of America will never again be the image of revolution, freedom, and democracy, but the image of violence and militarism."

In sports, "nice guys finish last," a quote attributed to Leo Durocher, Hall of Fame baseball player and manager. Nice guys don't win wars of aggression either—they do their best to stop them. Nice guys who are familiar with Muhammad's Five Pillars of Islam know to say no and set limits with people who act selfishly and aggressively (third base of the Golden Rule).

Nice guys get to reflect upon their lives positively, regardless of whether others perceive them to be on the winning side or the losing side. Nice guys realize that they are members of the 4-23 Club and, as such, are aware that there really aren't winning and losing sides; we are all on this planet together. Since humans are 24-7 thinking machines, success is not about finishing first or winning; it's about enjoying your thoughts—which nice guys get to do more of the time.

Born Again

Nice guys don't start life as nice guys. Thanks to four billion years of evolution, we all start as selfish DNA-incubating machines. Evolution doesn't care how much you suffer or how much suffering you cause others. What evolution cares about is your ability to get your strands of DNA copied into future generations. Evolution demands that you battle others for supremacy. Survival of the fittest is based on the premise that resources are limited and you can never have too much of these resources because nobody knows what catastrophic situation lies ahead.

Evolution demands that you fight for every possible advantage for your DNA. Qualities such as sharing, compassion, and love serve only as veils to camouflage your true motive, which is to advantage your DNA. If you convince others that you care about them, they'll let their guards down. Then you can dupe them into helping you get needed resources for your DNA's future survival—which, in turn, could limit the resources available to their DNA.

Existence as nothing more than a DNA-incubating machine is not a pretty picture, but that's how you are born. That's why it's so important to be born again with a spiritual life independent of your DNA. A spiritual life needs no resources, now or in the future, and it supplies you with information undetected by your five senses. A spiritual life allows you to get beyond the fear engendered by evolution's question "What if there are not enough resources to go around?" A spiritual life helps you realize that there are enough resources on this earth for everyone to raise a healthy family. Nobody's survival depends on being better or more deserving than anyone else, if we'll plan, share, cooperate, be considerate, and limit pollution.

What does it mean to be born again? In Christian orthodoxy, you are born again when Christ enters your life. But here's my expanded definition: You are born again when the four bases of the Golden Rule become the primary mover and shaker of your actions. For this to happen, you need to participate in any of the four spiritual acts with emphasis on altruism, which includes asking Christ to enter your life. The four bases of the Golden Rule and four spiritual acts include many ways to create a spiritual life, and they greatly limit the space used by your subordinate state as a DNA-incubating machine.

Free Will

People make their own choice about acting selfishly or kindly, based on their own psychological pressures and insecurities. Others' selfish or unkind behaviors toward us are not based on our own imperfections or past lives. Selfish, unkind behaviors are typical of people who have yet to realize that they are already good enough. No action that violates the Golden Rule will bear fruit or bring joy into a person's life. In fact, when we violate the Golden Rule, we actually cause misery for ourselves. As Jesus said, "Father, forgive them, for they know not what they are doing" (Luke 23:34 NIV).

Selfish or unkind behaviors only make life worse for the agents of these behaviors. Each time you act without considering the feelings of others, you build one more selfish memory that will resonate in your subconscious. As selfish memories accumulate in both quantity and intensity, so does the internal pressure—the need to prove something, get something, fantasize about something, or control something to think that your life is on track and that you are better than those whom you judge not good enough.

With selfish memories floating around in your subconscious, there is no contentment. It's hard to distract yourself from thinking about past selfish behaviors, so you get bored or lonely more easily and are more prone to abuse substances. You might even begin to feel misunderstood by others, but you're just reacting to the fear associated with thinking that maybe you aren't good enough. You're afraid that if there's a critical shortage of vital necessities such as food, water, and shelter, you might end up in the group that gets left out. It's hard to enjoy life when you think that you are not good enough to attract the people or groups you find attractive.

As hard as it is to distract yourself from unpleasant memories, it's even harder to accept that your lack of insight is responsible for much of your misery. Without insight, it's easy to think negatively or judge others in a way that raises your status by lowering theirs. All this negativity, however, can reach a tipping point where you can't handle it any longer. You'll start denying that you ever thought of yourself as not good enough or that you repeatedly acted selfishly. You'll project your own selfish behaviors and feelings of insecurity onto others and blame them for causing your misery.

Hidden Agendas

When you plan to violate one or more of the four bases of the Golden Rule, you're never sure if people are aware of your hidden agenda. If we think they may know about our hidden agenda, our Trojan horse, won't they try to get us before we get them? Thus, the safest approach to preventing what goes around from coming around is to have as much control and power as possible over others. The pharaoh, despite the warning of ten plagues, couldn't let go of his control over Moses and the Israelites. Like the pharaoh, if you're planning to stand out at the expense of others to gratify your ego or to fight in a war of aggression to prove your valor, then you have a lot to fear. However, if you practice the four bases of the Golden Rule, you have much less to fear since your true intentions are an open book and are nonjudgmental.

The pharaoh failed to touch the fourth base of the Golden Rule, "Never judge others to be undeserving of your kindness," despite God's attempts, with the ten plagues, to awaken him to a better way. People act selfishly when they don't yet realize that their lives can work out just fine without the need to stand out in some culturally desirable way and even without needing to hold the prevailing values of their culture, which typically favor some people over others. Furthermore, we don't need to experience as much sensual pleasure as possible to experience a most glorious life.

Each of us is a collection of memories. Do you realize that when your thoughts are based on memories of being kind, they bring you far greater satisfaction than when your thoughts are based on memories of your accomplishments or past pleasures? If your goal is to enjoy your consciousness, then you should avoid locking horns with someone just to prove that you're stronger. Unfortunately, many people behave like bulls by competing to be the most powerful, attractive, or praiseworthy.

The Dynamic of Envy

An interesting dynamic occurs when we become envious of those who appear to be the most powerful, wealthy, attractive, and praiseworthy. Envious people will sometimes develop subcultures by establishing alternative sets of values that allow them to stand out in the most desirable ways. Kids do this all the time when they form cliques. With the advent of the internet, a clique's new set of values can be advertised and its membership enlarged; Emo subcultures and Bronies are good example of this. Gang members and people involved in organized crime consider a different set of values to be praiseworthy, and the same is true of the military, police, sports teams, or members of any fraternal or professional organization.

Envy can also account for the development of grander organizations than cliques, gangs, and even governments. It has even been hypothesized that monotheism has its roots in this dynamic. Slaves from the land of Judah were envious of the life of the pharaoh and the wealth of his privileged class. The Egyptians worshipped many gods, so the enslaved Jews formed a belief in one God. In the Jewish religion, wealthy people have as much chance of getting into heaven as a camel has of getting through the eye of a needle, whereas the meek, lowly slaves inherit the Promised Land.

Underlying envy is the idea that people are either winners or losers and that the winners deserve to be valued more than the losers. The truth is that we all have value and deserve to be treated compassionately. Furthermore, by maintaining a compassionate viewpoint, you also learn that your own body is worthy of the self-discipline it takes to maintain its vitality.

Joshua Simon, MD, EdD

Does Evil Exist?

By maintaining a compassionate viewpoint, we can tackle any problem and arrive at a viable solution that is sensitive to all people and all of God's creation. Furthermore, with a compassionate attitude, we will realize that there is no such thing as evil—unless evil is defined as people reacting to fear while ignoring the feelings of other people or judging them to be undeserving of love and respect.

When we don't feel connected to a loving spirit, it's easy to react to fear in an "evil way." It's easy to think that others are doing a better job of preparing for the uncertainties that we may face in the future. It makes us uncomfortable to think that we're more vulnerable than others, so we look to join groups—a country, union, professional organization, gang, race, gender, or religious denomination, for example—where the nonmembers are the more vulnerable ones. The important thing is that the group's purpose is to enhance its members' ability to compete and if discrimination achieves its purpose, so be it.

We can compete more easily, whether individually or in a group, if we're seen in a positive light by other people, so we want to know what others are thinking. Do they approve of our views on marriage, disciplining children, race relations, taxes, religion, gun control, marijuana legalization, climate change, or even our definition of evil? To prevent others from gaining a competitive advantage over us, we try to get them to agree with our point of view. People who are less inclined to think independently often fall prey to "herd mentality" and conform to what members of the most powerful group are thinking. But no matter how successful we are, we will witness the loss of loved ones and our bodies will eventually crumble and die. We know from history (and this week's news) that some people suffer terribly through no fault of their own. Everyone is vulnerable.

Distractions and Escape

Rather than confronting our feelings of vulnerability, we often choose to escape by distracting ourselves and filling our lives with unhealthy, overly indulgent, or meaningless activities (the list of sixteen distractions), many for which we're willing to pay a lot of money:

1. Drugs
2. Alcohol
3. Food
4. Promiscuity
5. Attention-seeking behavior
6. Gossip
7. Idle chitchat
8. Hanging out with the crowd
9. Changing jobs or settings frequently
10. Risk-taking adventures
11. Mindless entertainment
12. Fantasy (including superstitions and some religious and political ideologies)
13. Shopping
14. Games and gambling[95]
15. Sporting events
16. Fashion

Distractions and Procrastination

We often are faced with choices. Do I do what needs to be done or get absorbed in a favorite distraction? Do I go to the gym or find something interesting on the internet? Do I eat a snack or

---

[95] Sports and games become distractions when the outcome matters or affects our mood.

stay focused on losing the weight I've recently gained? Do I give away things that I hardly use anymore or keep myself amused with shopping? Do I pay the bills or call a friend to chat?

Choose the more difficult path, provided that it doesn't impose unnecessary danger. Be mindful that even though you may experience some discomfort while on the more difficult path, you're just as safe or safer as when you're engaged in your favorite distraction. With this kind of thinking or mindfulness, you stay in touch with your inner feelings. Soon you'll realize that staying in touch with these feelings is a relatively easy thing to do. Procrastination will become a thing of the past.

Staying in Touch with Your Feelings

How do you develop confidence that your life will work out just fine, despite knowing that you are vulnerable and that things don't always work out the way they should? You could be victimized through no fault of our own. The tragedy of 9/11 and children killed in wars are prime examples. It would be nice to believe that there are ways to protect yourself in any situation. That is just not possible. Yet how many people get drawn into the fantasy that there is or should be an authority right now—a God, a religion, a country, a military—that has the power to protect us from all harm and give us advantages for fulfilling our desires in this life or in an afterlife?

If you could show me a culture built upon the Golden Rule, as opposed to cultures that evolved from a survival-of-the-fittest mentality, then maybe it wouldn't just be a fantasy that people could feel fully protected from man's inhumanity to man, and then too maybe the second coming of Christ could also become a reality. But right now that Golden Rule culture is only in its infancy. We remain too insensitive to our fellow human beings and continue to lack the confidence that we need.

Thought Patterns That Desensitize

People can develop confidence in the face of difficulties. We can evolve into a species wherein most of us can develop a healthy self-esteem, but that requires following the guidance of a loving force. That means using the four bases of the Golden Rule to solve problems and not losing sight of the feelings of vulnerability that arise within ourselves and others.

Unfortunately, because we are 24/7 thinking machines, thoughts can and do get in the way of staying in touch with our feelings of vulnerability. Many thought patterns, such as rationalizations, anger, criticism, and fantasy can actually desensitize us to feelings. One thought leads to another, and then another … and soon we have a whole bunch of ideas in our heads, but we've lost sight of our sense of vulnerability; we have lost sight of which of the four basic fears stimulated the whole process of thinking in the first place:

1. Fear of pain, discomfort, or death in the present moment and the unpleasantness of dealing with cultural norms that are highly critical of others.
2. Fear of pain, discomfort, or death in the future—for example, the fear that our basic needs will not be met, which is why we go to work to make money.
3. Fear that others do not understand how or why we think and feel the way we do. We socialize, in good part, to get feedback that we are reasonable and that others understand how we think and feel. As such, we are validated and feel worthy of acceptance, protection, and inclusion.

4. Fear of boredom and loneliness or a life without meaning, adventure, excitement, or pleasure, including the excitement and pleasure associated with dating.

Football

Let's say Bob is worried about having the approval of his father, and this initial feeling of vulnerability sets into motion all sorts of thoughts and actions. Bob worries that if he is unworthy of his father's approval, he could be cut off from food, shelter, and clothing (first and second fears). His father might also stop giving him money for fun activities or ground him and make him stay home all day (fourth fear).

Bob's father is interested in football, so Bob decides to try out for the varsity team. He now shares a common activity with other people, playing football and rooting for their favorite teams. This shared interest gives Bob a sense of approval or validation, counteracting the third fear, since he is doing what a lot of other people find interesting.

Football begins to shape Bob's values, and he gets upset when there's talk of dropping the high school football program because of budgetary constraints. He says that football is just as important as anything else at school because it involves getting into good physical condition, teamwork and camaraderie, strategy, and intelligence. This is a rationalization, since schools can function just fine without football. Is Bob aware that there are plenty of other ways to achieve these same results without playing high school football, and that his argument about the importance of football is just a rationalization?

Bob fantasizes about being a star, so it angers him when another player outperforms him at his position on the field. When he doesn't make the starting squad, he criticizes the coach and the player starting in his position. After a game in which he hardly plays, he escapes and distracts himself from his feelings of not being good enough by drinking with his buddies at a popular hangout. Does Bob know why he fantasizes about being a star, criticizes the coach, or gets angry on the field? Does he understand why he escapes with alcohol and doesn't feel content, even though it was quite an achievement just to make the team?

Bob doesn't understand that his relationship with football is about trying to win the approval of his father. The whole process of thinking about football started with Bob's fear of what could happen to him if he doesn't get his dad's approval (all four fears). If he's ever going to find lasting happiness and contentment, Bob will need to think that he's good enough. He'll need confidence that when the time comes to move out of his home, he'll find his way in this world.

Ideally Bob will have his father's approval in all aspects of his life except when he's acting selfishly. In this way Bob's dad will think that Bob is good enough whether or not he plays football, and Bob will have no doubts about being loved. Like most adolescents, however, Bob will carry into his early adult life the following beliefs: what he achieves, how he differs from others, and how he fits in with cultural norms will determine whether he will experience a good life.

Exercise: Can you remember your fears or unpleasant thoughts intensifying when you displeased a parent? If one of your deepest secrets was made public, do you know what you would fear and why? Keeping in my mind the relationship between fear and rejection, can you see how fear of revealing a secret would fall into one or more of the four basic fears?

Joshua Simon, MD, EdD

The Insecure Household

Some families hardly ever talk about their feelings in their own home, so Bob might not realize that he already has his dad's approval. Ideally, Bob's father already thinks his son is good enough, no matter what. But some children, through no fault of their own, have a parent who doesn't think their child is good enough. Parents sometimes pressure their children to stand out in some way, such as displaying impeccable manners, thereby proving to the world that they—the parents—must be good enough since they produced such outstanding children.

Some parents are too self-absorbed to provide meaningful guidance regarding the emotions that arise within their children. Instead those parents focus on activities that they like to do, rather than what their children enjoy. It's up to their children to show an interest in activities that their parents enjoy or associate with status. When their children get into trouble, the parents involve themselves only for the purposes of minimizing blame and financial loss. Children of self-absorbed parents are good at attracting negative attention.

If one or more of your family members is insecure, don't fret. This is the rule rather than the exception. The truly well-adjusted family is not nearly as common as we think. Furthermore, whether you are born into a well-adjusted family or not, nobody escapes from having to deal with difficult circumstances and emotions.

Other people might define us by our circumstances, such as whether we're rich or poor, pretty or ugly, educated or uneducated, or by factors such as our skin color, nationality, religion, or sexual orientation. These identifications don't take into account the most important factors of all—we all share the same feelings of vulnerability, and we're all motivated by the same four basic fears. Since we all have bodies that are going to fail one day, and since we can anticipate that failure, we will always, to some extent, feel vulnerable.

Sometimes our circumstances create such intense feelings of vulnerability that we feel overwhelmed. Keep in mind that these feelings have been experienced by others. Experiencing intense negative feelings doesn't mean that there's anything wrong with you or your life. We do not live in a Garden of Eden. The important thing is to stay in touch with your feelings. Don't use rationalizations, anger, criticism, or fantasy to desensitize yourself. Figure out which of the four basic fears is making you feel insecure. Then you'll realize that other people must have dealt with the same problem that's affecting you. In doing so, you will feel a connection to those others. Feelings of connectedness reduce loneliness and foster optimism and hope. Furthermore, a solution or even several solutions for your problem exist that take into account your feelings and the feelings of everybody else.

Use your spiritual or humanistic beliefs to strengthen your connection to a loving, guiding presence. If you associate a lot of hypocrisy with organizations purporting to know the ways of a loving God, consider taking another look. Abraham asked God to do that same thing, when he learned that God was about to destroy Sodom and Gomorrah: "Then Abraham approached Him and said, 'Will you sweep away the righteous with the wicked?'" (Genesis 18:23 NIV) In other words, don't throw the baby out with the bathwater. Don't write off the existence of God because of religion's association with war and other atrocities and misfortunes. These associations are based on misrepresentations of God by people who are guided by self-interest.

Essentially, a spiritual relationship gets started by maintaining an open mind and grateful heart while asking in earnest for a loving spirit, commonly referred to as God, to enter your presence and guide you eternally. When I experienced this entering into my life, God was named "Jesus, Our Lord." There are probably other ways to get in touch with our Creator's loving presence or the collective consciousness of humanity, but opening my heart to Jesus is the only way that I have personally experienced.

I was raised in a Jewish family by parents who were atheists, but here I am speaking of Jesus, Our Lord. I have many friends and some family members who are also guided by a loving force who never referred to God as Jesus, Our Lord. I believe that these friends, family, and I are guided by the same loving force, even though we may give it a different name. Yet, some of these very caring friends and family members are angered and think it disloyal for someone of their heritage to refer to God by a name not used by that heritage. Fortunately, the ones of whom I speak are guided by a loving force and as such know not to make plans or act while angry.

How to Handle Anger

Everyone gets angry. Sometimes we get angered when we think someone is working against us when previously we thought they were on our side; we are angered, as just mentioned, by disloyalty. Sometimes we get angered when we are slowed down while anticipating something more pleasurable than what we are feeling in the present moment. Sometimes we are angered when someone simply says no. This anger should let you know that you are feeling vulnerable. The important thing is to cool off. If you make plans while you're angry, don't act on them. Catch yourself when angered. Get in touch with your feelings. Think about which one of the four basic fears has you worried. Remind yourself to problem solve with insight and thoughtfulness.

Whatever problem your current circumstances have created, truly solving the problem and not creating more problems means your solution must take into account everyone's feelings. Therefore, do not act on a solution that judges others to be unworthy of your kindness. Also, keep in mind that pleasing others is not necessarily an act of kindness. If someone asks you to go along with their selfish plans (or asks you to do for them what they can to do for themselves), the caring and kind response is to say no. Also remember that sharing, cooperation, and inclusion take into account everyone's feelings; competing to have exclusive access or membership does not.

Let's say Mary asks Liz to go to a party. Then Liz says, "What about Judy?" Mary does not want to invite Judy and tells Liz that Judy isn't cool. Why would Mary say this about Judy? Perhaps Mary is fearful that her life is without meaning, excitement or adventure (the fourth basic fear) and having exclusive access to Liz's friendship gives Mary a purpose. Without Judy around, there would be less competition for the attention of a boy they might meet at the party. A romantic relationship is also an avenue for excitement and adventure. Perhaps Mary thinks Judy does not agree with her use of alcohol or sexy style of dress. Having Judy around could remind her that others don't understand why she thinks, feels, or acts the way she does, which is the third basic fear. Perhaps Judy might not be so tight lipped when Mary and Liz have a few drinks before heading to the party. If Judy somehow knows what Mary really thinks of her, what's to prevent Judy from retaliating by telling Mary's parents that she witnessed Mary drinking alcohol? Mary is anticipating being punished and having to deal with unpleasant emotions when confronted by her parents, which is the second basic fear.

If any of these scenarios that Mary worries about do in fact happen, she will have more memories to file away under the category "not good enough." Just the anticipation of them will intensify Mary's previous unpleasant memories. When Liz does not agree with

Mary to exclude Judy, yet another memory will be filed under the category "not good enough," because Mary will think she is not good enough at influencing others. With these memories of not being good enough, it will be easy for Mary to think that she is at a disadvantage in a competitive world and that because of this disadvantage she'll have difficulty attracting a desirable mate. If she becomes a mother, she may want badly to have her children stand out as proof to the world that she is good enough. Mary is setting herself up to be a self-absorbed parent.

If Mary persuades Liz to exclude Judy, how will Judy feel? Will Judy begin to believe that she needs to prove to the world that she is better than others or that she possesses those things that her family or culture value so that she will be valued and validated?

The perception that there is not enough for everyone underlies why Mary does not want Judy to be included. The perception that there is not enough for everyone sets into motion all kinds of activities that can cause pain and suffering to others such as Mary's rejection of Judy. Given that we are inhabitants of the only available planet that supports life, I ask, "How can we minimize unnecessary pain, discomfort, and suffering?" My answer envisions us getting better and better at sharing, which fosters inclusion, which in turn relieves our doubts about whether we are good enough. Below is a little mnemonic for remembering four important ways to share:

The T.R.E.E. of Life

Share your **T**houghts
Share your **R**esources
Share your **E**motions
Share your **E**xperiences

The Tree of Life is a symbol with imagery used in many religions. In Judaism, the Torah, or first five books of the Bible (Genesis, Exodus, Leviticus, Numbers, and Deuteronomy), are known as the Laws of Moses and given this symbol. The Tree of Life also represents the interconnectedness of the ten Sefirot as seen with the dotted lines in figure 1 that appears at the front of this book. These connections form the "spiritual arteries" of the primordial man.

When we are too fearful to share ideas and emotions, or when we take more than we need, it clogs our spiritual arteries; the flow of communication among the ten Sefirot becomes obstructed. It is this flow that nourishes our feelings of contentment. Blockages also form when we become desirous by attaching our self-worth to possessions or status symbols. Our spiritual circulation, most of all, is impeded when we don't realize or fail to remember that we are already good enough without having to prove anything to anybody. Sharing thoughts, resources, emotions, and experiences removes the blockages, barriers, or impediments within the circulation of the Tree of Life.

In Exodus 16:19 Moses warns us to take only enough resources to get us through any given day, with the exception of doubling up on the day before the Sabbath: "Then Moses said to them [the people following him to the Promised Land], 'No one may keep any of it [manna, the food sent from God to the desert] until morning" (Exodus 16:19 NIV).

If we lived in a world where all resources were shared, there would be enough "manna" available each and every day. However, when we live in a world where people hoard resources, then sharing becomes a much more difficult task. A faith or confidence in the earth's ability to meet our daily needs on a daily basis is greatly diminished when hoarding occurs. Hoarding is exemplified by a small percentage of the population controlling a large percentage of the wealth and resources. Unfortunately, the current state of affairs shows that the sixty-two richest people in the world have as much wealth as the 3.7 billion poorest.[96] The three wealthiest Americans—Bill Gates, Warren Buffet, and Jeff Bezos—possess more riches than the bottom 50 percent of the American population combined.[97]

When we live or strive to live in a world where people do share, it becomes much easier to let down our guard or shield—a guard or shield created in response to thoughts of inadequacy and the anticipation that we won't have enough resources to meet future needs. If you believe that a future in which the needs of some people will be ignored is not the kind of future you want to live in, then your shield or guard will dissolve. The dissolution of your guard or shield allows your authentic self to freely interact with the beauty in nature that our Creator has put before us. Your five senses become fully engaged. When you no longer worry that only a certain image of yourself will find acceptance by others, you will experience the beauty found in your heart and in the hearts of others.

Exodus 16:19 also points out the importance of deferring gratification. It is tempting to take more than what you truly need for today. It takes discipline to resist this temptation. It is easy to be tempted by the desire to accumulate wealth, tempted by the desire to stand out compared with others, or tempted by any of the sixteen distractions. These temptations take away valuable time that can be shared with loved ones or time for participation in any of the four spiritual acts. It takes discipline to raise your awareness of the importance of the four spiritual acts to your health and happiness. With this awareness it is easier to know that you are already good enough, which in turn

---

[96] https://www.oxfam.org/en/pressroom/pressreleases/2016-01-18/62-people-own-same-half-world-reveals-oxfam-davos-report.
[97] https://www.forbes.com/sites/noahkirsch/2017/11/09/the-3-richest-americans-hold-more-wealth-than-bottom-50-of-country-study-finds/.

makes it easier to avoid temptations whose purpose is to provide relief from the feeling that you are not good enough.

It is interesting to think of time as a resource as tangible as food, for example. We can ask, "Do I take too much time for my own personal needs of self-gratification? Do I tend to be self-absorbed and as a consequence less available to my family? Do I rush through my chores at home and at work because I cannot resist taking more 'time' for myself?" If you give of your time to others, you may think that you will not have enough time for yourself to do the things you like to do. As long as you remember not to do for others what they can to do for themselves, it is likely that you will need very little time for self-gratifying activities such as spectator sports, fashion, mindless entertainment, and enhancing your wealth. By being available to your family and by helping those truly in need of your services, you will experience so much intrinsic reward that the time needed to escape reality or pamper yourself or pursue extrinsic or materialistic rewards will seem quite immaterial.

Many Factors Affect Why We Do What We Do

Bob is quite focused on extrinsic, materialistic rewards. He fantasizes about all the recognition he will get if his football team wins the division championship. Recall that Bob's relationship with his father was cited as the primary motivator for his playing football in the first place. But Bob's life is not only about his relationship with his father. He has a mother and siblings. He has friends. He is interested in dating. He thinks about his future a lot and about what he thinks others think about him. He has a past that at times was quite unpleasant. Many factors contribute to Bob's playing football.

Football is risky. People get hurt playing football. Can you think of why Bob might take this risk even if he knew that his father thinks he is good enough? The answer lies in the four basic fears.

The high school football player may think he is not deserving of other people's attention, including a potential date, unless he can distinguish himself from others in a competitive way. This thought is based in cultural norms. This attention is called glory. If he doesn't get other people's attention, he may worry that he does not think and feel like other people (third fear). Furthermore, if he doesn't play football, he might think he is an oddball—a geek. He might think he'll be excluded from fun and exciting activities and that those peers he finds attractive will view him undesirably (fourth fear). He may even think that unless he excels on the football field, he is not worthy of approval from authority figures such as his parents, teachers, the coach, and even God. Without their approval, he may think he will not have their protection and that without this protection harm will come to him now or in the future (first and second fears).

Playing football is exciting. It can be dangerous. Like participation in the X Games, it gets the adrenaline flowing. It keeps the player focused on trying to avoid physical harm. This intense focus on avoiding injury, as well as on excelling by observing the movements of the other players on the field, can take his mind off all his other worries. In other words, football can provide a distraction that allows him to escape from his worries. While playing football, Bob may not have a single unpleasant memory enter his mind or thoughts about not measuring up to others in the classroom or rejection in social settings. It feels good to get relief from anxiety. Playing football, when it provides relief from anxiety, is fun. Fun relieves boredom (fourth fear). The player may feel connected with his teammates and thus feel accepted by others (third fear).

Bob may think that others are going to bully him unless he shows that he can be tough on the football field (first fear). Furthermore, he may hope to play football professionally and have doubts about his ability to make a living unless he excels at football (second fear).

Just like Bob experienced, thoughts about fear, failure, and not fitting in are occurring throughout much of our waking day, though most of the time they occur subconsciously. We all share feelings of vulnerability. These anxieties and related thoughts provide the motivation for Bob to play football and risk physical harm. Yet most boys would be hard pressed to explain why they choose to play football other than saying, "It's fun."

Fifth commandment: "Thou shalt not kill." Instead, thou shalt love. If someone wants to kill another, then someone is fearful and lacks awareness in these four ways: (1) awareness that he or she is already good enough, (2) awareness that he or she need not prove anything to experience a beautiful life, (3) awareness that other people's lives are as important as his or her own, and (4) awareness that there are enough resources for everybody to have what they need to raise a healthy family.

6

Tif'eret—Beauty

Practically every description of the "authentic person" extant implies that such a person, by virtue of what he has become, assumes a new relation to his society and indeed, to society in general. He not only transcends himself in various ways; he also transcends his culture.

—Abraham H. Maslow, *Toward a Psychology of Being* (1968)

Faith, unaccompanied by rigorous skepticism, is a recipe for myopia and foolishness.

—Joe Klein, *Bush's Last Days: The Lamest Duck*[98]

Tif'eret, meaning "glory" or "beauty," is about balance. It is the perfectly balanced union of love (Hesed) and fear (Gevurah). Another name for Tif'eret is "the Holy One, blessed be He." Tif'eret forms the spine of the primal Adam and unites the other nine Sefirot. More than any other Sefirah, Tif'eret is the aspect of God we worship and emulate. The Bible character it is most associated with is Jacob. Its direction is east. Its letter is *vav*.[99]

---

[98] *Time* (November 26, 2008).
[99] Arthur Goldwag, *The Beliefnet Guide to Kabbalah* (Three Leaves Press, 2005).

The earth, with its tilt of twenty-three degrees, infuses nature with the perfect balance of four glorious seasons, four glorious looks of nature in which winter balances summer and fall the spring. For the baby boomers, Bob Dylan's poetry provided balance to an otherwise overly rosy, self-serving picture we Americans have often had of ourselves. As America was building up its arsenal of weapons of mass destruction, Dylan asked in 1962, "How many times must the cannon balls fly before they are forever banned?" The answer to this question, once again, is "Blowin' in the Wind."

Many of us thought, as we headed off to college, that we could find the answer that had been blowin' in the wind. We were going to light up the world with our youthful enthusiasm and idealism. However, instead of answers, we found other questions: "How does it feel to be on your own?" Without the comforts of home, parents to keep us on track, or best friends to prop up our fragile egos, it was not difficult to feel disillusioned shortly after moving into the college dorm. Bob Dylan, the recipient of the 2016 Nobel Prize for Literature, won this award in part because he captured the worry, anxiety, and trepidations from our youth with his penetrating, insightful lyrics as found in *Rolling Stone* magazine's pick as the greatest song of all time, "Like a Rolling Stone": "how does it feel to be on your own, no direction known, like a complete unknown, like a rolling stone?"

In my first semester of college, I had no known direction and received four Cs and a D. The seven semesters that followed were not much better. I graduated as such a complete unknown that my school's official college transcript recorded that I had majored in geology when in fact it was geography. Geology, geography, geometry—what's the difference?

I imagine the Buddha, the son of a king, felt disillusioned too when he left his privileged home at age twenty-nine and saw more of the world. But unlike the college-age baby boomers who worried about whether their grades were good enough or they had a date to take to a frat party, the Buddha feels disturbed, as does Dylan, by the inevitability of aging, disease, suffering, death, and the sense of disconnection from those around us. The Buddha wonders how anyone could be relaxed, knowing the fate that awaits us all. But then he meets a monk, who appears to be so at peace with himself and the world that it inspires the Buddha to begin his journey. Along the way, he uncovers the Four Noble Truths. [100]

> First Noble Truth—Life is suffering; life includes pain, getting old, disease, and ultimately death. We also endure psychological suffering—loneliness, frustration, boredom, fear, embarrassment, disappointment, and anger.
>
> Second Noble Truth—Suffering is caused by craving and the need to control things. It can take many forms, among them the desire for fame and the desire to avoid unpleasant emotions, such as fear, anger, or jealousy.
>
> Third Noble Truth—Suffering can be overcome and happiness can be obtained; true happiness and contentment are possible. If we let go of our craving and learn to live each day, one day at a time (not dwelling in the past or the imagined future), we can become happy and free, then we have more time and energy to help others. This is nirvana.
>
> Fourth Noble Truth—The Noble Eightfold Path leads to the end of suffering: right view (understanding), right thought, right speech, right action, right livelihood, right effort, right mindfulness, and right contemplation (concentration).

---

[100] Mandy Barrow, "World Religions: Buddhism Religion," http://www.primaryhomeworkhelp.co.uk/religion/buddhism.htm.

The Buddha's Eightfold Path emphasizes the significance of the first base of the Golden Rule. When you are aware of and sensitive to how your actions affect the feelings of others, your views, thoughts, speech, actions, livelihood, effort, mindfulness, and contemplations will be "right." Furthermore, when you are aware of and sensitive to how your actions affect the feelings of others, you won't judge them to be undeserving of your kindness. When your views, thoughts, speech, actions, livelihood, effort, mindfulness, and contemplations are right, you won't do for others what they can to do for themselves and you will say no and set limits with people who act selfishly.

To learn the Noble Eightfold Path, at age sixteen I began my training as a monk in Japan at a Zen Buddhist temple. Wake-up time was 3:00 a.m. A bowl of rice was followed by meditation. Lunch consisted of another bowl of rice, followed by meditation. Dinner was yet another bowl of rice, although this time pickles were added, and was followed by further meditation. Then it was off to bed, to repeat the cycle the next day. I lasted two days. Actually, two days was all we had on our itinerary.

It was the summer of '67, and I was traveling with a group of fifty Americans that included my parents and various middle-aged couples. A few singles were thrown in, as well as two other teenagers. We were divided into two groups of twenty-five. I was the only teen in my group. We were all members of an organization called Servas.

Servas is Esperanto for "to serve." Esperanto was to be the universal second language, based on a blending of several common European languages. The concept was that if Esperanto could become everybody's second language everywhere in the world, there would no longer be communication barriers. As a consequence, we would all get along better. In other words, Esperanto was meant to promote peace and understanding between people of difficult cultures. Good luck getting Americans to learn a second language.

Joshua Simon, MD, EdD

Even without the use of Esperanto, however, Servas is able to promote peace and understanding between people of different cultures by using a system of hosts and travelers. Rather than staying in a hotel in a touristy, commercially oriented district, Servas arranges for travelers to be housed by individuals and families. Visitors get a much greater understanding, a real down-to-earth view of day-to-day life in the host country without a hotel bill. I think Americans will go for that. Hosts have the benefit of meeting people and learning about life in other parts of the world without having to travel.

So there I was in a Zen temple, sixteen years old, sitting in the lotus position on a tatami mat, trying to maintain proper spinal alignment without fidgeting in an attempt to meditate while my mind was busy trying to find a way to keep itself occupied. My brain waves naturally drifted to baseball. I thought about the lineups from the 1958 Braves, 1962 Giants, 1963 Dodgers, and the current New York teams, the Yankees and Mets. I went through each lineup umpteen times. Finally the gong sounded and the agony was over. We could open our eyes and look up, at which point the head monk walked right over to me. I was thinking positively: *he's going to let the other twenty-four Americans know what a good job I did, particularly since I'm the youngest person in the room.*

The night before, we had arrived late to the temple. We had eaten our dinner of rice and pickles, watched a short video about what to expect during our stay, and gone to sleep. As demonstrated in the introductory video, the head monk approaches each person at the end of a meditation session and taps them on the shoulder with a stick. The monk-in-training then lowers himself or herself and awaits the head monk's judgment. Another light touch of the stick indicates a good meditation. Two hard whacks across your back lets you know the head monk disapproves.

When the head monk approached me first and tapped my shoulder, I lowered myself, awaiting his tap of approval. Instead, two sharp whacks struck my back. There were gasps of disbelief in the room. Though we had seen the training film, we were tourists: surely they weren't going to discipline us like real monks-in-training. I immediately sat up and made eye contact with my parents and smiled, letting them know I was okay. Then the monk crossed over to the other side of the circle and tapped my father. Two whacks came down on his back too. The head monk then approached a woman. She sat up and waved her hands, saying, "No, you're not going to hit me." She got up and left the room. At that point the head monk walked out and so did we. Day two at the monastery ended rather abruptly.

In Buddhism success is a state of mind in which we are free from attachment. When we attach our ego to any person or object, it disrupts the object's natural presentation—a presentation that naturally already shines with radiance, harmony, and beauty. Our ego only gets in the way of the beauty. Apparently, at sixteen I was too attached to baseball.

By age sixteen I already had plenty of memories filed away under the category of "not good enough." Yet, when I think back to the head monk disciplining me because my meditation was not "good enough," this memory does not feel at all like I was not good enough. It didn't feel like criticism. The head monk did his best to bring my life into balance. He acted from his heart. After the two whacks on my back, I looked up with a broad smile on my face.

By referring to Figure 1, "the primordial man," at the beginning of this book, we see that Tif'eret is near the level of our heart. The takeaway message is that when we tune in to the information that our heart sends to our brain, we bring judgment and love into balance. Should we evaluate someone's performance, whether it be a good act or a bad act, the evaluation will be accepted with gratitude, provided that our evaluation is heartfelt.

The four bases of the Golden Rule also exemplify the balance and beauty of Tif'eret. Two bases from Hesed (love) are balanced by two bases from Gevurah (fear or judgment). Never judge someone to be undeserving of your kindness, and always maintain a heightened awareness of and sensitivity to how your actions affect the feelings of others: those expressions are steeped in love, or Hesed. Don't do for others what they can to do for themselves, and say no and set limits with people who act selfishly require judgment: those two concepts represent Gevurah. The more you practice these four "balanced" principles, the more beautiful life becomes and the easier it becomes to stay in touch with your heart. It also becomes easier for your spine to stay in proper alignment, which at age sixteen was quite difficult for me to do.

Still today I am working on keeping my spine in proper alignment and meditating more often to stay in touch with Tif'eret. Fittingly, I believe my first love, Elizabeth, was also making an effort to stay in touch with Tif'eret when we met up on March 13, 1996. On that day during a heartfelt conversation I interjected, "I know you love me, but you have never told me you love me."

Elizabeth had used the word *love* when signing off on letters or notes while we saw each other in college, but she had never spoken it to me. Elizabeth was in disbelief. Knowing how she felt for me at that moment and how she felt for me while we were dating twenty-four years earlier, she couldn't imagine that she had never spoken the word to me. At that point, as tears ran down my cheeks like the ones I'd cried at age ten while watching Lou Gehrig in *Pride of the Yankees*, Elizabeth said, "I love you. I love you."

It was my mother who aroused my suspicion that Elizabeth had been holding in her words of love. About a week before Elizabeth's declaration of love, my mom and I had watched the Keanu Reeves movie *A Walk in the Clouds* (1995), which was based on an Italian movie, *Four Steps in the Clouds*, released in 1942, the same year as *Pride of the Yankees*. My mom commented to me that the Hispanic father (played by Giancarlo Gianinni) loves Victoria, his daughter (played by Aitana Sanchez-Gijon), but never tells her.

Those three magical words, *I love you*, and again, *I love you*, facilitated the sensing of an energy that heretofore had passed me by. Perhaps this energy lit up the part of my brain where poetry resides. Within a week after hearing "I love you, I love you," a poem burst forth.

> Love, a flower
>   slowly unfolds
> Colors, aroma
>   senses behold
>
> Petals soft
>   feelings of ease
> Garden delights
>   essence to please
>
> Blossoms open
>   sunlight reveals
> Evening's secrets
>   darkness concealed
>
> Fragrant spirits
>   linger with night
> Sweeten dreams
>   of morning's light

Joshua Simon, MD, EdD

>Awaken gently
> feelings untold
>Love, a flower
> slowly unfolds

Two months later Elizabeth and I met up again in friendship. What's utterly fascinating is that she commented that I looked like Keanu Reeves. Yet I had not mentioned anything about the movie I had watched with my mom.

What did I perceive when I heard her say, "I love you"? Was it more than vibrations set in motion by vocal cords that struck my eardrums? Was some other kind of energy transmitted with these words, and if so, how did I sense or perceive it? Alternately, do we usually sense only some of the energy at any given moment and at this particular instance did I perceive more than the usual amount? Did I sense some kind of "spiritual" or "mystical" energy?

Perception and Health

It is clear that we possess receptive organs and a brain that can receive and perceive energy (sight, sound, touch, taste, smell) in a four-dimensional space-time continuum, but is it possible that under some circumstances, we may even possess a receptive sensor that defies the currently understood laws of physics by allowing us to sense spiritual or mystical energy as well? In the 2011 documentary movie *I Am*, Tom Shadyac cites several observations that defy scientific explanation. Yogurt is affected by human emotions, as measured by electrodes placed in the yogurt. Random number generators stop being random when news of a catastrophic event, such as 9/11 or the 2004 tsunami, travels around the world. These phenomena suggest that there are forces that are not easily explained by current scientific mechanisms.

The critical question is not whether we receive energy in all its known and unknown mystical or spiritual forms, but how we interpret this energy once it is perceived. For example, I might perceive or interpret a painting as beautiful, whereas someone else might see the same painting as ugly. I might perceive John Doe to be friendly; someone standing right next to me might regard the same John Doe with suspicion. These different perceptions or interpretations can have a profound effect on our health.

How Perceptions Affect Our Health

In *The Biology of Belief*, geneticist Bruce H. Lipton gives an elegant, detailed explanation of how perceptions affect genetic expression.[101] Accordingly, our brain can send different signals to the cells throughout our body by way of nerve connections and hormones. Which nerve signals and hormones are stimulated by our brain depends on how we interpret our interactions with other people and how we interpret other issues or stressors such as the weather or an upcoming test, for example.

These neurotransmitters and hormones affect the contents of the fluids that interact with the proteins embedded in each cell's membrane in the various organs throughout our body. The cell membrane proteins, in turn, can alter the internal environment of the cell, which will affect the unfolding of our set of twenty-three chromosomes. How our chromosomes unfold will affect which proteins are made. These proteins then affect just about every function of the body, from digestion to fighting disease.

If I perceive John Doe to be a suspicious character, for whatever the reason, it will set off a stress reaction. If I perceive John Doe to be

---

[101] Bruce H. Lipton, *The Biology of Belief: Unleashing the Power of Consciousness, Matter, and Miracles* (Hay House, 2008).

friendly, an entirely different set of signals will be sent to my cells. This will affect which proteins are made. No matter what situation I face, if I feel confident that somehow things will work out just fine, my brain will communicate with my cells differently from how they will if I think I must always be doing more to please others or to prepare for potential problems, or that I need more influence and control over the people around me.

Feeling confident, in general, will reduce the level of stress we perceive in any given situation. During those periods of our development when we relied almost exclusively on an instinctually driven brain—one that directs us toward pleasure and away from pain—it is unlikely that we would have had the insight to realize that we can develop a sense of utmost confidence not from accomplishments or status but from simply letting others know that their feelings matter to us. What better way is there to acknowledge the feelings of others than to follow the four bases of the Golden Rule! When you acknowledge others' feelings, you feel connected to them. These connections, in turn, form a spiritually driven support system that inspires confidence. With these connections you will sense that you are not alone, no matter what problems you face.

When you do not recognize the value in connecting to others through awareness and sensitivity, you will likely think that you need to prove something to yourself and others before your life will work out. Under the latter circumstance, achieving goals and obsessing over what you think others think about you becomes the focus of your conscious and subconscious mind. You will also focus on how you can influence others so that others will help you reach your goals, or at least not slow you down. Achieving these goals, in turn, will let you think (finally!) that you are good enough and that you have value, since now you possess the attributes or material things that others value. But does it?

We are programmed genetically, as I said before, to want to stand out and be the strongest bull in the meadow or the most desirable cow that attracts the strongest bull. Yet, like the bull or the cow, no matter how many successes we have had in our past, every other cow and bull in the present moment will continue to appear as a potential challenger. You can't rest on your laurels. The peace of mind that you think will be there when you achieve your goals is never really there. "I thought I had it made when I got into the college of my choice. I thought I had it made when I got into graduate school. I thought I had it made when I found the right person to marry. I thought I had it made when I got my first professional job. I thought I had it made when I got promoted. I thought I had it made when another company wooed me and gave me a large increase in salary. I thought I had it made when I moved into a better home and neighborhood. I thought I had it made when I put enough money away for retirement. Yet I still wished that I had put more money away and had fewer inches on my waist."

Instincts, Desire, Perceived Influence, and the Pecking Order

Underlying our inability to feel content are our instincts of survival and sexual reproduction. Our subconscious constantly asks, "What have you done lately to improve your position in society?" Do you stand out enough compared with others? Are you a winner or a loser? Are you outstanding or ordinary? If you think you're a winner or outstanding, you can more readily believe that you are deserving of safety, protection, and limited resources compared with those who you see as losers or just plain ordinary.

When you think you're a winner or a member of some kind of exclusive group, you'll also likely think that you're more capable of attracting those people who attract you. Essentially, without outstanding qualities or membership in an outstanding group, you will think that you are at a disadvantage when it comes to your ability to influence others to view you in a favorable light. Your subconscious mind works tirelessly by analyzing how much influence you think you have over others. Perceived influence may be the most powerful factor affecting your subconscious assessment of where you stand in the pecking order.

Yet, you do not need to stand out or please or influence others to feel safe and deserving of a beautiful life. To repeat, this book's mantra is that simply because you are human, you deserve a beautiful life and access to basic needs and protections. Rather than achievement, acts of kindness[102] bring to your consciousness all the beauty that our Creator has placed around you and in your heart. Also, as stated repeatedly, you do not need to prove anything to anyone to be deserving of this awareness and sensitivity. The more you let others know they do not need to prove anything to be the recipient of your kindness, the less you will think consciously or subconsciously that you need to do more before you can feel good about yourself. In other words, you can enjoy the moment right now simply by thinking others are good enough, no proof needed. When you drop the "proof" requirement, your experiences with friends and family become more enjoyable and form lasting moments of happiness.

Nature versus Nurture

In *The Biology of Belief*, Lipton makes the case that nurture has a much greater effect on the disease process than previously thought. He estimates that only about 2 percent of diseases can be attributed to dysfunctional genes from birth. Ninety-eight percent of diseases occur in people born with fully functioning genes. It is how our genes express themselves that will determine why one person dies at age thirty-seven from a heart attack, cancer, ALS, or even suicide,

---

[102] Kindness is synonymous with the four bases of the Golden Rule.

whereas another person with essentially the same set of genes lives to ninety-five. As previously stated, how our genes express themselves is influenced primarily by how we interpret the information picked up by our sensors or nervous system.

Stress Is the Killer

Stress is the killer. When we perceive John Doe to be a suspicious character rather than friendly, it sets off a stress response that affects neural activity and hormonal levels. This response includes cortisol release, which then suppresses immune function. It includes catecholamine (adrenaline and noradrenaline) release, which then elevates one's heart rate and blood pressure. These elevated hormonal levels in our circulation are sensed by our cell membranes, which communicate this information to the nucleus inside the cell. The protein-making apparatus in the nucleus, in turn, will be stimulated to make more proteins for future fight-or-flight responses. As a consequence, fewer proteins are made that can repair cells damaged by toxins or oxidants as well as fewer proteins that can strengthen other areas of our immune system.

Another factor is that in preparation for the fight-or-flight response, circulation to the muscles is enhanced for the delivery of nutrients and the removal of waste products at the expense of decreased circulation to other vital organs. Furthermore, stress induces changes in nerve tissue in our brain that have lasting effects on our mood and memory function.[103]

This situation in the cell is analogous to the rulers of a society activating a stress response when they perceive people who do not share their beliefs as competitors—competitors who could lower their

---

[103] Robert Sapolsky, *Biology and Human Behavior: The Neurological Origins of Individuality*, 2nd ed., The Great Courses (Chantilly, VA: The Teaching Co., 2005).

position in the pecking order. During this kind of stress response, more of the society's resources (analogous to cellular proteins) are devoted to building or acquiring weapons, armies, internal security forces, and detention centers. Perhaps the most troubling stress responses are those that devote resources to "spinning the news" and propaganda that is designed to combat the supposed "corrupting influence" of different points of view.

Because the rulers do not perceive "others" to be friendly, fewer resources are available for "society's immune system," which includes infrastructure; education; health, science, and environmental activities; spiritual centers; and the arts. Other "immune functions" are suppressed, such as individual artists and civic organizations (including open-minded journalists, legislators, and judges) that do not openly praise the ruling party's point of view. Though the rulers think their efforts make them safer from attack, in fact, they become more and more vulnerable because of the unrest from "their people," who are suffering because of a lack of both basic services and spiritual-humanitarian outlets.

It's all about perception. If people perceive others with differing views as potential collaborators on a better society, fewer resources are needed for the stress response. If we can accept that each of the four different ways of interpreting scripture[104] adds useful knowledge and wisdom for developing a healthier society, we should be able to accept that there are probably at least four valuable methods or ways of looking at economic theory; energy and environmental issues; the role of religion and government; justice and the rehabilitation of criminals; the role of the military, police, and gun ownership; sexual mores and birth control; tobacco, alcohol, and drug use; parenting styles; educational methods; medical treatments; diet and nutrition; and so on. As a society we will likely be a lot healthier when our

---

[104] Literally, allegorically, philosophically, and mystically.

leaders learn how to recognize that their point of view is just one part of the solution, not the entire solution.

This need to have influence over others and the degree to which we feel threatened if others don't espouse the same point of view as ourselves is directly proportional to (1) our history of acting without awareness of and sensitivity to the feelings of others (selfishness) and (2) the degree to which we feel inadequate or not good enough in some way. Our memories of selfishness and our thoughts of inadequacy cause us to believe that we do need to prove our worthiness. Thus we arrive at the need to have influence, since influence provides the proof we are looking for. After all, why would anyone let us influence them unless our opinion or objectives were valued? Furthermore, if my opinions or objectives are valued, then I must be valued! The pattern of thinking that creates the need to have influence does not take into account the truth, which is that we already have all the value we will ever need simply because we are human. When we recognize this truth, different points of view will not feel threatening just because they are different.

Are traditional values in America threatened when people oppose a Christmas display on public land? Does marriage between gay men or lesbian women threaten family or religious values? Because our subconscious associates how much influence we have in society with our place in the pecking order, it is hard to let go of matters in which we can influence others. I'm not making a case for or against traditional marriage or a Christmas display. However, the likely reason people use such emotionally laden words as *threatened* when discussing these kinds of issues is that they feel threatened individually, albeit primarily subconsciously, by a potential loss of status if others do not agree with them.

No one can stop an individual from envisioning or thinking about marriage, Christmas, or other topics in the way they choose to think about them. Do we really need others to validate our visions, ideas, and objectives to believe in the value of these visions, ideas, or objectives? We don't, and therefore we need not attach such emotionally laden language, the language of fear, when analyzing the effects of different points of view—that is, unless our vision is to see ourselves as having more influence, more value, or more status than others.

Stress and Observations

As I observe John and Jane Doe, for example, I notice their tattoos and piercings. If I think there is probably an interesting reason or story behind them, or John and Jane had an understandable urge to make a change to find acceptance, for example, within the group with whom they identify, then their presentations will not elicit a stress response. On the other hand, if I associate all sorts of negatives with tattoos and piercings, they will elicit a stress response. The bottom line is that the more judgmental you are, the greater the stress response.

If I look at tattooed and nose-ring-wearing men or women and they smile warmly, they have acknowledged that my feelings matter. The underlying message conveyed by this smile is that I do not need to worry that they may think I'm not good enough to be deserving of their respect. The simple act of smiling prevents a stress response.

Without a stress response, my brain will not send signals to the cells throughout my body to prepare for a fight-or-flight response. On the other hand, if I look at John Doe and he says, "What the f*#% are you looking at!" it will be difficult, although not impossible, to avoid a stress response. We can still respond to this situation with compassion by thinking that it's too bad this man perceives a threat where none exists. If he balls up his fist after cursing at me, then let the stress response begin. It's time to let my instinct for self-preservation take over. Regardless of the response that gets elicited, it will be a joint decision between the activity of a few conscious thoughts and a million times that activity in my subconscious brain.

So what can we do to influence our subconscious, which can greatly affect whether we perceive the universe as friendly? To answer this question we must first have a good grasp of why we think.

Why We Think

"I think, therefore I am." Rene Descartes is not alone. Thinking is intriguing. We have all wondered what people, ideas, and activities are truly meaningful. We frequently ask teens what they plan to do with their life. Most teens don't have much of an answer other than that they plan to go to college or get a job. However, if we don't find meaning in our life by middle age, the proverbial midlife crisis arrives.

Living a life without purpose or meaning is one of the four basic fears. Alternatively, a life with purpose and meaning is one of the four basic loves. To understand the meaning of life, we need to understand what truly motivates us. What do we expect to accomplish, and why do we have those expectations in the first place? Is there more to life than survival? From a practical point of view, how can we simplify or enhance our daily routine so that we spend more time on what really matters? Which people, activities, or ideas deserve our attention? What are our priorities? These are important questions.

What if you don't really know how to set priorities—priorities that are meant to bring you a measure of success? What if you don't know what activities, people, and ideas are important? What if you have a clear set of priorities but don't think you have the ability or resources to successfully act on them? Then what? Then you stagnate and procrastinate. You fill your life with meaningless activities and distractions. You escape. As mentioned in the third chapter, the list of distractions is quite extensive (four by four):

>Drugs
>Alcohol
>Food
>Promiscuity
>Attention-seeking behavior
>Gossip
>Idle chitchat
>Hanging out with the crowd
>Changing jobs or settings frequently
>Risk-taking adventures
>Mindless entertainment
>Fantasy
>Shopping
>Games and gambling
>Sporting events
>Fashion

The Definition of Success

I intend for the ideas presented here to make it easier for you to set priorities and find meaning in your life. This will allow you to sidestep the pitfalls created by a society filled with distractions. In addition, success will be defined not by results, but rather by the degree to which you can maintain a heightened awareness of how your actions affect the well-being of your body and the well-being of others. This heightened awareness and sensitivity is the essential component that underlies the development of confidence—confidence that life has a way of working out just fine no matter what problems you inherited or created through your own actions that were guided by ignorance rather than by the insight you now possess. To obtain this heightened awareness and sensitivity, to live positively on "4th Street," you must first understand what thinking is really about and its relationship to your emotions.

Fitting In

From an early age, you observed what was going on around you and tried to fit in. You modeled what you saw. You did this much of the time without your conscious awareness. As an adult, you try to fit in with those with whom you live and work and with your cultural values in general. "Not fitting in" causes unpleasant emotions. Ask kids what hurts the most, and they will say, "Being excluded by other kids."

According to Lawrence J. Kirmayer, psychiatric anthropologist, in trying to fit in, "We are unconscious of many of our own motivations and patterns of thought and behavior until they are reflected back to us by others ... We are unconscious of our cultural background, knowledge and assumptions ... Each society tends to cultivate blind spots around the specific forms of social suffering that it produces."[105] Colonialism and "white man's burden" blinded itself to the talents, abilities, and intellect of indigenous populations around the globe. Affirmative action blinded itself from the maxim that two wrongs (a new way to discriminate based on skin color to compensate for an old way to discriminate) don't make a right. We surely know how colonialism and discrimination causes suffering.

Joseph Campbell, famed mythologist of the PBS series *The Power of Myth* hosted by Bill Moyers, offered a way of thinking that would

---

[105] Laurence Kirmayer, *Psychiatry*, eds. Allan Tasman et al. (2008).

go a long way in eradicating the "planet of the blind spots": "[What] society has to talk about is the society of the planet and until that gets going, you don't have anything."

Once you realize that you have nothing to prove and that you are already good enough to deserve and experience a beautiful life, you will also realize that you are a member of each and all societies, for in reality, there is only one society. We are all members of the 4-23 Club; as stated previously, anyone who has four nucleic acids encoding a set of twenty-three chromosomes and lives with four seasons on a planet tilted twenty-three degrees is a member of the club. Furthermore, the Buddha, with Four Noble Truths, and Muhammad, with twenty-three years of revelations, showed us that by using a heightened awareness and sensitivity and the power of faith, you can protect yourself from the blind spots created by your own feelings of vulnerability as well as blind spots created by the rich and powerful. But if we are ever going to eliminate blind spots, we must all come together and realize that each person's needs are as important as those of any other person, regardless of his or her cultural values, family background, or place on the map. Furthermore, we need not blind ourselves to the ways in which our culture supports our involvement with the list of sixteen distractions.

Most of us participate in only a few of these distractions, but when we take into account the many subcultures in a population of more than three hundred million Americans, everything on the list of distractions is important among some sizable group. There are people who have staked their livelihood on you spending time and money on these distractions. If we consider distractions blind spots, it follows that "we are unconscious of our cultural background, knowledge and assumptions" that may lead us to these distractions in the first place. It is as if we are drawn to these distractions while our mind is on autopilot.

Problems and Disappointment

Automatic thinking underlies our daily routine, our mannerisms in social settings, our attractions and distractions, and especially our fantasies. We shift out of automatic thinking when we sense problems or disappointments. Problems or disappointments in the present moment bring us out of our fantasy world and back into reality, where we become much more aware of what is causing us to think. We are more attentive to our thoughts when we think others might disagree with or criticize us. Similarly, we attend consciously to our thoughts when we are disappointed or think we need to make a change. As a result, many people see their life primarily as a series of disappointments, regrets, misunderstandings, and lost opportunities. When not thinking about problems, our brain likes to shift us back into activities, such as watching sports or leafing through fashion magazines, activities where we can run on autopilot and that can engage us in fantasies that lessen our feelings of vulnerability.

In his best-selling book *The Power of Now* (1997), Eckart Tolle draws upon spiritual philosophies to teach us that most of what happens in this universe has little to do with problems or our negative thoughts of disappointment. If we can train our brain to stop running on autopilot, we will see that "nondisappointing" events occur all around us—events of beauty, harmony, creativity, and love. But to connect to these "nondisappointing" or "problem-free" events, we need to rid ourselves of the judgments and assumptions that are woven into the fabric of our society—judgments and assumptions based on biases that are meant to protect our ego from thinking we are not good enough when we compare ourselves with others. The truth of the matter is that we are good enough and do not need to compare ourselves or prove anything to know it. But until our self-esteem matures out of its egocentric viewpoint, we will think that we do need to prove something. Thus disappointment awaits us.

Our Universe's Message of Love

Even the most selfless, spiritually minded person whose ego is so intact that it needs little attention will experience disappointments and difficulties. But the time and intensity of these disappointments are greatly diminished when we reconnect to our universe's loving message. For those of us whose beliefs include one indivisible God, this is my interpretation of God's loving message—our universe's message. For those without a belief in God, it's my theory of how humanitarian ideals influence perception. It is relatively simple. What is our universe's message of love? It's the four bases of the Golden Rule:

1. Thou shalt develop and maintain a heightened awareness of and sensitivity to how your actions affect the feelings of others, as well as the well-being of your body.
2. Thou shalt not do for others what they can to do for themselves.
3. Thou shalt say no to people who demand that or ask us to go along with their selfish plans.
4. Thou shalt not judge others to be undeserving of your kindness or generosity.

This loving message is always available to us. Therefore, no matter what circumstances you find yourself in today, joy, happiness, contentment, and even ecstatic moments can be encountered at every corner with greater and greater frequency. By understanding how and why you feel and think the way you do, you can connect more easily to our creator's loving message embodied in the Golden Rule. Moses asks us to strengthen this connection by using the

Ten Commandments, Buddha by the act of meditation, Jesus by accepting his role as savior and source of unconditional love, and Muhammad by the use of daily prayer and the goal of uniting all of humankind. Humanitarians, who may be agnostic or atheistic, ask us to use the Golden Rule as well because it embodies compassion and makes sense logically in that no belief system is needed to see its benefits. When the Golden Rule is incorporated into our decision making, our brain and body reward us with greater wellness and contentment.

When the four bases of the Golden Rule are firmly embodied in our laws, in our sense of justice, and in our avenues of opportunity, we will have positioned ourselves to be on the pathway toward greater happiness and greater clarity of purpose. Furthermore, this pathway is lined with meaning, excitement, adventure, and sensual delights. When we declare that "all men and women are created equal," we are well on our way down the long and winding road that leads to the Promised Land. But watch out for the potholes, shortcuts, and bridges to nowhere.

Beware of cultural values that tangibly reward us for standing out. Any desire to stand out in a culturally (or subculturally) desirable way, no matter how well intentioned, will create distractions, intense disappointments, and negative judgments, and lead us off the path of happiness. This relationship between desire and suffering is central to Buddhist thought. This relationship can also be understood from the wisdom spread by God's three principal messengers: Moses, Jesus, and Mohammad.

Sixth commandment: "Thou shalt not commit adultery." Rather than an act guided by desire, when guided by a spiritual, compassionate force, physical love is an act of care and commitment. It is an act in which we communicate thoughtfulness with our sense of touch. Honesty is the most important aspect to a caring relationship with others. Adultery makes use of our sense of touch without care and commitment and most often without honesty. Be honest and open about your current sexual life with people with whom you are close enough to touch. To do otherwise would be thoughtless.

7

Netzach—Endurance

These human problems, these problems in society [such as weapons of mass destruction, corporate scandals, and environmental decay] don't appear from nowhere. They are created by human beings and arise from the same problems all individuals have. But collectively, on a wider scale, there is an additive effect ... If these problems in society are to get better, it is not enough that a few experts discuss these things. Every individual has to change. And the only way to do this is for ordinary people to have greater awareness of the bigger problem, an understanding of what creates the problem, and the desire to change things, person by person.

—The Dalai Lama, in conversation with Howard Cutler in *The Art of Happiness at Work* (2004)

Jesus says that it's natural to love those who love us. The Mafia, for instance, has perfected that concept. The good stuff, the destiny-defining stuff, happens as we take chances in loving those outside of that circle.

—David Schmelzer, *Not the Religious Type* (2008)

Netzach generally translates as "eternity," and in the context of kabbalah refers to "perpetuity," "victory," or "triumph." Netzach is also "endurance," the fortitude and patience to follow through on your passions and to inspire others to a cause and motivate them to act; it is the earthly counterpart to Hesed. It is the right leg of the primal Adam and is associated with Moses. Netzach represents prophecy, God's active grace in this world, and His limitless mercy. Netzach is where the urge to "repair the world" comes from, the aspiration to right wrongs and institute better social systems. Netzach is also the source of the messianic urge.[106]

Netzach asks us to institute better social systems. It asks us to triumph by changing the self-serving structures that are deeply ingrained in our culture. Judging by the quotes above, the Dalai Lama and David Schmelzer have felt the presence of Netzach and the urge to repair the world.

Netzach is eternal. It exists without the need for a physical body. It resides in the spirit or soul. The antithesis of Netzach is the fear that arises from the limited life of our bodies. Thus there are two major spheres of influence affecting the way we think and feel. One sphere is instinctual or fear based; the other is spiritual or love based. They exert two totally different types of pressure on the way we problem solve.

The instinctual sphere accounts for your competitive nature and why you sense fear when you anticipate that your survival or your offspring's survival is threatened. Your instinctual existence is encoded in your DNA and passed down genetically to each succeeding generation. Whether your spiritual side is also codified in your DNA is not as clear. Regardless, to strengthen your spiritual sphere, you need to learn how to lead a spiritual existence from the writings, actions, oral accounts, or artistic expressions of "enlightened" others as well as

---

[106] Arthur Goldwag, *The Beliefnet Guide to Kabbalah* (Three Leaves Press, 2005).

from your own heartfelt insights. However, who is enlightened and what is truly heartfelt is open to debate.

The instinctual side to the human condition is perhaps less controversial and easier to understand than your spiritual side, so let's explore your instinctual nature first. To help with this exploration, I'd like you to begin with a clean slate.

Clean Slate

Disregard every judgment you hold. Place no value on anything that has come before. Don't think positively or negatively about the human condition or any of its social conventions or social structures. Do not rely on any previous thinking about what is right and what is wrong. Disregard everything associated with your self-esteem and everything you expect of others. Let's begin with a clean slate.

Four Basic Competitive Drives

With a clean slate, use your five senses to observe and make sense of the world before you. What are the insects up to? The females dart as quickly as possible across the lake looking for a favorable spot to lay eggs and to attract a male to fertilize them. The slower-moving members of any insect species are at a great disadvantage. Insects find food and water and avoid, as best they can, being eaten by predators. We do not judge insects for doing what they do. What they do is obvious. Without judging human activity, what humans do is obvious, too. We compete in the same four ways that insects do, for sex, favorable habitats, harm avoidance, and speed:

1. We compete for sex and for the enhanced sex appeal that accompanies wealth, power, influence, and/or increased

visibility at public venues, in the media, or on the internet, for example.
2. We compete both individually and collectively for exclusive access to plots of earth and sea with habitats favorable to finding food, shelter, and fuel as well as habitats where the chances of experiencing draught, famine, floods, and other natural disasters are minimized.
3. We compete to avoid harm by seeking exclusive access to plots of earth and sea that are strategically located in the event of war and with materials and energy needed for defenses and weapons. Also to avoid harm, we compete for higher-paying jobs that are safer and less stressful, with health benefits, as well as for premium opportunities that hold the potential for greater wealth, power, and media exposure—opportunities whose additional resources could minimize the negative effect of foreseeable and unforeseeable hardships and enhance our sex appeal.
4. We compete to be faster at travel and to quicken the completion of any task with tools and machines. The faster we are at completing a task, the more time we have for pleasure. We compete for plots of land and sea for the raw materials and energy needed to build and power these tools and machines.

With this instinctual view of human behavior, it is easy to explain why I grew up where I did. In May 1951, two months before I was born, my parents and two sisters moved twenty miles from Brooklyn to Great Neck, Long Island. The main reason for the move was to give us, the three children, access to an excellent public school system. This education would give my parents' children a greater competitive advantage in finding a desirable occupation—an occupation that pays well, provides job security, and minimizes the types of stress or dangers that could shorten one's life. With a desirable occupation and the contacts to be made along the way, each child would have a greater chance of attracting a desirable, healthy spouse, which in turn would give rise to healthy grandchildren.

Two educated or well-connected parents would have the means to avoid hardships that shorten one's life and the means to provide for their parents' grandchildren. Furthermore, educated parents would be more likely to pass down to the next generation the importance of an education. This would facilitate the chances of my parents' lineage continuing.

Leaving a financial inheritance to our children and grandchildren serves the same purpose as an education; an inheritance gives our offspring more of what they need to attract a desirable mate and/or the means to provide for children. Education and wealth decrease the chances that our female relatives will suffer from famine or disease that could disrupt fertility. Our male relatives, with their wealth and education, will remain sexually attractive for longer periods of time as well.

Educational Systems and Instinctual Drives

A major purpose of an educational facility, and likely the most emphasized purpose, is to impart knowledge that ultimately relates to the four ways in which we compete. Think of how much activity in our society is organized for the purpose of imparting knowledge that will facilitate the skills to provide food, shelter, and clothing; ways to extract mineral wealth or access energy and harness it to facilitate transportation (speed of movement) and other time-saving devices (such as computers) or comfort features (indoor climate controls, for example); child and health care; and awareness of forces that could harm us, including legal entanglements. Even a religious education is designed to teach us how to defend ourselves from a nonspiritual life and from the harm that awaits those who lack this religious education. All this knowledge relates to survival. It also relates to sexuality. Those who appear better equipped for survival and capable of imparting useful skills to potential offspring will be more attractive from a sexual standpoint as well. Then there is knowledge about fashion, physical fitness to sculpt our physique, and beauty school, all of which is designed to increase our attractiveness.

People with wealth have greater access to time-saving vehicles and devices and a greater ability to provide comfort and get basic needs met during periods of shortage. Being an excellent provider adds to one's sexual attractiveness. People of wealth have greater access to fashion, beauticians, fitness centers, and cosmetic surgery. Thus it is not surprising that because of their sexual and survival instincts people try to accumulate wealth and seek out knowledge for this purpose.

There are industries, legal and illegal, whose primary aim is to get money and/or invest it to make more money. Unfortunately, if the focus is to accumulate wealth or turn a profit for owners and shareholders, as opposed to providing a service that truly helps others, then temptations will abound—temptations that ignore others' feelings (first base of the Golden Rule) as well as the environment. Deception, threats, violence, pollution, unsafe jobs, and unsafe products invade society when we fail to use the Golden Rule to guide our goal-directed activities, especially the goal of accumulating wealth.

Then there is the whole field of marketing to show us how to set up a business that entices people to spend their money on things they don't really need, many of which relate to the sixteen distractions previously mentioned. Sometimes we denote people in these types of businesses as pitchmen or hucksters—the infamous P. T. Barnum comes to mind—and if they break the law, it's fraud. We refer to those who are extremely skillful at making and accumulating money without providing a useful service as greedy. We also refer to those who provide a useful service but have large profit margins as greedy.

Fortunately, when people tap into their spirituality, it tempers their instinctual drives. This allows morals, ethics, and how we find meaning to influence us. We can find someone attractive, not so much because of their physical beauty or wealth, but rather because we sense their loving spirit. We can treat people the way we would like to be treated (Golden Rule), not because we fear that to do otherwise would violate a law and we could be punished, but rather because we act with sensitivity to feelings of vulnerability and are aware of how our actions affect others. Yet, even with our spirituality, why is it that, when given the opportunity, we tend to be greedy?

Greed

Greed is defined as the excessive desire for wealth or possessions. How does greed relate to competitive drives? We don't ordinarily think of other animals, which act on their instinctual drives, as greedy.

What if an insect, for example, was greedy? What if some female insects could attract many males to fertilize their eggs and fly faster than the others to be the first to reach the most favorable habitats and laid a gazillion eggs? What if by the time the male insects finished fertilizing the eggs from the most attractive females, they died before many of the other females insects could get their eggs fertilized? What if the fast-flying insects with their payload of eggs left little favorable habit for the slower females to lay their eggs? Are the "fast-flying great layers of eggs" greedy?

Do we judge negatively the insect that is better at getting its eggs fertilized and better at laying its eggs in a rich environment? No. So why do we judge some humans as greedy? Or, when it comes to sex, judge them as having "loose" morals?

Judgment and Competition

If there was ever a man who would be described as greedy, it would be Bernie Madoff, the former chairman of the NASDAQ stock market and convicted Ponzi-scheme swindler who defrauded investors of billions of dollars. A nonjudgmental, spiritual viewpoint understands that greed, envy, or jealousy primarily relate to self-esteem issues or the degree of doubt we have about whether others value us, which usually turns out to be a reflection of how much we value others. Therefore, I speculate that Madoff's excessive desire for money, power, and influence was driven by his low self-esteem.

Bernie Madoff was caught in a downward spiral. Every time he deceived someone for his own personal gain, a negative memory of himself formed in his subconscious, which, in turn, created an even greater need to cling to the things that he thought others valued in order to think he would be valued. With his money and his reputation as a brilliant investor (a reputation gained by hiding his Ponzi scheme), he could now think he was a valued member of society.

Do you think Bernie Madoff was aware that, with each encounter in which he misled another investor, his subconscious brain would lower his value one more notch by adding one more memory of himself that displeased his conscience? His lack of awareness, along with the increasing number of acts of deception, in turn, created an ever-increasing psychological drive to attach himself to things of even greater value, which, for Bernie Madoff, meant amassing even more wealth and status. His need for more wealth would, in turn, motivate him to deceive even more people to invest their money with him.

To reiterate, Bernie Madoff was caught in a downward spiral. The takeaway lesson is to realize that the degree to which you suffer, according to Buddhism, is proportional to the degree to which you cling to material possessions or other forms of status (which can include individual relationships with other people). Furthermore, the degree to which you cling to material possessions and other forms of status is directly proportional to the selfish acts deposited in your memory bank as well as to the selfish thoughts you may hold in your consciousness.

How could Bernie Madoff value himself while continuing to act or planning to act deceitfully? He couldn't unless he rationalized that having others believe that he was smart and rich was more important than following the Golden Rule! Bernie Madoff cultivated an image that was admired by many. People far and wide sought him out for financial advice. Think about all the sports heroes, rock stars, movie stars, and charismatic leaders that children, teens, and even adults seek out who fail at letting the Golden Rule guide their actions.

In sum, Bernie Madoff was driven to attach himself to money and an exalted position on the stock exchange, the things he thought others would admire. By standing out and having the admiration of others, he could think that he is worthy and that violating the Golden Rule was a justifiable means to achieve desirable goals.

We typically do not think of ourselves as selfish when our selfish acts accomplish very desirable goals. The ends justify the means. In addition to the example of Bernie Madoff, the robber barons of the industrial age—such as John D. Rockefeller, Andrew Carnegie, Cornelius Vanderbilt—often used cutthroat competitive practices and low-waged workers. These so-called robber barons amassed enormous wealth and became philanthropists admired for their business acumen and their philanthropic endowments to education and the arts. I doubt the Rockefellers, Carnegies, and Vanderbilts ever contemplated that following the Golden Rule would result in more happiness than competing and winning at or in business ventures.

It is easy to deny responsibility for failing to follow the Golden Rule. It is easy to rationalize that it is okay to take advantage of others because that is the way the system is set up. Then there is the reality that those who capitalize on favorable circumstance or opportunities are behaving no differently from how others, including the critics of such behavior, would have acted if faced with similar opportunities. We all can be tempted by the seven deadly sins.

We live in a society in which rewards are usually materialistic. This in turn reinforces materialistic goal oriented behavior. What is the reward for making sure that we do not take advantage of others? The answer is trust and favorable karma—being comfortable in your own skin. Unfortunately, the rewards for following the Golden Rule usually get overshadowed by materialistic rewards, status and ego-stroking recognition.

I speculate that Muhammad recognized how reinforcement shapes behavior. Thus he made prayer five times daily a requirement of a spiritual life so that by praying we would contemplate the highest ideals of humankind (ideals that bring us closer to God). In this way the reward for following the Golden Rule will be strengthened, and the reward for materialistic gain will be weakened. Through prayer, our conscious and subconscious memories of loving acts are activated. Acting with love, acting in step with the Golden Rule is its own reward. It creates memories that feel good. It is your karma.

By analyzing the current state of affairs of humankind, it still appears that, despite thousands of years of so-called progress, the intrinsic rewards for following the Golden Rule remain overshadowed by the extrinsic rewards of material gain and status; people continue to let materialism and status override their "better angels" at the expense of cooperation, caring, and sharing. If collectively the consciences of the individuals in our society are not strengthened, then we will remain guided by essentially the same four competitive impulses that guide insects. Doesn't that bug you?

Your conscience will not be pleased no matter what you accomplish, gain, or achieve should you do it while violating the Golden Rule. There is no contentment when our conscience is displeased. We can live in denial, live with rationalizations, project our thoughts about ourselves onto others and find all sorts of ways to keep our displeasure hidden from our conscious awareness, not only with the list of sixteen distractions but also with thoughts such as *Am I not lucky to be popular or to live in a big house, or am I not deserving, as a consequence of all my hard work and training, to be on the cover of* Sports Illustrated, Time, *or* Rolling Stone?

Displeasure from your conscience sets into motion brain activity in your subconscious mind, which has thousands, maybe even millions, more instances of neural activity than your conscious mind. The subconscious mind is almost totally subservient to instinctual drives unless you make a conscious effort to stay connected to your conscience. Without strengthening your conscience by participating in the four spiritual acts—meditation; altruism and prayer; attention to creativity in nature, science, and the arts; the joy of movement—our motivations and goals will remain under the direction of our instinctual drives.

Without an intervening conscience, we will remain on autopilot for the purpose of finding pleasure and avoiding physical and emotional pain. We will remain on autopilot for the purpose of avoiding the unpleasant thoughts that accompany our memories of physical and emotional pain. We will perceive anything that can distract us or shield us from these unpleasant thoughts as pleasurable. Thus the defense mechanism of denial is pleasurable because it shields us from unpleasant thoughts. Denial can become a group identity. There are groups that deny the holocaust or the genocide against the Armenians in Turkey, for example.

Without an intervening conscience, you will continually seek distractions or feel a need to raise your status to get respect. However, you can never get enough of what you never needed in the first place. What you do need to do is realize that you were always deserving of respect just by being human. You also need to forgive yourself for not knowing what you know today, which is that any action or thought not guided by the Golden Rule will ultimately prove fruitless.

What you also now know is that to experience the beautiful life you deserve, you need to get better and better at letting the four bases of the Golden Rule guide your behavior. Develop faith that by following the Golden Rule, you will be valued by our society. Furthermore, because we take care of the things we value, and we value people who follow the Golden Rule, develop faith that following the Golden Rule means you will be cared for. Our society most commonly provides this care in the form of opportunities to earn money. Who wouldn't want to hire or work with a person who follows the Golden Rule? Only someone who is up to no good—and what a blessing it is not be involved with such people. As we go about the business of earning money to gather basic necessities for ourselves and family, those of us who follow the Golden Rule will lead joyous and meaningful lives.

Netzach: The Altruism Revolution

Thus far humankind has experienced three revolutions: the Agricultural Revolution, the Industrial Revolution, and most recently the Digital Revolution or Information Era. However, if humankind is ever going to change course to avoid the seemingly inevitable cataclysmic ending foreseen in the Bible's book of Revelation and indicated currently by an ever increasing world population, weapons of mass destruction, the rise of disinformation, and dwindling resources caused by the pollution of our air, water, and land, then a fourth revolution is needed: the Altruism Revolution. By incorporating the four bases of the Golden Rule into your everyday thinking, the Altruism Revolution will be well underway.

Let Your Conscience Be Your Guide

Maybe, with the exception of those of us who were born with brain damage or were later damaged by trauma or disease, everyone has a conscience, and when we do wrong, we know it. But if we have not strengthened our conscience by participating in the four spiritual acts, we will often fail to heed its message. Bernie Madoff most likely realized early on that he had fallen prey to the temptation of getting rich at the expense of others and that what he was doing was unconscionable. At that point he could have straightened out his life by returning the money to the first few investors he was bilking. Instead he procrastinated and remained crooked. He likely thought it would be too humiliating to admit that he was acting fraudulently. So when he wasn't busy trying to prevent others from finding out that he was a fake, he likely found all sorts of ways to distract himself from his unpleasant thoughts with gala events, luxurious homes, yachts, and just chatting with all the people around him.

It is too bad that Bernie Madoff did not realize that everyone, including himself, had all the value they would ever need. If happiness and a life of fulfillment is your goal, then you need not attach yourself to the man-made gods of wealth, status, and privilege. Everyone already has the God-given right to think and feel that they deserve to live a beautiful life filled with beautiful thoughts without having to prove anything to anyone.

Because you don't have to prove anything, the beauty of life will enter your consciousness whenever you free yourself from the desires associated with wealth, status, and privilege. With the benefit of meditation, altruistic prayers, and/or self-reflection, you can keep these desires, which we all have, from dominating your thoughts and actions. However, when you don't exert control over your instinctual drives and selfish behaviors, negative thinking will arise and lead to low self-esteem and the perception that life is unfair. Your instinctual drives make it easy to think that others will reject you because you are flawed or not good enough when you compare yourself with people who stand out.

Helping Harm-Doers

How can we help Bernie Madoff and other harm-doers develop a healthy sense of self-esteem? With a healthy self-esteem, harm-doers stop doing harm and start doing good. The first helpful step is to forgive Madoff for not knowing that he already has value and is valued and never needed to attach himself to material things. Keep in mind that forgiveness is not trust. Trust comes only to those who act with kindness consistently.

The second step in helping harm-doers improve their self-esteem is to stop them from harming more people and/or animals, destroying property, polluting the environment, and disrupting fragile ecosystems. I emphasize that the second step to improving the lives of harm-doers is to stop them. The first step is to "forgive them … for they do not know what they are doing" (Luke 23:34 NIV). They don't know that selfish acts lead to their own psychological and emotional discontent. As we follow through on the second step by stopping them, it is of utmost importance to let the harm-doer know that their feelings still deserve respect even though they have done harm, and that we may need to restrict their freedom.

More often than not, however, we take a judgmental view of those who are greedy or harm others. Why is this? There is much more to the answer than just the utility of using judgment and the corresponding shame and punishment as a deterrent. Judgment confers status. If you are judged favorably, your status is elevated. If you are judged negatively, your status is lowered. When you judge Bernie Madoff or a tobacco company CEO, for example, as greedy, you are, in effect, raising your own status and implying that you are different from the likes of a Bernie Madoff or a tobacco company executive. But we are not different from the likes of a Bernie Madoff or a tobacco company executive. We only have had different circumstances or different temptations to contend with. Would you turn down a million-dollar yearly salary to run a perfectly legal enterprise such as a tobacco company?

By making judgments that others are wrong, we create the perception that we must be right, which raises our status. By raising our status, we think that others will view us more favorably. The more favorable others' views of us, the more favorable the chances that we will get what we want. Thus, the tendency to be judgmental is driven by our instinctual drive to obtain a competitive advantage for the things we typically compete for. Because of instinctual drives, our mind wants us to have even greater status today than we had yesterday. *What have I done lately to raise my status?* becomes a part of our subconscious thought patterns.

Joshua Simon, MD, EdD

The Quickest Way to Raise Your Status

The quickest way to raise your status is to form judgments that are critical of others. That is why children ridicule other children. That is why we gossip, criticize others with our blogging, and watch biased news/talk shows. You want to get confirmation that your judgments are valid. It is your competitive instincts that lead you to believe that your own values are better than those of the people who disagree with you.

You don't even have to think or talk about what your own values are as long as you demonize someone else (a strategy that politicians often use with negative campaigning). It is hard not to think that you are better and more deserving than those who are maligned and denigrated. At a subconscious level, you may think that you are more deserving than others simply because your views are in line with a revered political or economic philosophy or because you follow the tenets of the religion to which you ascribe. All this thinking is driven by desire—the desire to hold competitive advantages and its offshoot: the desire to marginalize, minimize, or negate those people who you perceive are getting in your way.

The Bible points out the errors in our ways when we think or take action while believing we are more deserving than others. "Do nothing out of selfish ambition or vain conceit. Rather, in humility value others above yourselves, not looking to your own interests but each of you to the interests of the others" (Philippians 2:3–4 NIV).

The logic that our point of view makes us more deserving extends to personal relationships as well. Our mind wants us to believe that because we think we care about a certain person more than others do, we deserve more of that person's attention and affection. There are countless love songs with lyrics ("Stop in the Name of Love" by the Supremes, and "La La Means I Love You" by the Delfonics, for example) in which the pursuer extols his or her care for the love object as greater than that of his or her rivals. By identifying with the lyrics—which many of us do, and that's why these songs are so popular—we reinforce beliefs and fantasies that we are the most deserving of our love object's attention and affection.

The belief that we are more caring than others is another example of how we raise our status to get what we want. Keep in mind that this kind of thinking applies to this writer as well. As much as I am trying to be unbiased in my presentation and telling you that we all have value, it is quite possible that my purported view of reality is just an attempt to validate my judgments and elevate my status. I say "purported" since I might be trying to deceive you into thinking that I am more caring than I really am. Therefore, I remind you to challenge everything I postulate and to remember that actions speak louder than words. So far all you know of me is words.

Relative Caring

Our status, our place in the pecking order, can be raised by the perception that we care more than others, also known as "relative caring." We often try hard to appear that we care more than others. The "art of deception" is the human way of camouflaging our true intentions. The appearance of caring can fool people into thinking we are acting altruistically and with such noble motivations that it's difficult for others to see through our facade to our true motives, which could very likely be about some form of selfish gain.

When our image of caring is effective, it becomes easier to obtain the trust of others. This trust then allows us to influence others in a way that makes it easier to gratify our own desires. Because all these connections between "caring" and getting what we want are mostly subconscious, it's hard to know whether it is our instinctual competitive side or our spiritual altruistic side that gets us to donate to charities and participate in activities associated with caring such as those sponsored by various religious and civic organizations. The Bible warns us of our subconscious motives: "But when you give to the needy, do not let your left hand know what you right hand is doing" (Matthew 6:3 NIV).

Our mind thinks that if others can see our charitable, civic, and religious participation, and it's greater than that of the person next to us, it will raise our "relative caring" status. As a consequence, the image we are trying to project will be viewed more favorably. This increased status or favorable image could then provide us with a competitive advantage. Relative caring implies that by participating in a religious or civic organization, charities, or the like, we are more deserving than those who donate less time or money or are not involved at all. However, as previously stated on numerous occasions, we are all already deserving of a most beautiful life without having to prove anything to anybody.

Do you see the irony in the fact that many of Bernie Madoff's biggest paydays were found among those people who represented religious and charitable organizations? Can you see the wisdom in the biblical advice in the Gospel of Matthew about how to make charity a spiritual act? True charity is giving without drawing attention to yourself or to the organizations you associate with:

> So when you give to the needy, do not announce it with trumpets, as the hypocrites do in the synagogues and on the streets, to be honored by others. Truly I tell you, they have received their reward in full. (Matthew 6:2 NIV)

Judgments While in College

As I said earlier, I grew up in Great Neck, Long Island, a community noted for its excellent public school system. Much emphasis was placed on getting good grades and scoring high on achievement tests. In my mind the perception of being smart was the most important priority. There were quite a few wealthy families in Great Neck, but to me intelligence was far more desirable than wealth. My father's interest in sports led me to believe that excelling in sports was another way to get approval. So the people I wanted to be friends with were smart and/or good athletes. The pretty girls interested me too, and I didn't mind if someone "popular" spent time with me, since "popular" translates into being desirable. So I grew up focused on status because I had yet to learn that true self-worth comes from caring about other people's feelings.

If you had asked me at age eighteen what it would take to feel good about myself, I would have said, get good grades, live in or near a city with an active nightlife, possess the best stereo equipment, be on the basketball or baseball team, and have a pretty girlfriend and a group of friends with whom to do fun things. To be of service to others would not have entered my mind at age eighteen.

At age twenty, I met my fourth girlfriend, Elizabeth, in college. She was a sophomore and I was a junior. There was plenty of attraction. She was physically beautiful and athletic, and she got good grades. She was energetic and fun to be with. Many other boys let me know that they thought she was beautiful and sexy. *Aha, you see I have a girlfriend who is desirable in the eyes of others. She is desirable and chooses to have me as her boyfriend, so I must be desirable too. Therefore, I must have value. I must be good enough; otherwise why would such a desirable girl choose me?*

During the first few weeks of our relationship, however, I was constantly judging her. I still wondered what others thought of her and what they thought of me since I was her boyfriend. As I said earlier, I wondered if she was smart enough to be my girlfriend. Keep in mind that my issue with Elizabeth being "smart enough" really had to do with the projection of my insecurities onto her. I had doubts about whether I appeared smart enough. Perhaps my barely passing grades in college added to this insecurity.

With the army waiting to draft me as soon as I graduated (number 4 in the draft), it was difficult to see the relevance of a college education. Add to this outlook my propensity to goof off, and that there were plenty of other students ready to goof off with me, I didn't attend half my classes. At this time getting a grade above a C was not easy unless you took "gut" courses, which I didn't. The gut courses were in the curriculum to prevent student-athletes from losing their eligibility because of poor grades. In addition, some professors were known to be easy graders to prevent students from flunking out and losing their student deferment from the draft. Some teachers thought it was their moral duty to keep whomever they could from ending up in Vietnam.

My grades and other possible sources of subconscious doubt about my worthiness easily translated into conscious doubts about whether Elizabeth was the right girl for me. When I would visit her at her dorm, I would check out the other girls. Whether she knew it or not, Elizabeth was competing with them for my attention. During those first few weeks of dating, I often thought about breaking up with her, but I didn't want to give up my access to the girls' dorm, and I enjoyed Elizabeth's physical affection, a mind-set similar to "quit your current job only when you have secured your next job."

Relating to and caring about my girlfriend's feelings was not in the picture at the time. I was too busy dealing with competitive drives and related insecurities to pay full attention to the feelings of others. I was busy trying to find value by attaching myself to things and people I thought had value. That is exactly what social climbing is about. But if you had asked me at age twenty if I was a social climber, I would have said, "You're crazy." I would have told you that social climbers are people in the mainstream culture. I was a counterculture hippie, a free-spirited antiwar protester. "Me, a social climber? You've got to be kidding. I can't stand snobs. If you want to see social climbers, check out the fraternities and sororities. I would never join a frat!"

When we have yet to learn how to be sensitive to and aware of how our actions affect the feelings of others, or able to value that in ourselves, we become social climbers, living in the United *Status* of America. When we are not social climbing in the mainstream culture, we will do it in a subculture. Regardless of the culture where we choose to find value, we will think its values are superior to those of other cultures.

During the 1960s and '70s, the image of the leaders protesting the war in Vietnam was far more pleasing to many of us than the image of the leaders supporting the war. (Picture an image of an antiwar protester holding a peace sign versus General Alexander Haig Jr. in military regalia.) Some people joined the peace movement not because of a commitment to nonviolence but because it was cool (cool = more attractive) to be against the war. It was our competitive drive to raise our status by having the approval or acceptance of others that led many to choose sides during the Vietnam War. The people in the peace movement were better than the people supporting the war. Of course, the other side thought that those supporting the war effort were more deserving than those opposed to it. In reality, both sides were deserving of understanding and compassion.

If you identify yourself as a law-abiding citizen, what kind of judgments do you make about someone who breaks the law? If you identify yourself as a conservative, what kind of judgments do you make about those who identify themselves as liberal, and vice versa? If you have certain religious beliefs, what kind of judgments do you make about those who don't identify with those beliefs—or with any religion, for that matter? Our subconscious connects these kinds of judgments to consequences that could affect our ability to attain status, achieve goals, and obtain the approval of others.

Judgments are inextricably intertwined with status. Our status goes up if we are judged positively or others are judged negatively and vice versa. As our status rises, we can believe that we are more deserving of a love object or more entitled to limited resources. Our instinctual brain, using its subconscious neural circuits, makes most of these judgments without being guided by the four bases of the Golden Rule. Consequently, these judgments of right (or positive) and wrong (or negative) are not really judgments of right or wrong but rationalizations meant to give us competitive advantages. These so-called judgments of right and wrong are motivated by the same competitive factors that motivate insects, or any animal, for that matter: avoidance of harm, sexual desire, favorable habitats, and the speed to be first. If insects could judge, they would.

Nonjudgmental Assessment of Right and Wrong

Rather than judging others, why not see human behavior in these terms. Are the actions of others motivated by love or by fear? If others are motivated by love, then join in. If others are motivated by fear, don't join in. If others are motivated by a mixture of both, divide your support accordingly.

Show those motivated by fear that they can approach their problems with solutions that are guided by love—solutions that are nonjudgmental. Have empathy for people like Bernie Madoff, who make the most common mistake of all, which is not realizing that their lives would have worked out so much better if they had only been caring and sensitive to feelings of others.

When we are caring and sensitive to the feelings of others, the following good things happen: (1) our mind generates pleasant thoughts, more pleasant than would be generated by achieving goals; (2) we sense the beauty in and around us; (3) we know we are worthy without feeling the need to prove it to others; and (4) we develop the utmost confidence that our life will work out just fine no matter who chooses to spend time or who chooses not to spend time with us, no matter what difficulties or circumstances we were born into, and no matter what circumstances or difficulties we aggravated or created by our previous lack of insight and awareness.

People who act selfishly need a caring person to tell them no. To be caring is to be strong and firm. Selfish people need limits set so they will not commit further acts of selfishness. We can treat people who act selfishly with kindness. We don't need to take a harsh tone when setting limits, just a firm one.

When a parent picks up a child who is writing on the walls with crayons, the child kicks and screams and holds on to the crayons as tightly as possible. Even though we are not doing what the child would like us to do, we still care about our child as we remove the crayons and give them a time-out. We can do the same with older children and adults. We can show them that we care about them every step of the way as we stop them from doing further harm, even as we send them to prison if need be. But if we judge harm-doers to be undeserving of our kindness, we miss an opportunity to show them a better way to solve the problems that inevitably arise from the same four basic fears that we all hold in common.

Picture the judge who says to the nineteen-year-old criminal, "You are a despicable, reprehensible scourge on society. I am sorry that the laws limit my sentencing of you to ten years in prison. If it were up to me, I'd lock you up and throw away the key." Now picture the judge who says, "I hope that by the time you finish your ten-year sentence, you will have learned to be a more caring person and that how you treat others reflects what you think of yourself. You have already been forgiven by God and me for the mistakes you have made. When you get out, you will be twenty-nine. You will still have a long life ahead of you. You will make more mistakes, as will I. If you can learn from your mistakes, you will enjoy the life God has given you."

Judgment and Group Identity

Humans use judgments as a way to solidify their group identity. As a group of people who share the same judgments or "values," we typically try to punish and restrict those who do not agree with us. We particularly like to restrict any group that appears to enjoy life through activities that are not sanctioned by our culture. How dare those people enjoy themselves more than us when they hold inferior values (or commit sins)! How dare those people possess more of the things I want while they hold inferior values (or commit sins)!

With our outrage and resentment, we restrict groups with differing values or at least try to make them look inferior. With restrictions and/or the appearance of inferiority, these groups will be less able to take away from us the things we want, such as better jobs, attractive dates or mates, and fertile land. Once again, our judgments and so-called values are meant to give us a competitive advantage. The corollary is that if you help me get what I want or help me believe that I hold superior values, then I will make you a member of my group and/or judge you more favorably.

Group Membership and Circumstances

Our group identity changes as our circumstances change, just as the most favorable habitat for an insect changes as the environment changes. Groucho Marx put it this way: "Those are my principles, and if you don't like them, well … I've got others." Think of politicians who change their positions or even their parties or just want to rephrase what they just said because it didn't go over very well.

Think of Johnny Damon, who left the Boston Red Sox to join Boston's biggest rival, the New York Yankees, for a more lucrative contract. After his move to New York, the fans in Boston booed him more vociferously than the other Yankees because they had judged him as disloyal. Meanwhile, had Derek Jeter left the Yankees to join the Red Sox, those same fans would have cheered him, even though that move would have been just as disloyal. If Derek Jeter had joined the Red Sox, the fans in Boston wouldn't have judged him negatively, because he would have been helping the Boston fans get the championship they wanted. We use judgments as a tool to help us get the things we want.

In the fantasy world of reality TV, shows such as *Survivor* are based on shared and changing judgments as circumstances change. If you agree with me to vote the same person off the island, we are members of the same group. We have an alliance. Our group identity is based on the assumption that we can help each other get the things we each want. But if later I decide to vote you off the island, the previous group identity will have changed and the alliance will be broken. This kind of competitive behavior underlies most group formation in the "real" world as well. We form alliances and join groups and organizations to improve the chances of getting the things we want. And the things we want (such as wealth, status, sexual pleasure, comfort, recognition, safety, fast transportation, entertainment, tasty food) are programmed by our instinctual drives.

What People Want to Believe!

People want to believe that their judgments are right, they are right, and those who do not share their judgments are wrong. Furthermore, if people have an irrefutable authority that tells them in black and white what is right from wrong, such as a bible or "the founding fathers," they will be more assured that they must be right. Guess who decides what the irrefutable authority is? The choice is up to each individual, who will undoubtedly be influenced by the prevailing thoughts and promises of the surrounding authority figures of the time and era in which they happened to be born and raised.

Feelings of vulnerability are created by the four basic fears, regardless of the specific culture in which we were born. To cope with these feelings, we look for comfort, and what a relief it is to hear and learn from an irrefutable authority that guarantees protection from our greatest fears. For some that irrefutable authority will be science and logic. For others it will be God and religion or God and country. Though some of us will not feel threatened by people with different beliefs, others of us will.

If a more powerful group or tribe threatens us if we do not accept their belief system, we can renounce our current beliefs and join the more powerful group. Instantly, we will feel safer from harm. All of a sudden the belief system we resisted can seem like the truth since we are now safe from being attacked by the group we once resisted. If you can't beat them, join them, or in some cases pretend to join them to save your life and keep your real beliefs hidden. On the other hand, there were those whose beliefs may not have been based in fear but rather in love, a faith so convincing, with such little doubt, that even when faced with death, some of the early Christians for example, chose death rather than deny their beliefs.

From a purely "survival of the fittest" or evolutionary standpoint, why not choose a belief system, such as a religion and/or an economic theory such as capitalism or socialism, that will be perceived to enhance your status and thereby confer a competitive edge for living in safety or for looking desirable? It makes perfect sense from a survival point of view to find or choose an irrefutable authority. It makes no sense to question the choice once the choice has been made, because that will introduce doubt. Doubt raises the question "What if I am wrong?" It is a question raised by your conscience. But your subconscious has already wrapped itself around all the advantages we obtain by having an alliance with an irrefutable authority.

Our subconscious does not like doubt. Doubt allows us to hold two divergent views at the same time. Our subconscious doesn't like divergent views. Instead, it likes to think that its view of the world is superior, no doubt about it. These thoughts of superiority stem from the want of competitive advantages. Thus when it comes to discussing politics or religion with someone who has a divergent or contrary view, it is common to hear, "I can see that I'm not going to change your opinion and you're not going to change mine." When there is a change, we call it an epiphany!

Doubt

The more others support my beliefs—especially a belief in an irrefutable bible or other alleged powerful authority—the less doubt

I will have about holding wrong judgments and the more certain I will be that I am holding right judgments. By being right, it will be easier to get what I want, since "right" judgments raise my status and status begets competitive advantages. However, people who question my beliefs are in effect raising the possibility that I am wrong. By being wrong I am now at a competitive disadvantage. People who question the validity of my irrefutable source of knowing right from wrong lower my status and make me feel unsafe and undesirable.

It is relatively easy to tell which cultures and societies throughout the ages have had great difficulty dealing with doubt and respecting divergent views. The greater the secrecy, the greater the limitation of free speech, and the greater the public display of authority figures and symbols associated with them, the greater the difficulty with doubt and accepting that it is perfectly reasonable, understandable, and human to be curious about and question any statement of "truth" that has yet to be experienced directly or proven with the use of numbers, statistical analysis, or other objective scientific measures.

If we know God or a religion that presents an irrefutable code of conduct, why not be glad that we have found the truth? Why do we sometimes insist that others agree with our view of God or religion? If we know the truth about God, shouldn't it feel good just to explain as best we can what the truth is and how we know it to be the truth? Must we threaten those who do not adhere to our beliefs or code of conduct?

Can we problem solve tactfully by showing people "the way" while being respectful of the fact that others might have doubts about our explanations? How can other people's doubt about our explanations affect our relationship with God or our ability to know right from wrong? It can't, unless we are uncomfortable with doubt and want others to reassure us. How can other people's doubt about our explanations affect our relationship with God? It can't, unless we think that our relationship with God or our view of right from wrong is meant to give ourselves a competitive advantage over other groups.

CSNY Déjà vu is a documentary movie about Crosby, Stills, Nash, and Young's 2006 tour while George W. Bush was president. Their concert was a mix of their 1960s and '70s songs with new material about their opposition to the wars in Iraq and Afghanistan. The most poignant scene in the movie is during a concert in Atlanta while they are singing the following lyrics:

> Let's impeach the president for lying
> And misleading our country into war
> Abusing all the power that we gave him
> And shipping all our money out the door

The booing from the audience began, and it was loud. Hundreds of people got up and left even though they had probably paid a hefty price for tickets and travel expenses. Of these people who were interviewed on camera, the gist of their comments sounded like this: "I came to this concert because I like their music; I am not here to put up with their bullshit politics."

The explanation for this reaction is relatively simple. Many Americans believe that their president, especially one who shares their political affiliation, is dedicated to protecting them and working on behalf of Americans to be as competitive as possible in international arenas. These Americans understandably want to be safe, have decent jobs, and see their incomes grow. They judge their president favorably on these issues. As previously stated, we use judgments as a tool to get what we want. But the CSNY lyrics judge the president unfavorably. Quite logically, upon hearing the lyrics, those booing sense at some level that Crosby, Stills, Nash, and Young are not helping them get what they want. If the judgments in the lyrics are right, then those booing must be wrong. Our minds interpret being wrong as a competitive disadvantage. We boo to express our displeasure at being put at a competitive disadvantage, just as those in Boston booed Johnny Damon when he went to the Yankees.

What I Want!

Who would ever want to let go of an advantage that allows him or her to feel safe and desirable? If I am focused on getting what I want, then it is likely that I would prefer to hear ideas that support the way I judge what's happening in the world. If I could dominate others and prevent others from voicing their contrary opinion, wouldn't this give me a competitive advantage? Wouldn't this dominance be further proof that I must have been right in the first place? Wouldn't I much rather dominate others so that I'll think I'm going to get what I want than let those "questioners" put me at a competitive disadvantage? What do I want? I want what any self-respecting insect wants—a competitive advantage.

Might makes right! Either you are with me or against me! Here's a rally cry from the antiwar and civil rights movements of the 1960s and '70s: "If you are not part of the solution, then you are part of the problem!" Whose solution do I want you to be a part of? My solution, of course: a solution that agrees with my religious or political philosophy.

Here's a paragraph from Bill Moyers's 2008 book, *Moyers on Democracy*:

> In his book *In Praise of Religious Diversity,* James Wiggins reminds us that virtually every armed conflict occurring on the planet today is explicitly driven by religious motives or by memory traces

of persisting religious conflict. So we get Sunni Muslims in Afghanistan fighting a civil war with Shiite Muslims. We get fundamentalists in Algeria shooting teenage girls in the face for not wearing a veil and cutting professors' throats for teaching male and female students in the same classroom. We get Muslim suicide bombers killing busloads of Jews. And a fanatical Jewish doctor with a machine gun mowing down praying Muslims in a mosque. The young Orthodox Jew who assassinated Yitzak Rabin declares on television: "Everything I did, I did for the glory of God." In India, Hindus and Muslims kill one another. Here in America, Muslims bomb New York's World Trade Center to smite the Great Satan. Timothy McVeigh blows up the federal building in Oklahoma City, killing 168 people, in part as revenge against the government for killing David Koresh and his followers. Groups calling themselves the Christian Identity Movement and the Christian Patriot League collect arsenals, and at a political convention in Dallas not long ago, at a so-called Christian booth in the exhibit hall, you could buy an apron with two pockets—one for the Bible and one for a gun. (pp. 367–68)

The above paragraph postulates that "virtually every armed conflict on the planet today is explicitly driven by religious motives." However, in reality, it is each individual's four basic fears and four basic competitive drives that underlie every armed conflict, not religious motives per se. It is our competitive instincts that drive us to form or join religious organizations in the first place. Conflict is not religious. It's competitive. If religious organizations did not exist or attracted very few adherents, people would rely on other organizations or belief systems to help them get what they want.

Granted, it is hard to change the minds of people who believe that God favors them exclusively. Our instinctual nature pressures us into insisting, both consciously and subconsciously, that the group we identify with is right and that those who express a different viewpoint or lifestyle should be marginalized and have as little influence as possible. Our instinctual nature insists that those who have a different point of view must not be an impediment to our group's quest for land, material wealth, status, and enhanced sexual appeal.

Freedom

American people pride themselves on freedom. But are Americans any less competitive or any less judgmental than other nationalities? In the cause of reaching competitive goals, we are instinctually driven to form judgments. To do so is human nature. However, to spread freedom is to spread a nonjudgmental mind-set because judgments by their nature are meant to limit the freedom of, restrict, devalue, and marginalize those of us who are judged unfavorably.

It is our spiritual side that leads us to be nonjudgmental. The Bill of Rights in the United States Constitution is a spiritual document. It is meant to protect people's freedoms by limiting the restrictions that can be placed on those who are judged unfavorably by government officials. The Bill of Rights spreads freedom. The Bill of Rights hinders those who pray to the false gods of wealth, power, and status, and it does so without favoring one group over any other.

People will compete even beyond the instinct of self-preservation. Some of us compete for a coveted spot in the afterlife. The suicide bomber, I surmise, is fearful of what will happen to their soul if their deeds on earth don't measure up. Thus they perform their self-sacrificing act, a deed to put their soul in good stead. I further surmise that they must judge that hurting others (this judgment is a violation of the fourth base of the Golden Rule) with their suicide attack (a violation of the Golden Rule's first base) will somehow make the world a better place. Can you think of a category of people judged more negatively in American or Judeo-Christian culture than the suicide bomber? (Perhaps only the child molester.)

Is it possible to think about the suicide bomber and other harm-doers without negative judgments? To spread freedom and a nonjudgmental mind-set, it is important to recognize that it's easy to be judgmental when you anticipate feeling vulnerable. It's easy to be judgmental when anticipating physical or emotional pain, including, for some, pain in the afterlife. It's easy to be judgmental when you anticipate rejection, rumors, or mudslinging directed at you, or when your privacy is invaded. When fearful, it is easy to act selfishly because acting selfishly is instinctual. Is it possible to feel confident in such a way that we need not act selfishly except when we are in the grips of a physical attack, when it is indeed in our best interest to let our survival instinct take over? Is it possible to feel confident in such a way that we need not act instinctively or judgmentally when trying to solve problems that include, for example, the likelihood that at some future time there will be another attack by a suicide bomber, someone wielding a semiautomatic rifle, or someone in a truck mowing down pedestrians? Can't we use the four bases of the Golden Rule to protect ourselves and guide us to safety without judging others as undeserving of our kindness or generosity?

Actions motivated by instinct or feelings of vulnerability do not deserve negative judgments, nor do they deserve positive judgments. Freedom is the ability to be free of judgment. Judgment is trapped in fear. According to this logic, we are free only when we have no fear and form no judgments. Yet this nonjudgmental attitude still leaves us with the predicament of what to do with people who harm or plan to harm others.

Joshua Simon, MD, EdD

Dealing with Harm-Doers

How to deal with people who cause harm to others is a difficult subject. The number and complexity of legal statutes is mind-boggling. In 2008 America crossed a threshold: more than 1 percent of the American adult population was in prison.[107] Currently, there are well over a million convicts in our society, many of whom are repeat offenders. This is more than any other country and is five times the percentage of the population for Great Britain and ten times the percentage of the population for Denmark.[108] Furthermore, this 1 percent represents only those who have been caught. Many other harm-doers, especially harm-doers with wealth or in positions of authority, escape capture and prosecution. Jonathan Swift said it this way: "Our laws weave a web that catch the small flies, but the wasps and hornets get through."

Our state and federal judicial systems, as well as those systems in other countries, are in need of an attitude adjustment. As stated previously, when children act up and aren't fully aware of what they're doing, we set limits and restrict them. However, while setting these limits and enforcing our restrictions, we maintain a loving attitude. We believe these limits and restrictions are part of teaching our child to be more aware of and sensitive to how his or her actions affect the feelings of others. It is precisely this loving attitude that needs to be modeled by those of us who act on behalf of the state in our courts, jails, and prisons, and through law enforcement.

---

[107] Adam Liptak, "1 in 100 U.S. Adults Behind Bars, New Study Says," *New York Times* (February 28, 2008).
[108] https://www.vox.com/2016/6/16/11955484/mass-incarceration-stat.

Introspection, Ambivalence, and Doubt

The instinctual sphere can dominate the human condition. But we have a spiritual sphere of influence as well that encourages us to be more aware, to be more sensitive, to see with our hearts, and even to question our motives. As I am writing my ideas down, what is motivating me? Are my motivations competitive? For example, am I trying to enhance my status by demonstrating intelligence or enhance my status by accumulating wealth through book sales or speaker presentations? Am I writing to convince others that my opinions are right, hoping that by getting feedback that agrees with my opinions I will feel empowered to get the things or do the things I've always wanted to get or do? Am I simply responding to the third basic fear (fear of appearing unreasonable), worried that the way I look at the world, the way I related to Elizabeth, the way I experience God is or will be problematic unless others let me know I am reasonable and understandable? In other words, is this book simply just another example of how someone might go about looking for validation?

Am I trying to present myself in the most favorable light possible to mislead others into thinking that I am less selfish, more trustworthy, and more disciplined than most people, which, by the way, may or may not be the case? After all, I am human and, as such, likely to act out of pure self-interest when fearful, just like everyone else. Is my writing self-serving only, or can some things be both self-serving and helpful to others at the same time? Are my ideas meant to be of value to all people (not just myself and others of similar belief)? Is my writing meant to help me strengthen my faith so that I will be less fearful and inspired to develop greater discipline, sensitivity, and awareness?

I believe that this kind of introspection is not insect behavior, not motivated by the four basic competitive drives. Inviting others to question our motives, to question the truthfulness of our ideas, is truly spiritual. It is noncompetitive. It is saying that I can live with ambivalence. Though I think I am right, I recognize the possibility that my ideas may be wrong because there is always the possibility that they serve merely to disguise my selfishness; my ideas are my camouflage. I recognize that I may be both partly right and partly wrong. Most importantly, I welcome others to point out flaws in my logic and to point out when I am blinded by my own ego or competitive drives. My life will be improved if people can show me a clearer picture of reality by pointing out the inconsistencies and purely self-serving ideas in my thought patterns. This is my case as best as I can state it. Who can argue with me over this? If you can prove me wrong, then show me a better way to peace and contentment than the ideas presented in this book, for I would welcome a better way or even just a different way that is also beneficial. This is the message found in the book of Job.

As described in chapter l, I found a Bible[109] folded open at Numbers, chapters 18 and 19, with a ribbon in Job 13 at verses 18 and 19. Job 13:18–19 reads as follows: "This is my case: I know that I am righteous. Who can argue with me over this? If you could prove me wrong I would stop defending myself and die."

Do you believe there was some kind of divine intervention when the book of Job appeared on the side of the road after I had watched *The Passion of the Christ*? If you do, then perhaps you also believe that the words written here and the case I am making about the role played by Moses, the Buddha, Jesus, and Muhammad in the formulation

---

[109] Unfortunately, this Bible was lost with many others of my books when they were mailed with the United States Postal Service. This box of books broke in transit. However, photocopies of the pages exposed at Numbers and in Job remained in my possession. Thus far, I have been unable to match this Bible's wording to any of the Bibles referenced on various internet sites.

of the four bases of the Golden Rule are indeed righteous and would not exist if they were not true.

The Buddha says that the veracity of my words and ideas should not be affected in any way by whether you believe some kind of divine intervention contributed to the writing or endorsement of this book. The veracity of my words and their ideas can be known only by your use of them in such a way that you experience greater happiness without causing anyone to suffer.

Banning of the *New York Times*

The Chinese government has had issues with veracity and people trying to get at the truth. The rulers within the Chinese government on December 19, 2008, banned their citizens from having internet access to the *New York Times*. Why do you think these rulers did that? The *New York Times* likely prints ideas that question these rulers' opinions and actions. Contrary opinions raise doubt, and doubt is interpreted subconsciously as a competitive disadvantage. So what should we do with people who inhibit free speech? Let those who are free of competitive drives cast the first stones!

I welcome those of us who have formulated doubts about God's very existence. If God did not exist or had no influence on this earth, how would the world look different today? I think one could make a good argument for it not looking any different. I welcome those of us who believe in God but recognize that there is some level of uncertainty about how God influences us. I welcome those who have no doubts about God's existence and the ways He affects the human condition. Apparently, others are "welcoming" as well: "In June [2008], the Pew Forum on Religion and Public Life published a controversial survey in which 70 percent of Americans said that they believed religions other than theirs [including even those of no religious belief] could lead to eternal life."[110]

Our spiritual side is noncompetitive and inclusive. It lets us include others, even those who do not share the same religious beliefs as our own. Exclusivity, on the other hand, is clearly competitive and designed to give us advantages over those who are excluded.

What I Really Believe

I believe in the law of parsimony or Occam's razor: a simple model that can predict observed phenomena is more likely to be accurate than a complex model for the same phenomena. The classic example of this law is accepting the theory that the planets in our solar system revolve around the sun. The alternative theory was that all celestial objects revolve around the earth as once adhered to by religious authorities of the church. Ptolemy developed complex mathematical equations that did indeed predict the movements of the sun and other planets with the earth at the center. However, Copernicus's mathematical model was much simpler. His model postulated that the earth and other planets revolve around the sun.

In his 1979 Pulitzer Prize–winning book *On Human Nature*, E. O. Wilson makes the case that human behavior is 100 percent subservient to the "survival of the fittest" principle of evolution. Wilson's theory complements the purely biologic evolutionary theory expressed by Herman Pontzer in his February 2017 *Scientific American* article, "The Exercise Paradox." Pontzer purports that "life is essentially a game of turning energy into kids, and every trait is tuned by natural selection to maximize the evolutionary return on each calorie spent." These models of human activity certainly are parsimonious. Every family unit, as best it can, uses the social structures of their particular

---

[110] Charles M. Blow, Op-Ed, *New York Times* (December 27, 2008).

culture as well as their own individual efforts (energy expenditure) to benefit their family's strands of DNA—their family's own genetic pool. I am in almost total agreement with this model.

I believe that the overwhelming majority of human behavior (let's say 99 percent rather than 100 percent), including our daily routine and the fabric of society, is influenced primarily by instinctual drives and its derivative—the four basic fears. These fears allowed the more dominant, weaponized members to gain control and set up the rules, regulations, and cultural norms in a way that gave these dominant members and their offspring competitive advantages. Those not benefitting from the rules and regulations want new leaders who will change the rules and regulations to benefit them and the members of their tribe. In our daily lives, we are consumed by the ever-present influences of this pecking-order, wolf-pack mentality. The desire for this kind of change, in which we are the ones benefitting from the rules and regulations, underlies the political movement known as populism.

By acting on our competitive-instinctual drives, four basic fears, and tribal mentality, or consumed by our fantasies and the sixteen ways to distract ourselves, little time and energy is left. For the average Joe this leaves only about 1 percent, for argument's sake, of his time and energy for noninstinctual activities—time and energy that can be used to reflect on the four bases of the Golden Rule and for participating with undivided attention in one or more of the four spiritual acts. However, it is during these noninstinctual, spiritual moments (few though they may be) that we find hope, harmony, honesty, and a healing spirit despite living in an environment characterized by a continuous stream of unavoidable problems.

If we can reduce the amount of time and energy we spend on reacting to instinctual fears and on the sixteen distractions from 99 percent to 95 percent, we will have a fourfold increase in the number of moments we find lasting meaning in our lives—moments unrelated to rising or falling in the pecking order or escaping from any doubts about our self-worth or self-esteem. To the outside observer, the daily routine of people who act and distract themselves 99 percent of the time in instinctual ways will not appear much different from that of people who do the same thing but only 95 percent of the time. But those who change from 99 percent to 95 percent by tapping into their spiritual side more often will see a big fourfold increase in their happiness and contentment.

Winners versus Losers

Though competition gives us the thrill of victory, this thrill is really the avoidance of the agony of defeat. Competition, driven by the fear of failure, creates stress. Losing generates negative thoughts and feelings. Winning generates a temporary reprieve from this negativity.

We think the winners and losers are different and winners deserve to avoid the consequences of losing. What is the consequence of losing? It is the belief that we are "not good enough" and that the winners are good enough. At some level we sense that the winners are more deserving of limited resources. This is a distortion of reality. There are enough resources for all. We just have not done a very good job of creating a social fabric that allows all people to have access to needed resources.

We cannot pass laws that will get people to care. Beware of plans that offer solely a governmental solution for "spreading the wealth" or for instilling "family values." At the same time, embrace those who ask us to be more caring and concerned about the welfare of all people. When we get people to care about others and create an environment that runs on cooperation, our social fabric will contain fewer and fewer distractions. Without these distractions, we can focus on the work that needs to get done—and there is plenty of work that needs to get done, since there are plenty of people who are suffering needlessly right now.

Winners and losers are not different from each other. The same forces motivate both sides. When we connect to the spiritual aspect of our existence, we realize that competitive activities have little to do with feeling good about ourselves. Maybe there are winners and losers in an insect's life, but I'd like to think that there is more to life than being an insect, unless, of course, insects enjoy sharing with others outside their gene pool without the expectation of something in return.

It's the 1 to 5 percent of our existence, when we are not competing, that contains the joy of life. Noncompetitive activities allow us to feel connected to each other and see the beauty in and all around us. It allows us to have faith that our creator has put enough resources on this earth for all 7.6 billion of us to have what we need to raise healthy families. Furthermore, this faith will give us the insight to realize that we will all feel a lot safer if we learn how to protect our air, water, and arable land from man-made hazards as well as how to share these and other needed resources rather than compete for them.

Seventh commandment: "Thou shalt not steal." Stealing is an act in which we do not care about the feelings of those from whom we steal. If we don't steal because we are afraid of being caught, then it means that we would steal if we thought we could get away with it. However, in a state of spiritual enlightenment, we don't steal, not because we fear being caught but because we care about the feelings of others. When guided by a compassionate, spiritual force, we would not steal even if there were no rules or laws that said, "Thou shalt not steal."

8

Hod—Majesty

How is it that animate beings can come out of inanimate matter? What is a self, and how can a self come out of stuff that is as selfless as a stone or a puddle?

—Douglas R. Hofstadter, *Godel, Escher, and Bach: An Eternal Golden Braid* (Twentieth Anniversary Edition, 1999)

New ideas come into this world somewhat like falling meteors, with a flash and an explosion.

—Henry David Thoreau (1817–62)

Hod means "majesty," "awe." Hod is the earthly counterpart to Gevurah (power). It is the wisdom that pays homage to mystery, gratefully accepting its own limitations, accepting that some things in life cannot be changed or challenged. Hod is the left leg of the primal Adam; the biblical character it is most associated with is Moses's brother, Aaron.[111]

---

[111] Arthur Goldwag, *The Beliefnet Guide to Kabbalah* (Three Leaves Press, 2005).

"What about my brother, Aaron?" Moses responds when God asks him to lead the Jews out of Egypt. "He is so much more capable than me." Moses, lacking confidence, does not think he can rise to the challenge set before him. God, on the other hand, knows Moses's potential and through Moses delivers us to second base of the Golden Rule, "Don't do for others what others can do for themselves." God does not let Aaron do for Moses what Moses can do for himself.

God raises the importance of second base again with Moses when He chooses not to let Moses remain or return to Egypt. He does not let Moses teach the hard-hearted pharaoh and his people the immeasurable value of the Ten Commandments and the Golden Rule to which these commandments speak. Instead one could interpret that God knew it would be best if the Egyptians learned the importance of the Ten Commandments and the Golden Rule without significant help from Moses and the Israelites. In this way the Egyptians' self-esteem would be on equal footing with that of the Jews.

Moses, as a young man, was far more capable than he could ever have imagined. This often is the case for many of us as well. We typically have a limited understanding of our limits and potential. Moses did not realize that he already possessed all the abilities he would ever need to lead the Jews to the Promised Land. You, the reader, may already possess all the abilities you will ever need to lead the 7.6 billion people currently on the face of the earth to the Promised Land—a land where the four bases of the Golden Rule are the standard rather than the exception.

In addition to not realizing our full potential, particularly as teenagers, we often misjudge our limits in the other direction by believing we are invincible and possess unlimited power. When Aaron's rod strikes the rock and water gushes out to bring needed water to the Israelites, Aaron and Moses act as if they had the power to perform this feat. They do not acknowledge that the power to bring water from rock lies in the hands of God. As such Aaron's and Moses's egos get in their way and prevent them from entering the Promised Land.

It takes time and learning from mistakes to know the difference between what we can and cannot do or can and cannot change. Our ego often lacks the ability to accept limitations created by our circumstances—circumstances that most often include a brain and a body that is not smart enough, strong enough, beautiful enough, or talented enough to compete on an elite stage as well as circumstances in which we were or were not raised by wealthy, well-connected, or well-adjusted parents. But most importantly, what we often lack is the understanding that these kinds of circumstances can have little to do with how much joy and happiness we experience over the course of our lifetime.

Our circumstances also include a survival of the fittest mentality regardless of whether you believe in Darwin's theory of evolution. Humans since biblical times have continued to evolve into competitive groups with political and social structures that favor some families or gene pools over others. We have yet to incorporate into these social and political structures the realization that one day—and that day is now—there would be technological advances that could greatly prevent any region of the world or any group of people from suffering from a lack of basic resources caused by drought, famine, or other natural disasters, let alone prevent suffering from disasters caused by war, man-made pollutants, and the failure of our judicial systems to incorporate the four bases of the Golden Rule into our correctional facilities.

There is no real need anymore for humankind to organize in separate competitive units for the survival of our gene pool. There is enough for everyone to have what they need to raise a healthy family if we make use of our technological advances, limit environmental pollution, and, most importantly, share and cooperate. However, if humankind cannot replace status, attention from others, money, and material possessions as the way we measure success and reinforce behaviors, then our social and political structures will continue to accommodate war, greed, and the pollution of the environment as well as foster criminal activity.

Shortages of clean water, clean air, and untainted food will undoubtedly lead to more and more conflicts and catastrophes especially with the world's ever-increasing population, environmental pollution, and climate change. These apparently inevitable conflicts and catastrophes, the destruction of the world as predicted by the Bible's Revelation, can all be prevented if we find something better than status, attention from others, money, and material possessions as our measure of success. I am proposing that we follow the four bases of the Golden Rule as this better measure. With a faith in the existence of a loving force, the force that created the universe, areas of our brain will strengthen (so I hypothesize) whereby we will actually sense more pleasure from following the Golden Rule than by winning at games, garnering attention, or amassing status, money, and other possessions.

The consequence of our survival-of-the-fittest mentality and methods of measuring success have also led to widespread feelings of inadequacy; it easy to think that others do not think we are good enough. These thoughts reinforce the fear that we won't experience a wonderfully satisfying life unless we stand out. As such, while growing up, we "want it all." We want to live without fear so that we can leave no doubt that we are exceptional and among the best of the best. Boys and men (and to a lesser degree girls and women) risk injury and even death in all sorts of activities—on skateboards, in cars, on motorcycles, on football fields, mountain and rock climbing, boxing and engaging in martial arts—in large part to deny their feelings of fear and to stand out, to prove their mettle, and to be on a path where their dreams come true.

As it turns out, we can "get it all" where our dreams come true if we use the power of fantasy. With fantasy, we can dream up anything we choose. The power of fantasy extends especially to the games people play. Winning at games takes on special importance because winning is interpreted as a sign that our fantasies might come true; no matter what adversary we face, we will come out on top. Notice how upset people can get when they don't win, or their team doesn't.

Cultures all around the world have signs, omens, and superstitions that capitalize on our fantasy life. A lucky coin in our pocket, a horoscope, and a fortune reading are just a few examples of how our fantasy life maintains a hold on our thinking. It is no wonder that children (and some adults) cannot resist cheating at games (or political elections) rather than experience losing, since losing could undercut one's fantasy life.

By the time we are in our early teens, we have become somewhat more rational and the games we played when we were younger have lost some of their luster. However, with an infusion of sexual energy during puberty, dating picks up where games left off. Our first serious romantic relationship, our first love, powered by fantasy, will likely feel different from anything we have experienced. It becomes easy to think again, like we did as a child, that there is a way for everything to work out the way we would like it to—that is, provided the person we love will love us as much as we love them. Perhaps some of us use a concept of God like that of a romanticized partner: everything will work out fine, if only God will love me as much as I love God.

As most of us have probably experienced, it is nearly impossible to maintain our romantic fantasies when confronted by reality, let alone trying to satisfy someone else's fantasy life. Thus there are countless "love" songs testifying to an unfulfilled romantic fantasy. A few that come to mind, from an endless list, include Roy Orbison's "Crying," Harry Nilsson's "Without You" (written by Pete Ham and Tom Evans from the British rock group Badfinger), the iconic "Yesterday" by the Beatles, Burt Bacharach and Hal David's "Anyone Who Had a Heart" and "Walk on By" as sung by Dionne Warwick, the Skyliners singing "Since I Don't Have You," and the immortal Elvis Presley's "Don't Be Cruel" written by Otis Blackwell.

Even with a strong fantasy life, by the age of eight we are usually able to distinguish between fantasy and reality. By our teenage years, we usually know that life never works out exactly the way we would like it to. With the exception, perhaps, of the world's most spoiled child, every one of us experiences disappointment while growing up.

In response to disappointment, we typically think that if we were without flaws or imperfections or if we had just tried harder, we would have been successful and would not have had to experience the unpleasantness of our failures. Another response to disappointment is to think that we should have known better than to waste our time, money, or other resources on achieving a goal that was way too difficult or on trying to win the favor of a person who was not that interested in us. As such, we typically grow up thinking that we are flawed, lack fortitude, don't measure up compared with others, or are incapable of making sound decisions, and therefore, we carry into the present feelings that we are not good enough, like Moses did.

Joshua Simon, MD, EdD

Fantasy Formation

Though it is easy to think you are not good enough, paradoxically, it is hard to accept the feelings associated with this negativity. Yet these kinds of feelings are easily generated. It's tough being a Homo sapiens. Anytime you experience, remember, or anticipate not excelling in any of the four areas in which people compete (sex, habitat, safety, speed), you will likely generate unpleasant thoughts. You compound these unpleasant thoughts by thinking you are not good enough. Then to escape from the negative feelings associated with these negative thoughts, you easily shift into a fantasy life. As children, we pretend that the games we play are actually real. Fantasizing continues into our adolescence and adulthood as well. How many people at some point in their life dream of being rich, famous, and/or admired? In sum, we look to others to validate us, whether in reality or in our fantasies. We do so when we haven't yet realized that true self-worth comes to those who follow the Golden Rule.

Anytime you feel (1) unattractive or without sex appeal; (2) too poor to live in a favorable habitat or without access to plentiful amounts of food, shelter, clothing, and recreation; (3) incapable of avoiding harm; or (4) that you lack the speed to complete a task, you will have an unpleasant thought. Conversely, by excelling at any of those four basic competitive drives, you can think more readily or fantasize more readily that you have or will have more access and/or time to experience pleasure and can more easily avoid any painful situations. However, when our egos are not getting stroked by others or when our fantasies start to fail, which they usually do, frustration sets in, and we envy those who are perceived to be successful.

Envy

When you don't realize that you are already good enough, it is easy to envy those who you think do "measure up." Typical categories in American culture that affect our perceptions of who measures up (aside from racial, religious, nationalistic, and sexist prejudices) include physical attractiveness, educational and work-related credentials and skills, positions with rank and authority, creative talent, wealth, intelligence, physical strength, athletic ability, and devoutness to a religion, marriage, family, country, tribe, or philosophy. If you do not think you measure up in most of those categories (and who doesn't?) and have yet to develop a strong spiritual bearing, you will likely dwell on negative thoughts and have difficulty accepting that you, just like everyone else, are vulnerable.

It can be uncomfortable to feel or be aware of the fact that just by being alive you are always vulnerable. You are always moving a moment closer to your death, and you can feel pain at any moment along the way. These thoughts and feelings of vulnerability reside primarily in your subconscious. To prevent these subconscious thoughts and feelings from reaching your consciousness, you, like everyone else, use psychological defense mechanisms. These defenses can include denial, whereby you refuse to accept reality or fact and act as if a painful event or thought never existed. These defenses can also include projection, in which you project your unwanted thoughts about yourself onto others. You can also displace your anger from one situation onto another person or situation. Then there is the use of sublimation, a more mature defense than denial, projection, or displacement, whereby you channel your unacceptable impulses, thoughts, and emotions into more acceptable ones. The use of fantasy is an example of sublimation, as is humor.

Humor often allows us to make light of a situation that otherwise might elicit more dour emotions. For example, I slip while rounding first base, and everyone in the dugout starts laughing. At the moment I am intent on getting the most out of my at-bat, but slipping slows me down. The laughter from the dugout lets me know that it is not that serious, and I get up from the ground chuckling as well. Without the laughter, I could have thought the world was against me—only I would have fallen in such a situation.

The Best Defense against Boredom

People typically deal with boredom by finding distractions. However, distraction is not the only way to deal with boredom when you realize that the antecedents to boredom (as well as loneliness or unhappiness) are unwanted or unpleasant thoughts and memories. When you realize those are derived from doubts about whether you are good enough, you have positioned yourself to answer the following four questions positively:

1. Can I prevent the want of a distraction?
2. Can I prevent boredom, loneliness, or unhappiness?
3. Can I put an end to my doubts about thinking whether I am good enough?
4. Can I deal with life's inevitable difficulties and disappointments without forming or creating unpleasant, unwanted thoughts and memories and without resorting to activities tied to fantasies or the many other ways to find comfort by overindulging in food, drugs, alcohol, and the getting of attention from others?

As you let the four bases of the Golden Rule guide your actions, as you participate more often in the four spiritual acts, it will become easier to answer yes to the four questions above. Should you begin to procrastinate, dwell on the past, or start the process of looking for your next distraction, should you begin to err, sin, or slip, the four-by-four pursuit of happiness is there to grip the road and keep you on track.

By using the four bases of the Golden Rule as well as participating in the four spiritual acts (altruism; meditation/prayer; creativity in arts, science, and nature; physical movement), you strengthen your conscience, which puts the brakes on your instinctual drives. In this way you become more mindful of your thoughts and actions. Without this mindfulness, your instinctually driven subconscious will direct or control your thoughts and subsequent actions. It will be as if you are on autopilot, like a moth being drawn to a flame. Without developing your conscience, without mindfulness, you will be drawn into one activity of distraction after another.

When your distractions eventually fail to distract you from thinking about past failures or anticipating new failures, your next line of defense is to dull or numb your senses to all this negativity. Unfortunately, dulling or numbing the senses often leads to a negative mood (boredom, anger, irritability, depression, frustration). Without your awareness and sensitivity operating near their peak, it is difficult to sense other people's love and our creator's love and it is increasingly difficult to sense the beauty in nature and other creations.

Love and the perception of beauty dampen your body's stress response, which in turn strengthens your immune system and other defenses. This can correct insults felt by your nervous system, muscles, gut, and other organs, as explained in chapter 6. Aches and pains all over the body can indicate that your defenses are compromised. However, these kinds of aches and pains can often be prevented when we learn to say the following:

1. Yes, I can prevent the want of a distraction.
2. Yes, I can prevent boredom, loneliness, and unhappiness.

3. Yes, I can put an end to my doubts about thinking whether I am good enough.
4. Yes, I can deal with life's inevitable difficulties and disappointments without forming or creating unpleasant or unwanted thoughts and memories.

As explained previously, your subconscious brain navigates on autopilot. It uses instrumentation that measures pleasure (sex and food) and pain (physical and emotional). This pain includes any unpleasant emotion that forms when you do not get positive feedback (including feedback from your own self-reflections) on your efforts to excel in each of the four ways we compete (sexual attractiveness, favorable habitats, harm avoidance, speed for tasks). However, by partaking in the four spiritual acts, you can shift out of autopilot. By partaking in the four spiritual acts you strengthen your conscience, which, in essence, develops new and improved instrumentation that will guide you to the Promised Land. The stronger your conscience, the more you will know that you are already good enough, the more you will act with purpose, and the less you will search for a distraction.

Every time you follow the four bases of the Golden Rule, you create one more memory that feels good, one more memory that strengthens your conscience, one more memory that draws attention away from past disappointments. As more memories build up that feel good, you will be less likely to ruminate or dwell on an uncomfortable thought or memory. The smaller the percentage of uncomfortable thoughts bouncing around in your memory bank, the smaller your chances of procrastinating and the less likely you will be in need of a distraction. However, you may have been so good at distracting yourself, or so well "defended" psychologically, that you aren't fully aware that you possess a multitude of unpleasant thoughts. But trust me, chances are you do! You weren't born with insight, and therefore, chances are you had thousands upon thousands of interactions from your childhood into your adult life that occurred while you were unaware that you were already good enough.

Lighten Up and Stop Procrastinating

Procrastination is about letting the weight of your memories slow you down. With "heavy memories," memories that don't feel good, your mind dwells on the past or yesterday. "Yesterday" is the most covered song of all time. The original by the Beatles recorded on June 14, 1965, has been rerecorded by more than two thousand other artists. It ranks thirteenth on *Rolling Stone*'s 500 Greatest Songs of All Time 2004, and to put it in perspective, it has been recorded five times more than the second-most-covered song of all time, Ben E. King's "Stand by Me."[112] Apparently singers, who want to connect to their audience, realize how easy it is to relate to and dwell on past disappointments.

Ideally by now you can relate to the "Positively 4th Street" version of "Yesterday":

> Yesterday,
> I didn't know that I was good enough.
> Now I do, so I don't dwell on stuff.
> Oh, I'm so over
> Yesterday.

But when you have yet to learn that you are good enough, your mind easily gravitates toward any activity that can block your awareness of unpleasant memories. These activities are typically found on the list of sixteen distractions. Because these distractions block your

---

[112] "Stand by Me" is number 121 on *Rolling Stone*'s 500 Greatest Songs of All Time (2004). http://www.smoothradio.com/features/most-covered-song-ever/ (10/18/2017).

unpleasant memories more easily than the work that needs to get done, it will be more pleasurable to procrastinate than to stay focused on the task at hand.

Paradoxically, listening to a song like "Yesterday" can remind you that you are not alone. It can remind you that feeling lonely is universal. You are on equal footing with everyone else. There is actually no need to distract yourself from feeling this way. Let the feeling serve as a reminder that we are all together in this condition we call humanity and that we can work it out. So get to work: don't procrastinate, and stop distorting reality by thinking you are not good enough! If you have worked hard on "Takin' Care of Business,"[113] then follow your hard work with some relaxation. First comes the work and then comes the relaxation. Don't procrastinate on finding ways to relax, either. If you have ever practiced yoga, you know that almost every session ends with relaxation pose.

Being reminded of your highest ideals or even just your next most pressing priority will get you focused. This focus extends to the beauty of giving your undivided attention to the creativity of others. This creativity connects you to your source—the energy that created the universe. Let's thank Paul McCartney's creativity and the two thousand others who spread the word by recording "Yesterday."

The word is that you are already good enough to get done whatever needs to get done. You need not dwell on the past or form a fantasy to counteract your anticipation of future failure. The word is that you can live in the present, the only place where contentment can be found. Contentment is found right now by working on the things you know need to get done—activities that bring you happiness and don't cause others to suffer. That is the word *love*.

---

[113] "Takin' Care of Business" by Bachman-Turner Overdrive, released as a single in January 1974.

Memory Quotient

The key to happiness, the key to a life without procrastinating, the key to a life filled with meaning (and not filled from the list of sixteen distractions) is to "lighten up" your memories; you are not to carry that weight. There is a simple formula or ratio that measures the weight of your memories. It's your memory quotient. In the numerator are unhappy or unpleasant memories, and in the denominator are happy or pleasant ones. Some unhappy memories are much more intense than others, and they carry the most weight.

Memory Quotient

$$\text{Weight of Memories} = \frac{\text{Unpleasant Memories}}{\text{Pleasant Memories}}$$

Every time you follow the Golden Rule, you will add a pleasant memory to the denominator, which lessens the weight. Anytime an unpleasant memory arises into your consciousness, you have an opportunity to remove it from the numerator (which also lessens the weight) by realizing that it is unpleasant simply because at the time it was formed, you were incorrectly thinking that you were not good enough. As your memory quotient decreases, it becomes easier to turn off that part of the brain that likes to run on autopilot. Recall that while running on autopilot, your subconscious brain draws you into your favorite ways of procrastinating.

Remind yourself that most of your most intense unpleasant memories or disappointments were caused by the perception that others disapproved of you because they didn't think you were good enough. Remind yourself that just by being human, you are both *Yesterday and Today*[114] already good enough to deserve and experience a beautiful life. Unhappy memories can be thought of as simply learning experiences. Take them out of the numerator and lighten your load. Learn from your mistakes—the mistake of judging yourself or others as undeserving of your kindness or generosity.

God Is Action

According to Judaism, you benefit from God's love whenever your actions are guided by the Ten Commandments, regardless of the reasons you follow them. It doesn't matter whether you follow them because you fear God, act out of guilt, want to impress somebody, or want to show that a nonbeliever can be just as good as a believer, as long as your actions are in keeping with them. It's what you do that counts, regardless of the intellectual content of your beliefs. To my way of thinking, the four bases of the Golden Rule are in accordance with the Ten Commandments, and therefore, when guided by these 4 bases, it counts.

Also according to Judaism, God punishes those who violate His commandments. I don't believe there is a need for human involvement in this punishment. The punishment happens at the moment you transgress. By violating God's commandments or by failing to follow the Golden Rule you will be

1. stuck with one more unpleasant memory of yourself circulating in your subconscious, a memory that lowers your self-esteem and lowers your self-confidence;
2. distorted by thinking you are not good enough;

---

[114] *Yesterday and Today* (released June 20, 1966) is the album by the Beatles containing the song "Yesterday." This album was preceded by *Rubber Soul* and followed by *Revolver*.

3. possessed by bad karma: you anticipate that others will violate God's commandments when interacting with you, thereby adding to your anxieties and worries; and
4. pressured into thinking you need to obtain material things or status before you can be valued, so you end up dwelling on the past or focusing on what you think you need to prove or obtain in the future.

Being stuck, distorted, possessed, and pressured means the punishment is built in. You don't get to live in the present moment, the only place where joy and contentment can be found. The bottom line is that anyone who acts with compassion acts with God's love and is spared the negativity associated with violating His commandments. Anyone who acts without compassion is separated from God's love, or, for nonbelievers, separated from that mysterious force that formed the universe. Those of us who do not believe there is any connection between us and whatever force created the universe can still lighten our emotional load by creating far more pleasant memories, compared with unpleasant ones, as long as we are guided by the Golden Rule.

Forgiveness

Can we forgive people who focus on achieving goals and, while doing so, become insensitive to how their actions affect others? Can we forgive people who try to achieve goals or attain some level of status simply because they think they need to attach themselves to what they think others value in order to feel valued? Can we forgive people who are fearful of what they think happens to people who do not measure up compared with others? Can we forgive people for not knowing that everyone, including themselves, already has immeasurable value, deserves to experience a beautiful life, and doesn't need to stand out to experience it?

What about the unfairness of "circumstantial endowments" in which some children are born into privilege and others into poverty or some are genetically endowed with physical beauty, athletic prowess, genius intelligence, or creative talents, whereas others are just plain ordinary? How can we feel good about ourselves when others so easily get positive attention because of these genetic or circumstantial endowments? How can we feel good about ourselves when others so easily get positive attention because of their family's position in society while other families struggle to acquire basic necessities? What about survival of the fittest? Won't those people who are more "fit" be happier?

Spirituality and Circumstances

To help answer the last question, let's accept for a moment that there is a spiritual side to the human condition and that we can experience it. Does God give everyone, regardless of genetic or circumstantial endowments, the opportunity to enter through the doors of heaven—doors that may be open for moments and even possibly extended periods of time on this earth? For those of us who do not think in terms of "God" or "heaven," does love among people give us the opportunity to feel contentment and to sense meaning in our lives? If the answer to either of those questions is yes, then no matter what circumstances you were born into and no matter what circumstances you currently find yourself in, you have the opportunity to experience as much joy and happiness as anyone else. Granted, some situations (such as being born into abject poverty, living in a war-torn region of the world, raised in an abusive family) can create bigger hurdles to overcome before arriving at the wisdom of the Golden Rule, but this wisdom is available to everyone and includes the ability to problem solve while taking into account other people's feelings. This wisdom can bring you a sense of heaven on earth right now.

Two Very Important Questions

Question 1: What about problems where it is not possible to have a solution that takes into account other people's feelings?

How do I know what Billy the bully is feeling when he intimidates me? You know what the bully is feeling. Here is what you are feeling and what everybody else is feeling right now: we all feel vulnerable. Our mind is aware of many things that could go wrong, many things that could lead to unpleasant feelings, and many ways in which others could outperform us. Everybody feels vulnerable. Our mere existence is intertwined with problems.

When people are not acting in a loving manner, it is because they are feeling vulnerable, and more specifically, their behavior is being guided by one or more of the four basic fears. Billy may think others will harm him right now unless he shows he is tough (first basic fear: harm in the present moment) or sometime in the future (second basic fear: harm in the future). He may not understand why he thinks the way he does or that others don't understand why he thinks the way he does (third basic fear: not being understood) unless he gets a predictable response to intimidation, the way he responds when he is intimidated by an older brother, for example. He might find intimidating others exciting (fourth basic fear: a life without meaning, excitement, or pleasure).

Now that you know that Billy is fearful, there is a solution that takes into account his feelings; there is a way to apply the four bases of the Golden Rule. Begin with the third base. As best you can, set limits with Billy and protect yourself. By stopping Billy from acting selfishly, you are actually taking the first step in helping him. Then, if you are child or a teen in a structured setting, such as a school, inform an authority figure—a teacher, a parent, or an enforcement officer—that something must be bothering Billy because why else would he be bullying others? Best yet, also speak directly to Billy if at all possible. Let him know he deserves a beautiful life and that what he is doing is only making it more difficult to experience it. The same goes for adults in a company setting. Inform Billy, the person acting inappropriately, that you care and that that is why you are letting him know that he needs to be more considerate, more aware and sensitive. However, if you aren't comfortable speaking directly to the person or your discussion goes nowhere, then contact human resources. Ask human resources staff what can be done so that Billy won't be so bothersome. What can be done to help him feel better? What can be done to help him follow the Golden Rule more easily?

By handling Billy's inappropriate behavior with insight, we are, in effect, starting the process of teaching him that he is already good enough, despite what his experiences may have led him to believe. We are teaching Billy that life works out much better when one learns to follow the Golden Rule. He may need restrictions placed on his freedom for some time because he is disruptive or a danger to others, but his worthiness and value need never be questioned.

How often will another child or adult respond to Billy the bully with such insight and thoughtfulness? Unfortunately the answer for a child is hardly at all, and for an adult, only occasionally at best. Most responses to Billy the bully have a competitive underpinning: "Oh, Billy, you think you are going to have power and control over me or others? Well, I have news for you. We'll see who has the power and control! No way am I going to let you move past me in the pecking order or past those of us who follow the rules." The teacher, the parents, the enforcement officer are usually prepared to see to it that Billy is punished and shown who has the real power and control. "Billy you are going to move down, not up, in the pecking order, and if there is not enough to go around, you will be the one left out. You should be ashamed of yourself."

We do not need to respond to harm-doers in the competitive way described in the previous paragraph. Our creator has put on this earth enough resources for all 7.6 billion[115] of us to be able to raise healthy families. Since everyone can be included when it comes to basic necessities, it is logical to realize that the pecking order or the survival-of-the-fittest mentality need not be so prominent in human behavior and organization. Without the need for a pecking order, without humans needing to function at the emotional level of a pack of wolves, the world does not need to divide up into tribes or countries or emphasize power and control over those who fail to follow the rules or law. Your tribe, country, or religion does not need to be better than another to ensure that you have your basic needs met—just "Imagine," as John Lennon sang. Without a pecking-order mentality and all the competition that goes with it, we can arrive at solutions to our problems that take into account and validate everyone's feelings.

No one needs to suffer at the hands of others. Billy the bully can be treated with compassion as he is suspended from school or sent to jail. He can be reminded that he is good enough and that it is important to learn from your mistakes and that some people take longer to do that than others. But if he is going to learn, he will need to witness others, especially authority figures, being guided by compassion and the four bases of the Golden Rule.

The Attraction of the Bad Boy or Bad Girl Image

With so much of our brain's activity occurring subconsciously, whether we are aware of it or not, our minds are always thinking of ways to prevent physical harm, physical restrictions, and negative judgments. We also try to prevent ourselves from appearing unattractive to those people to whom we are attracted. Other times, rather than thinking

---

[115] World population as of May 2018: en.wikipedia.org/wiki/World_population.

about restrictions, we think about the pleasures we can experience when there are no restrictions. This is the appeal of the bad boy or bad girl image: no restrictions, only pleasure. It accounts for our fascination with pirates or tough-looking tattooed men and women on choppers—people who have carved out a life that we think might be free of the everyday frustrations experienced by those of us who abide by the rules, laws, and mores of the mainstream.

Everybody has the same unpleasant thoughts and feelings as well as the same anticipation of pleasure. We may differ from each other in the ways we try to protect ourselves and in the ways we try to appear attractive to those to whom we're attracted. We may differ in the degree to which we find some things pleasurable or repulsive since we have different tastes. However, the reasons why we do what we do are the same. We are drawn to pleasure and repelled by pain. Everybody is feeling vulnerable and acting on these feelings. We are all motivated by the same factors that underlie fear and competition in the animal kingdom.

Question 2: Why should I care about the feelings of someone who does not care about me?

What if a man is trying to kill me and I have a knife in my hands? How do I take his feelings into account? The Golden Rule and your instinct for survival are not at odds with each other in this situation. Use the third base and protect yourself. Don't contemplate. Just let your survival instinct take over. Then once you are safe, and assuming your attacker survives, put into motion a plan similar to the one discussed with Billy the bully; it shows you care about the attacker and his or her feelings of vulnerability as he or she is put behind bars. Wouldn't it be amazing and beneficial to everyone if our judges, police officers, and prison guards as well as victims all modeled the Golden Rule when dealing with lawbreakers and harm-doers?

As we grow up, we usually don't have the insight to realize that when something or someone is bothering us, there is a solution that takes into account not only our feelings, but the feelings and needs of others, including the person who is bothering us. Instead, we usually blame others with our judgments, and then we proceed to react with insensitivity and a lack of awareness. We react without trying to gain a greater understanding of our circumstances; we react without realizing that we are having another encounter with a person and often that person is our own ego—an ego that is impatient when anticipating something more pleasurable than the present moment. Other times we are reacting to someone who mistakenly, albeit understandably, feels they need to prove something or get something or is in need of a distraction. It is common to encounter people who don't yet know (or have lost sight of the realization) that they are already good enough to enjoy the moment right now.

Retaliation

If somebody punches us in the arm, we want to punch him or her back even harder. If somebody calls us a name, we call him or her a name. If somebody does us wrong, we want him or her punished; we want justice. If we think our parents are being unfair because we don't like to hear "no," then we may want to lower their status and make them feel worse than us by withholding our affection or disrupting their lives. Children, however, often misperceive situations. They are probably not being mistreated or treated unfairly; rather their parents, teachers, and even their peers are just pointing out to them that they have been acting selfishly and that steps are being taken to set limits and raise their awareness. If, however, these steps are conveyed with anger rather than with tact, the child will perceive that he or she is not good enough and your chance to raise their awareness and sensitivities will be lost.

Joshua Simon, MD, EdD

When We Think We Are Not Good Enough ...

When we think we are not good enough, we tend to think that the only way we are going to get what we want is by outperforming others, by being in control, or by intimidating or manipulating others. When we think we are not good enough, we think that those who are good enough will beat us to the finish line and get what we want, leaving us only unwanted scraps. "It's a hard world to get a break in / All the good things have been taken."[116]

When we don't realize we are already good enough, what other people think of us becomes more important than almost anything else; we can become obsessed with creating an image that will find acceptance by others. To this end, some of us text, tweet, Snapchat, and Facebook all day long. We may spend hours each day doing our hair and makeup or pumping iron. We may rely on one or two close friends, a leader of an organization, a romantic partner, a parent, a teacher, a sibling, or even public opinion to validate that our image is working. As young children, we sometimes use imaginary friends. It can be emotionally devastating when we are met with disapproval from someone who matters to us in some special way and has been propping up our ego.

Alternatively, when we think we are not good enough, we can get tired of failing to meet what we perceive to be the expectations of others. When that happens, we withdraw. We socialize less. We avoid situations that could remind us that we are not good enough. We stop trying because if we don't try, we won't be reminded as often that we are not good enough. This kind of reaction leads to depression with a loss of motivation. It can also lead to extreme nonconformity wherein someone might dress outlandishly so they will get a reaction that lets them believe they are being rejected solely because of the

---

[116] "It's My Life," by the Animals (1965). Lyrics by Roger Atkins and music by Carl D'Errico.

way they look. In this way, they do not risk being rejected by what they perceive to be the content of their character; rather it's because of something quite superficial, something prejudicial: their looks.

The Critical Issue: Transformation

How do we transform ourselves from teenagers, filled with insecurities about our own self-worth, to people who know we have value—not because we stand out but because we recognize the importance of empathy, prudence, forethought, and compassion, and, for those who believe in God, because we value all of God's creation? How do we transform ourselves from teens who have learned how to distract ourselves with activities (many of which are meaningless and sometimes destructive) to people engaged in meaningful activities that (1) show respect for the environment and the safety of others, (2) help ourselves and others gain access to the physical, emotional, intellectual, and spiritual resources needed to raise healthy families, (3) hold our undivided attention to the wonder of creation—through music, art, poetry, drama, comedy, nature, and scientific curiosity—and (4) foster ways in which we can experience the presence of a higher power?

What Is Success?

The transformation from superficial to meaningful activities forges ahead when success is defined as "being a better person than I used to be." Notice that in this definition, there are no comparisons to others, only to oneself. What is meant by *better* is that we are more sensitive and aware today than in the past to how our actions or inactions affect the feelings and needs of others. At age thirty we realize that there are plenty of things we did (and didn't do) at age eighteen that we would never consider doing (or not doing) again.

Why? Because at age thirty, we have a greater realization of how our actions affect other people and our own health. The same could be said for age sixty compared with age fifty, for example. As parents we are more aware of the mistakes we made as teenagers, mistakes that we wouldn't want our children to make. Yet we know that we are good enough despite having made these mistakes. So parents, relax! Our children will learn from their mistakes, too. As they learn the importance of letting the four bases of the Golden Rule guide their behavior, they'll engage in risky behaviors less often.

Forgiveness Is Wisdom

Throughout your life you will make mistake after mistake. That's an inevitable predicament that you cannot escape. It's not possible to possess the same level of awareness today as the one you will possess in the future. Therefore, you will act today (and so will others) to solve problems without all the knowledge and insight needed to find the absolute best solution. That is why it is so important to be able to forgive yourself and others for this predicament we all find ourselves in.

It is important that you learn how to forgive yourself and others for not knowing that the only true way to solve a problem, and not create more problems, is to take into consideration the feelings and needs of all others by letting the four bases of the Golden Rule guide your actions. Rarely do we see this problem-solving method used by leaders of countries or by the news pundits who support or criticize these leaders. The people who rise to positions of high status in government (as well as in all other fields such as education, entertainment, business, sports, science, or religion) are, as a rule, great competitors following the dictates of their subconscious brain. One's rise to a position of status often has little relationship to possessing a gracious attitude. Fortunately, however, most of us will interact with people in leadership positions who are exceptions to this rule.

Throughout your lifetime your mind will generate many more pleasant thoughts, feelings, and memories by being kind to others than by competing with others. Have you forgiven yourself for the things you did when you were younger, when you didn't have the awareness and sensitivity you have today? Have you forgiven others who acted without realizing that feeling good comes to those who care about the feelings of others? Have you forgiven those of us who did not realize that achievements play only a minor role in feeling that we deserve to be respected by other people? Have you forgiven yourself if you mistakenly thought you needed to have power and control to get others to include you or respect you? Keep in mind that forgiveness is not trust. Trust comes only to those who interact consistently with kindness.

Connectedness and Feelings of Vulnerability

Happiness comes from an appreciation of how beautiful yet fragile life is. Life is, by its very nature, vulnerable. As already stated, what all people have in common are the same four basic competitive drives and four basic fears that translate into feelings of vulnerability. With awareness and acceptance of these feelings of vulnerability, we naturally feel a connection to all people. You will realize that what other people are doing or have done relates to the very things you have felt in your life. Your feelings of vulnerability form a connection, a bond, to the activities that make up the entire history of humankind.

All of us at some point in our life have felt inadequate or not good enough. In this state of mind, you likely didn't know that it is okay to accept these feelings of vulnerability. Without this acceptance, people tend to distance themselves or form psychological walls around others who are perceived to be vulnerable. People prefer to think they are better than anyone whom they judge to be insecure.

When we don't realize that it is okay to feel vulnerable, we are attracted to those who appear to be invulnerable—people who show no fear. We may even be attracted to monsters who show no emotion except aggression. When we can't accept our feelings of vulnerability, we create the "dark side," a place where only the fiercest survive and those who care and share are weak. We like superheroes and superstars and tyrannosaurs. We may fantasize about being a king or queen, a fascination that may account for why people pay attention to the lives of royal families and movie stars. We will be attracted to people who have a belief system that will supposedly protect us from anything that goes wrong. Yet this is not reality. Life is filled with difficult times, including intense negative emotions, even for royalty, superstars, Tyrannosaurus rex, and the pope.

Intense Negative Emotions

It is important to realize that it is perfectly normal to have moments in which you feel intense unpleasant emotions. There is nothing wrong with you or your life if these kinds of feelings emerge. If you can be patient and accepting of your feelings of vulnerability, they will uncover the negative thought patterns that distort reality. Your deepest feelings will guide you to the reality that you are perfectly fine precisely because you are able to accept your feelings of vulnerability. It is the wanting to be invulnerable or our impatience with finding pleasurable activities that causes most of our emotional pain. By staying in touch with your feelings of vulnerability, you will also sense beauty in new ways. Your feelings will lead you to a greater awareness of the suffering of others. With your heightened awareness and sensitivities, it will be easier to problem solve in ways that will reduce your suffering without judging others as less deserving than you.

We don't live in the Garden of Eden. As a matter of belief, there is a far greater chance that something is wrong if you haven't had moments of great discomfort—moments in which grief overwhelmed your consciousness, you thought you did not fit in, or you thought your life was about to unfold in some kind of terrible way. It is hard for me think of anyone, except someone who lives a fantasy world, who has not experienced rejection by a friend, an intensely embarrassing situation, an untimely loss of a loved one, an abusive relationship, or other difficult moments and troubling feelings—personal experiences that can raise doubts about everything you hold dear to your heart. However, ideally you now realize that you were never truly alone during those times when you felt so alone. You are connected to all others through these feelings of vulnerability.

Eighth commandment: "Thou shalt not bear false witness." People lie for fear of what might or might not happen if they tell the truth. These fears relate to the belief that one's life will not work out—you will not achieve the goals or experience the pleasures that your instinctual drives would like you to achieve or experience. People who lie or bear false witness lack faith. Spirituality is based in faith—a faith that says that if you are caring and sensitive to how your actions affect the feelings and needs of others, then somehow and in some way, your needs will be met. Bearing false witness is clearly an insensitive action to the feelings and needs of others.

9

Yesod—Foundation

Ideas come in pairs and they contradict one another; their opposition is the principal engine of reflection.

—Jean-Paul Sartre (1905–80)

God is a concept by which we measure our pain.

—John Lennon (1940–80)

God is love.

—1 John 4:8

Love, therefore, is a concept by which we measure our pain.

The ninth Sefirah, Yesod (foundation) is the reconciliation of the opposite extremes of Netzach (changing wrongs into rights) and Hod (accepting things that cannot be changed). Yesod is frequently called Tzaddick or "the righteous one." Yesod is the circumcised phallus of the primal Adam, the conduit through which the divine, fructifying forces of the ninth Sefirah pass into the tenth Sefirah, Shekhinah, and then on to man. The biblical character associated with Yesod is Joseph; Yesod is also associated with peace, the covenant, and the

Tree of Life, and with redemption, remembrance, and the restoration of balance.[117]

Reconciliation of Opposite Extremes

My parents were content as atheists. My mother did not pray when my father was sent overseas to fight the Nazis. My father did not pray while in a foxhole facing enemy fire. I too was content (or at least I thought I was) to be an atheist, and while growing up, religious rituals struck me mostly as silly superstitions. Then to think that a ritual could bring one closer to God, a God that doesn't really exist, well, that fell in the realm of "what kind of fantasy world do you live in!" Yet, despite my parents' aversions to anything that had to do with religion, confoundedly they made sure that I was circumcised in accordance with the Bible: "For the generations to come every male among you who is eight days old must be circumcised" (Genesis 17:12 NIV).

So when I was eight days old, family members gathered around me in a ceremony known as a bris. A *mohel* (often a rabbi) then cut off my foreskin. Supposedly, this act formed a covenant between me and God. Was my bris an insurance policy given to me by my parents just in case there really is a God? If it was, then it seems that this covenant with God escaped my detection for eighteen years.

As explained earlier, I did not believe God existed until age eighteen when evangelists opened my heart to Christ's love, at which time I felt a warm energy, presumably the Holy Ghost, entering my body and, of all places, in my upper thighs or place of my circumcised phallus, the very site at which a Jewish boy forms a covenant with God. The area of the circumcised phallus is at Yesod, the ninth

---

[117] Arthur Goldwag, *The Beliefnet Guide to Kabbalah* (Three Leaves Press, 2005).

Sefirah, on the primordial man (see figure 1 in the introduction) and is, according to kabbalah, the foundation for insight.

Yesod, or "foundation," is associated with the Tree of Life. In chapter 5, this tree was introduced as a way to remember the importance of sharing your thoughts, resources, emotions, and experiences. Recall that in chapter 1, I found the foundation for Christianity, a Bible, after viewing *The Passion of the Christ.* This Bible directed me to Job 13:18, which says, "I know that I am righteous." Righteousness is yet another characteristic associated with the Sefirah Yesod. Expounding upon the quote from Sartre at the start of this chapter, Yesod balances forces that contradict one another, allowing us to reflect and gain insight. What a contradiction that my parents had me circumcised on the eighth day! Perhaps this was their way of balancing their atheistic stance with their awareness of the wisdom often found in Jewish traditions.

Speaking of balance, the numbers 4, 10, 18, and 23, which form the foundation of the four bases of the Golden Rule, are also in balance. Recall that Buddha's Four Noble Truths raise our awareness of and sensitivity to how our actions affect the feelings of others. Moses's Ten Commandments with his exodus from Egypt lets us know that we are not to do for others (for Moses these others were the Egyptians) what others can do for themselves; Jesus's eighteen, or the eternal chai, is a reminder that we are never to judge others to be undeserving of our kindness or generosity; and Muhammad's twenty-three years of revelation lets us know we have a divine right to say no and set limits with people or groups of people who judge us or others to be undeserving of kindness or generosity.

The Buddha's Four Noble Truths (first base) and Moses's Ten Commandments (second base) add to 14 (10-4, message received). Muhammad's twenty-three years of revelations (third base) and Jesus's eighteen for the eternal chai (Home) add to 41. The numbers

14 – 41 are balanced and read the same left to right as they do right to left. In each direction we see 10-4, message received. Conclusion: You will be hard pressed to find a more unifying, well-balanced message of love than the one embodied by the four bases of the Golden Rule.

The number 1441 also happens to be the exact number of days by which I am older than her majesty Minerva, my wife. Thus I will be hard pressed to find a more unifying, well-balanced message of love than the one embodied in Minerva. Furthermore, I would also like to believe that our marriage and parenting skills facilitated the development of two well-balanced children, Marianela and Joseph.

The Foundation for Insight

Yesod is the foundation for insight. But from where does insight come? Let's go back to our birth. We were born into the world a feeling organism. When we felt the pain of circumcision, we cried instinctively. When we felt cold or hunger, we cried instinctively. When we felt the pain of colic or a diaper rash, we cried instinctively. We took an innate action, crying, in an attempt to reduce an uncomfortable feeling.

While our caregiver interacted with us and relieved us of our pain, our innate thinking processes were active. We started making as many associations as possible between our five senses and our caregivers. We associated smells, sights, textures, sounds, and tastes with the caregiver. All five senses were at work, making us aware of when our caregiver was nearby, a condition of heightened sensitivity and awareness.

Soon we learned that crying got attention, which led to relief of pain. Attention from caregivers could relieve the physical discomforts of hunger, colic, skin irritation, and cold, for example. But do newborns know from birth that they are the ones making the crying noise?

Initially, newborns have little or no awareness of where the sound of crying is coming from. When newborns cry, they do so reflexively. It's instinctive. However, after they have been tended to many times, they make the association between crying and receiving attention. This association is a new awareness: whenever babies hear the crying noise, it means that relief or positive attention could be on the way. Making this association requires thinking. Just as newborns are innately programmed to cry when they feel uncomfortable, they are innately programmed to think.

As infants struggle with physical discomfort and pain, their brains are trying to understand the relationship between the actions of others and their pain. Thus, infants are demonstrating a most important lesson. When we are in touch with and sensitive to our feelings of pain (and fear), or when we are in touch with our feelings of vulnerability, thinking brings awareness. As we mature, "in touch" means that we keep asking ourselves why: *Why do I feel sad or angry* or, for example, *Why do I fantasize*? Ultimately when we keep asking ourselves why, we arrive at one or more of the four basic fears.

With time babies also connect the crying sound with their own bodily sensations. They feel tears running down their cheeks. They feel the muscles of the jaw flexing to keep their mouth wide open. They feel their chest expanding and contracting while hearing the crying noise. Then at some point a most magical moment occurs: the babies have a new awareness. They make the connection that they are the ones making the crying noise. They now have more than just an awareness of an association. They have an awareness of a cause-and-effect relationship: "I make the crying sound!"

Awareness of a cause-and-effect relationship is insight. This awareness also brings about our sense of self—"I am." This sense of self is confirmed by taking an action: "I acted to make the crying sound and this action led others to respond." Leading others to respond is empowerment, and empowerment lets us know that "I am," I exist. God's existence is through His action—the creation of the universe—and we are to respond.

Association versus Cause and Effect

We use two logical processes—association and cause and effect—to bring greater awareness and understanding of what is happening around us. However, only the cause-and-effect relationship is insight. For example, if infants connect their own bodily actions to the crying sound heard when uncomfortable, then they have gained insight. They now realize that they are the one causing the crying sound. A cause-and-effect relationship is much closer to reality than association because cause and effect addresses who or what is in control.

Once infants obtain this insight, they will assert greater control over whether to make the crying sound. On the other hand, the realization that crying causes others to give them attention does not assert control, and therefore is a distortion of reality. Infants cannot make someone give them attention. It is the attention giver who has control.

Pavlov

When we assume that an association is one of cause and effect, we distort reality. Let's evaluate the famous example of Ivan Pavlov ringing a bell every time he fed his dogs. After repeated exposure to food with the sound of a bell, Pavlov's dogs salivated when the bell was rung even when no food was served. Yet, if Pavlov's dogs were your only experience with dogs, you might incorrectly conclude that ringing a bell causes dogs to salivate.

We know that a Pavlov dog salivated reflexively because it had been conditioned to associate the bell with food. The bell is an association, not a cause. A bell will not cause your dog or my dog to salivate; it causes only the dogs conditioned by a bell to salivate.

Prejudice and Faulty Reasoning

Suppose that most of our experiences with people of color have shown that they occupy subservient roles or positions of low status and often live in poverty. We might then incorrectly conclude that being of color causes inferiority. We might conclude that people of color occupy inferior positions and live in poverty because they are inferior to others in some important way. The belief that people of color are inferior to others is clearly a rationalization. Prejudices are rationalizations and use faulty reasoning. In this case the faulting reasoning is taking an association and assuming a cause-and-effect relationship.

Until the late 1960s, the movie and television industry's portrayal of people of color in subservient roles likely reinforced this prejudice in our society. However, if our society did not use faulty reasoning, that is, assume an association was a cause-and-effect relationship, we would not have believed that people of color are inferior no matter what roles were portrayed in the movies or on TV. Hollywood did not cause prejudice; faulty reasoning was and is the cause of prejudice.

Currently, people of color are portrayed in the movies and television in both subservient and leadership positions. We have black and Hispanic months to celebrate great thinkers and achievers. The association between being of color and being inferior cannot be made as readily anymore. However, this increased awareness of great people of color does not correct the root cause of the problem, which is that faulty reasoning leads to faulty conclusions.

Though it may be more uncommon in our society today to apply this kind of faulty reasoning to issues of color, faulty reasoning continues in our culture in many other realms, leading to many other distortions of reality. A prime example of this kind of faulty reasoning is thinking that you have had and may continue to have unpleasant experiences because you are not good enough in some way. The real causes of unpleasant experiences, however, are actions that are not guided by the four bases of the Golden Rule—an action you committed or someone else committed or, which too often occurs, a group of people committed.

It seems that as groups, tribes, or political parties, we more easily validate and give license to each other's selfish behaviors and principles because we think they might help us gain or maintain an advantage—an advantage for winning a competition, for procuring wealth, status, safety, sex, or some other desired outcome, and, for some of us, for maintaining a childhood fantasy that we are special in some way. Thus it is no wonder that forty-one of America's fifty states at one time or another passed anti-miscegenation laws prohibiting interracial marriage.[118] As a result of these laws, white men could greatly limit competition from men of color for the more desirable women (more desirable because of prejudice): the white

---

[118] "Interracial Marriage in the United States," *Wikipedia*. The only states that have never had anti-miscegenation laws are Alaska, Connecticut, Hawaii, Minnesota, New Hampshire, New Jersey, New York, Vermont, and Wisconsin.

women.[119] Any man or boy of color who displayed or was accused of any kind of physical attraction toward a white woman often found himself in danger of white mob rule. As of 1967, twenty-five of these forty-one states had removed their anti-miscegenation laws. The sixteen remaining states, all in the South, had their laws declared unconstitutional by the United States Supreme Court on June 12, 1967, in the landmark case *Loving v. Virginia*.

Two Significant Distortions in Personal Relationships

To reiterate, we distort reality when we mistake associations for cause-and-effect relationships. These types of mistakes can interfere markedly with happiness in personal relationships by (1) thinking that actions associated with attention cause attention and (2) thinking that our feelings are hurt by a person whom we perceive to be rejecting us. Like Pavlov's dogs, these distortions are based in conditioning.

As babies and toddlers, we thought we created attention by crying. When we felt pain and cried, very often we did get attention. Soon we began to think it was a cause-and-effect relationship. Pain and crying would cause attention, just like the bell caused salivation in Pavlov's dogs. These associations between pain, crying, and getting attention are some of our very earliest thought patterns. Yet we know that crying does not necessarily cause attention. It is just an association. If no one had responded to our crying, there would have been no attention. Our crying and pain did not really cause the attention we often received.

---

[119] *Playboy* magazine began publication in December 1953. A hundred and twenty-one white women in a row appeared as the centerfold before the first nonwhite woman, who was Asian, showed up. Eight months later in March 1965 the first black woman appeared: https://en.wikipedia.org/wiki/Playboy_Playmate.

Relationship between Romantic Love and Bliss

The distortion of reality from our early childhood, that crying and pain somehow creates attention, has a lasting effect on our adult life and greatly interferes with happiness. This is why we cry when a romantic partner leaves us. Romantic love allows us to feel a childlike bliss. Romantic love brings back memories of our earliest feelings at a time when we were totally unaware that we were vulnerable to all sorts of dangers in the world. Romantic love acts like a shield, protecting us from any thought that could feel threatening. So when a romantic love breaks up with us, our bliss is shattered and we get re-exposed to all sorts of unpleasant thoughts.

As adults we feel vulnerable, but when we were infants, our ignorance often allowed us to feel free of any kind of danger. Without an awareness of danger, when we were free of physically painful feelings and not yet able to anticipate future painful feelings, we were in a state of bliss. Almost all of us have memories of these blissful feelings locked away, some of which may have formed while we were in the womb. Unfortunately, as adults it is difficult to feel blissful, especially as we approach our later years. Many of us are already experiencing the unpleasantness caused by the deterioration of our bodies with aging. Then, on top of our own personal discomforts, we are aware of many stressful, painful, dangerous, and hideous things that are happening right now and conceivably could happen to us.

How is it possible to feel bliss now that we no longer live in the Garden of Eden? For infants, bliss is found in ignorance. In our preteen years, it is often found in the belief that our parents can protect us from danger. For teenagers and adults, it is found in romantic love. For some it is found in a faith in God, a belief that we are protected by God and His angels. For others, thoughts of superiority over others can relieve feelings of vulnerability and provide opportunities for bliss. Then there is the use of mind-altering substances. The current opiate-heroin abuse epidemic is caused, in part, by people trying to find bliss by turning off that part of the brain that keeps us aware of our feelings of vulnerability, especially those created by thoughts of not being good enough!

The Bliss of Romantic Love

Romantic love rekindles our memories associated with the feelings of bliss from our infancy that usually remain locked away. These locked-away feelings have no thoughts attached to them. Therefore, they cannot be remembered consciously. They can only be sensed subconsciously. When we are in love, it may be because somehow or in some way our romantic partner evokes these subconscious memories of blissful feelings.

We experience bliss when we don't feel vulnerable. Feeling vulnerable is not pleasant. It does not feel all right. But by having our romantic partner's undivided attention, we can fantasize that "It's All Right."[120] The fantasies attached to the object of our love allow us to feel bliss over and over again because this romanticized, fantasized love shields us from feeling vulnerable. It's similar to a child clinging to a teddy bear.

If we cannot get the attention of our loved one, so that we can feel like a blissful baby, we will act and feel like a baby who is not getting what he or she wants. We cry. When we perceive rejection by a romantic partner, we will, without thinking, feel emotional pain and start crying. Just as when we were a baby, our crying and painful feelings will be intense. It is difficult to minimize the pain when we feel like a baby because in this state our brains are unable to tap into our more mature thought patterns that more readily allow us to cope and/or distract ourselves from unpleasant feelings.

---

[120] "It's All Right," by Curtis Mayfield and the Impressions (1963).

Furthermore, just like a baby, we associate feeling pain and crying with getting attention. We want to get the attention of our once romantic partner, so we cry and cry and feel pain and more pain.

In our infancy, when we felt discomfort and pain, a short time would elapse, we would cry, and then a little longer time would elapse before our caregiver responded. Before getting relief, we almost always experienced discomfort. Through classical conditioning, we associated discomfort and pain with getting attention from a caregiver. If the caretaker had insight into what was causing our discomfort, he or she could do something to relieve it. As an infant this was our primary way of getting attention that would bring relief from discomfort.

When whining, you feel just like you did when you cried as an infant. However, with language you are able to communicate more precisely what you want your caretaker to do to relieve your discomfort. The crier or whiner makes demands. Although adults don't need to use this way of getting attention to relieve discomfort, classical conditioning means you end up repeating this infantile pattern over and over. However, with maturity, you do not have to depend on others to provide relief. You can initiate your own actions to bring relief. Therefore, only for an instant do you have to feel or anticipate pain or discomfort before you take an action that brings relief. If you are hungry, you can feed yourself. If you are bored, you can find an activity of interest or call a friend or, better yet, remind yourself that you are good enough and enjoy the moment.

As an adult, you often subconsciously think that before someone takes a helpful action, you have to feel pain and express discomfort. At times you might express this pain by crying, moping, or feeling hurt. Other times you might express it by whining, yelling, screaming, or letting others know you are angry. These infantile patterns may be even more striking if you were raised by a caregiver who let you cry and feel discomfort for longer periods of time before comforting you. If, for example, your primary caregiver was depressed or anxious when you were an infant, he or she may have been less attentive to your needs or too anxious to take a moment to figure out why you were crying. Thus you would have cried for longer periods of time before finally getting some relief. Can you imagine how long you might have been left crying if your primary caregiver was uninterested in being a caregiver?

It's important to recognize this pattern of feeling unhappy, sad, or angry before you begin to believe that you can do something to improve your life. If you can catch yourself in this pattern, you can tell yourself, *I don't need to feel miserable before I can do something to improve my life or the life of someone else. I can skip all the miserable feelings and get right to the actions.* You might simply need a mindful thought: the realization that you are already good enough. As an adult ideally you are capable of changing your own proverbial diapers. You don't have to lie around in the proverbial crib crying for half an hour, half a day, half a decade, or half a century before you think it's time for a change.

Asking for Help

Sometimes a problem cannot be handled individually, such as a flood or forest fire, when many people need to cooperate to reduce the burden on those affected. Likewise, it takes more than one person to move some pieces of furniture and similar items. Other times we don't have the knowledge or equipment to solve a problem, and we require the assistance of someone who does. Unfortunately, there are plenty of times when we don't ask for help even though we could use a helping hand. Our infantile behaviors and memories may underlie the reason why we sometimes hesitate to ask for help with a problem.

Cognitive Distortions

Before caretakers attended to our needs, we often felt pain and discomfort. Furthermore, we felt dependent on the caretaker to do for us what needed to be done. We associate the need for help, and asking for it, with pain and discomfort. All of this is going on at a subconscious level. However, when we ask for help as adults, we have conscious thoughts that match the underlying subconscious uncomfortable feelings. Therefore, our thoughts will be negative. This is called a cognitive distortion.

Some typical negative thoughts or cognitive distortions might be that the person we ask for help disapproves of us. Other typical negative thoughts might be that the person we ask for help thinks we are a burden or incapable of taking care of things we should be able to take care of and that therefore, we are incompetent. To avoid feeling the emotional discomfort associated with these thoughts, we might avoid asking for help altogether.

All too often, we would rather live with the discomfort of an unsolved problem than face the discomfort of asking for help. The irony is that the more we act in this avoidant way, the more we could benefit from the help we're so desperately trying to avoid. Cognitive distortions such as "I'm not good enough if I need help" contribute to the stigma associated with psychological therapy. Yet we are acting with intelligence when we ask a therapist to help us understand our thoughts and feelings.

We also make cognitive distortions about positive feelings. In romantic love, we rekindle our subconscious memories of blissful feelings from our infancy. In infancy we did not attach thoughts (or if we did, we don't remember them) to those blissful feelings, but as adults we do attach thoughts, and we remember them. We attribute all sorts of wonderful qualities to our romantic partner. For example, they are the sweetest, most caring, most attractive, most competent, smartest, brightest, or wittiest; they just know what to do; they have the best judgment; and so on. We use these favorable cognitive distortions not only to set our romantic partner apart from others but, more importantly, to set ourselves apart from others. We think that because we see our romantic partner in this special way, we are most deserving of their attention.

We separate our romantic partner from others because he or she meets our expectations of what we think a romantic partner should be. These expectations are a result of family and cultural circumstances and conditioning, as well as genetic programming designed to propagate the species, that is, to be attracted to healthy women and men who look fertile or virile, respectively, and possess the means, emotional stability, and intelligence to be good providers and caregivers.

Four Questions Raised by Hurt Feelings

If a romantic partner, friend, coworker, or family member chooses not to spend time with you, does not agree with your plans, or mentions something about you that you do not like, you may think they have hurt your feelings. In reality, they have not hurt your feelings. What they have done is raise the following four questions for you to contemplate:

1. Have they given you more information about who they really are and where their interests lie?
2. Have they let you know that you may have feelings you don't understand?
3. Have they pointed out that you may be dealing ineffectively with your four basic fears and lack confidence?

4. Have you been failing to meet reasonable expectations (honesty, cooperation, sharing, tactfulness) in the role you play with that particular romantic partner, friend, coworker, or family member?

At a subconscious level, perceptions of rejection often let you feel exposed to the fear that you have little worth and that other people don't understand why you think and feel the way you do. "How could anybody question my actions or behavior when my intent is always to be the best person I could possibly be? Who could possibly understand why I love somebody who does not love me?" These questions raise doubt about whether others see you as reasonable. Being perceived as unreasonable will raise fears related to your two basic instinctual drives: propagation of the species and survival. If you're perceived as unreasonable, who would want to mate with you or offer you a job that provides for basic necessities?

Alternatively, when your feelings are hurt, you may immediately revert to a state of anger. Anger deadens your feelings. Anger desensitizes you to your feelings and the feelings of others. Instead of gaining insight into why you feel hurt with any of the four questions as just previously mentioned, you can avoid confronting feelings of vulnerability by becoming angry and/or by becoming highly critical of others.

When it comes to your perceptions of rejection from a romantic partner and the bliss you experienced in that relationship, you may feel that the rejection is caused not by your failings but by the failings of your partner. Your former partner is not living up to all the wonderful qualities you believe they possess. These qualities, of course, are in large part cognitive distortions. Furthermore, if they don't live up to all these cognitively distorted wonderful qualities, you will be exposed and your so-called rejecting romantic partner will be exposed to all the dangers that were protected by these wonderful qualities. With this line of reasoning you can believe that not only will you be happier, but your partner will be happier if a reunification takes place; a reunification would indicate that your partner is back in touch with all of their "wonderful qualities."

Stated once again, your so-called rejecting friend, family member, or romantic partner is not hurting your feelings. To think that they are hurting your feelings is a rationalization, an association. Instead, your emotional pain is caused by the loss of a positive cognitive distortion: "I am with the most wonderful person, and therefore, I must be wonderful too." When you're rejected, you can no longer maintain the cognitive distortion that once shielded you from thinking about the ways in which you may have felt vulnerable or not good enough.

It is not uncommon for people to deny their feelings of vulnerability. For example, when I worked for the Veterans Administration, every now and then I came across a veteran claiming, "I had no fear [when I was in combat]."

I would ask, "If you had no fear, why didn't you just lay down your rifle and walk away?" Obviously, this vet didn't realize, until I pointed it out to him, that he had been in denial of his fear while in combat.

Another way to deny fear is to develop a fantasy in which you are fully protected and then to believe in it by thinking something such as "God is on my side." Alternatively, rather than deny feeling vulnerable, we simply do something to distract ourselves from these unwanted thoughts; we whistle a happy tune, or an army marches to the beat of drummers or bagpipes, for example. By the time the soldiers realize that they have only been distracting themselves, they may find themselves within short range of the enemy, with no way out but to fight.

The Role of Anger

When you are unaware that you have doubts about your self-worth, it is easy to get angry. It's as if a switch is flipped to anger mode when anything reminds you that you are vulnerable or not good enough. Anger desensitizes you to feelings that you don't want to feel. Anger dulls your awareness not only of your own feelings of vulnerability but of those feelings in others as well. It is hard to feel empathic when angry. Anger prepares you emotionally to inflict pain and harm. It prepares you to do battle with the competing bull.

We often get angry or frustrated when slowed down, such as when we're stuck in traffic or misplace something we need. Subconsciously, we think that being slowed down means we will have less time to experience pleasure. We don't like to miss out on pleasure. Furthermore, the experience of pleasure, as will be explained shortly, can play a major role in relieving doubt about whether you are good enough.

Life is good while experiencing pleasure. It indicates that your position in society's hierarchy can't be that bad. Like that of a wolf within the hierarchy of the wolf pack, the experience of pleasure indicates that your position in the pack—your place in the pecking order—is high enough such that when your pack takes down the proverbial "deer," there will still be food left on the carcass when it is your turn to eat. Without this status or rank, there would be no food left when it's your turn, and therefore no pleasure.

The experience of pleasure becomes associated subconsciously with the thought that you have enough status and rank. Status and rank often translate into pleasurable thoughts. It's good to be the king. We anticipate that rising through the ranks of any organization will lead to increased opportunities for pleasure. Thus, we often fantasize about occupying positions of power.

It's relatively easy to think that others experience more pleasure than we do. We see people with homes with grander views and money for gourmet meals. Others have more physically attractive features. Others don't abide by the rules, laws, mores, and customs that sanction "recreational" sexual behavior and the recreational use of drugs and alcohol. Therefore, it is common to fantasize about being wealthier, more attractive, and having fewer inhibitions. The movie industry is well aware of these fantasies.

It is not hard to think that you will be happier when your achievements bring you more money, power, status, and other forms of recognition—when your achievements raise your position in the pecking order. It is hard not to fantasize about what life will be like once you've achieved your goals. But if your plan for reaching your goals is to prove to yourself and the world that you are indeed good enough, that you are indeed worthy, then reaching them won't work.

Unfortunately, there is no way to satisfy instinctual drives. There is no contentment in achievements. There will always be other people with things you want but don't have. Thinking instinctually ultimately leads to the conclusion that you still are not quite good enough.

The problem has never been that you are not good enough; the problem has always been letting your instinctual brain dominate, letting it interpret your circumstances. For argument's sake, let's say 99 percent of the time your instinctual brain is directing your thoughts as opposed to 100 percent which is the case made by E. O. Wilson as cited in chapter 7. This leaves only 1 percent for spiritually guided thinking.

Obviously, thinking instinctually is your dominant mode of thought. You do want to survive, and you wouldn't exist if parents hadn't had sex. But if you can think outside the instinctual box, let's say 5 percent rather than only 1 percent of the time, you will see a big change. What is this big change? The big change is that you will know "often enough" that in reality you were yesterday, are today, and will be tomorrow "good enough" to experience a beautifully satisfying, meaningful life. "All I Really Want to Do"[121] and all you really need to do is let the four bases of the Golden Rule guide your thoughts enough of the time.

We all know that there is work to be done, not only to provide basic necessities and a healthy environment for yourself and your family, but to see to it that others have opportunities to provide the same for their family. Since humankind has not been guided by spiritual thinking much of the time, we have a lot of problems to overcome, including prejudice and discrimination. To provide opportunities for all, we need to level the playing field by using a level playing field.

To level the playing field by using a level playing field, we need to understand the root causes that underlie our problems—problems that get in the way of health and opportunity for each and every family now and for future generations. As touched upon briefly in the introduction, the human species maintains two fundamental flaws that affect the ways we problem solve:

1. Thinking that we are not good enough
2. Acting selfishly by acting instinctively, rather than spiritually, too much of the time

If you recognize these two flaws, you will know the way to greater joy, contentment, and meaning, both individually and for society as a whole. Every field of action has the potential to be an even playing field once you find the diamond in the rough—a diamond whose facets are formed by the four bases of the Golden Rule:

---

[121] "All I Really Want to Do" is the first track on Dylan's fourth studio album, *Another Side of Bob Dylan*, released August 8, 1964.

First Base:	Be aware of and sensitive to how your actions affect the feelings of others.
Second Base:	Don't do for others what others can do for themselves.
Third Base:	Say no and set limits with those who act selfishly; protect yourself.
Home:	Never judge someone to be undeserving of your kindness or generosity.

Direction

Like a rolling stone, all of us need direction and would benefit from strengthening our conscience or "compass," so that when we are on autopilot (thinking instinctually), we are headed in the right direction (thinking spiritually) by solving our problems on a level playing field. Recall that life is a continuous stream of problems. Problems are what stimulate us to think. I think, therefore I am. But with spiritual thought making up perhaps only 1 percent of our time, our compass is far too insensitive. We get lost all too frequently, resulting in bigger problems. "How many times must the cannon balls fly, before they are forever banned?" So asked Bob Dylan in 1962 in his song "Blowin' in the Wind." Now we have weapons of mass destruction to contend with all over the world! Now we have new questions for Dylan to sing about. How many times must the greenhouse gases fly, before they are forever limited?

If you try to solve a problem with an action that reinforces an uneven playing field, an action that violates one or more of the four bases of the Golden Rule, you will not have solved the problem. Instead you will have only compounded it with additional problems. Humankind, starting in the Garden of Eden, has a history of compounding problems that has only worsened over the years. It's no wonder Revelation predicts our destruction.

Fortunately, we still have a chance to restore humankind to a place where we no longer compound our problems. The "Time Has Come Today"[122] to perform mitzvahs (good deeds). The time has come today for you and me to solve our problems without creating additional ones. The time has come today to make plans while following the four bases of the Golden Rule. The time has come today to think spiritually at least 5 percent of the time. The time has come today for our plans to hatch while using our spiritually driven brain. The time has come today to elevate our "5 percenters" to leadership roles in every facet of society.

Owing to the proliferation of nuclear weapons, rising greenhouse gases, and disinformation campaigns, combined with a decline in leadership, we have moved ever closer to fulfilling Revelation's apocalyptic prophecy:

> The Doomsday Clock, a potent symbol of scientific concerns about humanity's possible annihilation, was advanced by 30 seconds on Thursday [1/25/18], to 2 minutes to midnight, the Bulletin of the Atomic Scientist announced in Washington. The last time the clock was moved so close to midnight was in 1953, during the cold war.[123]

---

[122] "The Time Has Come Today," by the Chambers Brothers, is from their 1967 album, *The Time Has Come Today*.
[123] Sewell Chan, "Doomsday Clock Is Set at 2 Minutes to Midnight, Closest Since 1950s," *New York Times* (January 25, 2018).

Joshua Simon, MD, EdD

The time has come today to follow the Golden Rule.

Should you think you are a "1 percenter" and have difficulty following the four bases of the Golden Rule, then call on the four spiritual acts to strengthen your conscience—your compass. Spend time (1) in meditation or prayer, (2) doing physical activities and other forms of movement, (3) attending to the creativity found in the natural world and in the arts and sciences, (4) and acting with kindness or altruism. Go ahead, leaders of the world, do the four spiritual acts and circle the bases. You might even lead the league in scoring, and if you don't, you'll know it doesn't matter because you don't need to be the best, just good enough.

Be warned, however, that instead of enhancing your awareness and sensitivity through the four spiritual acts, you can always choose to go in the opposite direction by diminishing your awareness and sensitivity with alcohol and drugs. You can also distract yourself by fantasizing about a perfect union with a romantic partner or with God. In short, your instinctual drives make you desirous. Desire, like a fantasy or drugs, diminishes your sensitivity and awareness. When desirous, people gravitate toward power and pleasure (look at all the sexually scandalous behavior of people in positions of power), and when you don't get what you want, you feel angry or frustrated. This frustration and anger, tragically, readies us to inflict pain on others (look at all the wars and mass killings perpetuated or encouraged by frustrated men and women).

Instead of acting on desires when feeling vulnerable, it is better to realize that the other 7.6 billion people on the face of the earth are feeling vulnerable too. You are not alone when you feel vulnerable. Can you humble yourself and ask what makes you so special that you should not feel vulnerable? When you can humble yourself in this way, you will sense the love and security provided by your faith in God or the collective goodwill of millions upon millions of men and women around the world. This faith or humanitarian spirit is strengthened by the four-by-four pursuit of happiness and fosters the wisdom, discipline, and strength necessary to steer clear of the "Ring of Fire,"[124] that deadly sin known as desire.

Instead of letting desire guide your actions, you can tune in to the feelings of vulnerability that emanate from all living things and focus on taking a harmonious action that will help reduce some of the needless suffering that exists today. You can be a teacher, a nurse, a garbage man or woman, something that serves society and doesn't take advantage of people's weaknesses—weaknesses that are often created by our wanting to be desired by others.

The suffering in and around us can be explained in large part by people competing with one another for objects of desire, competing to stand out from others. These desires end up distracting us from and desensitizing us to our feelings of vulnerability. However, if you are humble enough to accept that you are vulnerable, then almost paradoxically your feelings of vulnerability will gain protection. For when you humble yourself before God—or, if without a belief in God, you humble yourself to the mysteries of this universe—a door opens from which a guiding, loving light emanates—the light needed to uncover the root cause of your problems, the root cause of your self-doubt. With this knowledge, the process of truly solving your problems can begin. This light led me to the conclusion that the root cause of my feelings of vulnerability were (1) thinking I was not good enough and (2) having had a history of not knowing the importance of following the four bases of the Golden Rule.

At age thirty-five, I entered medical school. When I was introduced to psychiatry, my eyes opened wide. Psychiatry must be the most prestigious field of medicine. You have to know the functioning of

---

[124] "Ring of Fire," recorded by Johnny Cash in 1963, is number 87 on *Rolling Stone*'s 500 Great Songs of All Time (2004).

not only the body but also the mind. How naive I was when I entered medical school in 1986. Back then psychiatry was considered one of the least desirable fields of medicine. However, in recent years this specialty has increased in prestige—at least that's my perception. But what really attracted me to psychiatry was the fact that it took into account feelings and those aspects of the human condition that do not readily lend themselves to measurement. How do you measure love? I knew that love was important in whatever I did.

Ninth commandment: "Thou shalt not covet thy neighbor's wife." Covetousness or desire can occur only when we lose focus on our greater purpose, which is to be of service to others. Those who are guided by a spiritual, compassionate force greatly diminish their feelings of desire. Those who are guided or, more accurately, misguided by their instinctual drives will have no end to the number of things they desire or covet.

10

Shekhinah—Presence

The end of all our exploring will be to arrive where we started and know the place for the first time.

—T. S. Eliot, *Four Quartets* (1943)

I have a great deal of sympathy for any cockamamie theory that tries to find meaning in randomness.

—Elizabeth Gilbert, author of *Eat, Pray, Love*

Shekhinah means "that which dwells," referring to the tabernacle of God. Shekhinah is the female vessel into which God pours his generative energies. Shekhinah is also called Malkhut, or "the kingdom," the place where the king presides in perfect peace, harmony, and fulfillment, a place we can easily associate with the Promised Land. When we shake in the face of the *mysterium tremendum*, a Latin term that Christian mystics use to denote "overwhelming mystery," we feel her "presence." Shekhinah is the mouth of the primal Adam: she is associated with King David and the matriarch Rachel. Her letter is *hey*.[125] "Hey Jude"![126]

The Number 4

In October 1958, while watching the World Series between the New York Yankees and Milwaukee Braves, Sam Simon, my dad, could sense the *mysterium tremendum*, my excitement when Hank Aaron, wearing the number 44, stepped up to the plate. Why I latched on to Hank, I will never know for sure. Be that as it may, with my interest in baseball in full force, my dad gave me the 1959 edition of *Big-Time Baseball* by Ben Olan. I pored over the statistics. I clearly remember that the stats that stood out the most were the four top home run hitters, the Big Boppers:

1. Babe Ruth — 714 home runs
2. Jimmy Foxx — 534 round-trippers
3. Mel Ott — 511 dingers
4. Lou Gehrig — 493 four-baggers

There they were, the four heavy hitters, the greatest sluggers of all time. I followed number 44 Hank Aaron's career to see where he would be in the end.

At age ten in the spring of 1962, I got my chance to hit my own home runs when I joined the Little League and played shortstop for the Great Neck Estates Dodgers wearing the number 4. In the meantime Hank had had some pretty darn good years. In 1959 he batted .355 to lead the league and had 400 total bases with 39 home

---

[125] Arthur Goldwag, *The Beliefnet Guide to Kabbalah* (Three Leaves Press, 2005).
[126] "Hey Jude," recorded by the Beatles in 1970, is eighth on *Rolling Stone*'s 500 Greatest Songs of All Time (2004).

runs. In 1959 he also began a string of five consecutive years with at least 120 runs batted in.

Though number 44 Hank Aaron would end up hitting forty-four home runs four times, and though number 4 Lou Gehrig's July 4 farewell address touched my heart at just about the time I began wearing the number 4 in Little League, the significance of the number 4 in my life remained below the radar, that is until July 1, 1970. That was the day when all American XY chromosomes (males) born in 1951 would get their draft number—one that would greatly determine this boy's risk of being sent into the inferno called Vietnam. The lower the number, the greater was the risk. As of the summer of 1970, the US Army was not drafting boys with numbers above 125. Any number above 200 was considered safe, and above 250 was really safe. A number at or above 300 was like rolling twelve strikes in a row—perfect!

So on the afternoon of July 1, 1970, I would drive my car home from my summer job while tuned to New York's all-news radio, 1010[127] WINS, and think positively. *Just give me a number like the one I got in the first lottery.* After all, my birthday is July 29, 1951, and in the lottery held earlier for those born in or before 1950, July 29 came up at number 270—safe at home!

Needless to say, with the lottery potentially changing the course of thousands of eighteen- and nineteen-year-old boys' lives, the Selective Service System's lottery was big news. Although the radio news stations were not about to read off all 365 numbers with their corresponding birthdays, they did announce the first ten. A newscaster in his patented newscaster-type voice began the count.

"Number 1 is July"—my heart starting pounding—"9." Whoa, that was a close call. "Number 2 is December 24." No sweat. "Number

---

[127] Hank Aaron "WINS" his only World Series on 1010: October 10, 1957.

3 is July" … "twenty" …, now I was getting really scared—"five." Whoa, that was a really close call—too close. July had already given its fair share of low numbers. The law of averages predicted that the other months would now be getting the low numbers. In retrospect, I should have known better. The law of averages doesn't work. Just the same, at this point I was still feeling really positive. "Number 4 is July"—my heart was thumping … "twenty" …, but I told myself to stay positive—"nine." There it was! The moment I received the number 4, I was telling myself to stay positive, and I was on a street in my car—"Positively 4th Street."

Until the day of that lottery, I had had only one girlfriend, Marsha, a summer of '69 romance at Camp Echo. Number 2 rolled in around two years later during a weeklong conference for student representatives to the Council on International Relationships and United Nations Affairs. The keynote speaker at this conference was George H. W. Bush, who was the ambassador to the United Nations. Girl number 2 lived in St. Louis—my apologies to her since her name escapes me. During the following summer, as my roommate, Sam, and I traveled across the country, we stopped in St. Louis and I met up with my second girlfriend. However, the spark was no longer there.

About a year and half later, my third girlfriend (my apologies to her as well, since I can't recall her name) entered the picture. We had met at a disco sometime in December 1971 and saw each other on weekends. While we were dating, my dorm buddies and I had already planned to throw the greatest dorm party of all time, a party whose aftermath would steer my life in a new direction. There would be another girl.

Sam was in charge of the beer, I was in charge of promotion, and others were responsible for securing the venue, the music, and handling the finances. Then there was the matter of timing. Timing, as any comedian or dorm-party thrower knows, is everything. We realized that nothing would be better than registration week. All the students would be on campus but no courses would be in session—no tests, no papers, no morning classes, no anything that could distract an able-bodied student from their God-given right to party. Wednesday, February 2, the second-to-last day of registration, would be perfect.

To be the greatest, our dorm party had to have live music, and we needed something novel. Once again, our timing couldn't have been better. Not only was this Groundhog Day, but Matt Brewing Company in nearby Utica, New York, had just released Maximus Super, a beer with a much higher alcohol content than most American beers.

Fliers were distributed all over campus inviting students and groundhogs to our Maximus Super Party. But these were no ordinary fliers. Two of our buddies, both of whom were named Leroy, were amazing artists and created an R. Crumb–like comic strip[128] detailing why you wouldn't want to miss this party. Tens of hundreds into the thousands jammed the cafeteria that night. The beer flowed, the music rocked, and oh, how we danced.

By the time I awoke from my drunken stupor on Thursday, it was already a quarter to noon. "Oh, my God, I was supposed to be at registration at eleven thirty." I was scheduled to register with the second-to-last group, not a favorable position, since the best courses and times usually filled up on the first or second day and were closed by the third day, never mind eleven thirty on the fourth day. Furthermore, if I didn't get through the gym's doors by noon, I would miss registration altogether and hello, draft board!

---

[128] Robert Dennis Crumb (R. Crumb), born August 30, 1943, is an American cartoonist most noted for his *Fritz the Cat*, *Mr. Natural*, and *Keep on Truckin'* comic strips.

I dressed quickly and raced into the winter. When I arrived at the gym, it was just after noon. I had blown it. I was a bad boy. I had slept through registration. As my college's registration personnel looked in their file for my IBM registration punch card, I was told I wouldn't be able to enter the gym. They started to explain what I would need to do to stay enrolled. But they could not find my registration card. They tracked down the head of registration on the other side of the gym. I followed behind and seized the day—carpe diem. "Sir, how was I supposed to sign up for courses without my registration card?" Now the staff thought they were at fault for my registration difficulties. As a consequence, I was given special permission to sign up for any course, even if it had been closed. Furthermore, in their haste they issued me a meal card but didn't ask for payment. However, about a month later the school sent my parents the bill.

Later that day, excited by my good fortune, and thinking I had just eaten the first of many meals for free, I went to a friend's dorm room to tell my registration story. But each time I began to tell it, somebody would enter the room with their own agenda and interrupt me. So I would begin all over again to set the stage. I must have started and stopped three or four times before finally getting to the finish. Elizabeth, who happened to be in the room before I arrived, was the only one who paid attention to each retelling. Needless to say, our presence "registered" with each other, and the rest is history.

I didn't know at the time that Elizabeth would be my fourth girlfriend (and first love) or even years later that my wife, Minerva, in the end would be the all-important fourth love. I wasn't counting. I didn't know while watching the 1958 World Series that Hank Aaron and then later while watching *Pride of the Yankees* that both he and Lou Gehrig would capture my boyhood heart. I didn't know that the four bases touched by each of their home runs, when totaled, in some mysterious way would identify the girl who would break my heart. I didn't know that in 1959 when I first studied the home run records to see where Hank Aaron stood that the number of home runs that separated the top four hitters on this list, Ruth, Foxx, Ott, and Gehrig, would identify the numbers 10, 18, and 23 in addition to emphasizing the number 4 for each of the four bases touched in a home run. I didn't know that these four numbers would align with Moses's Ten Commandments, the Buddha's Four Noble Truths, Christ's eternal chai, eighteen, and Muhammad's twenty-three years of revelations.

I didn't know when I first listened to Dylan's "Positively 4th Street" that it was recorded on my fourteenth birthday or that it would be ranked at 0203 on the list of the 500 greatest rock songs of all time, thus pointing out February 3 (0203) once again. I didn't know that on July 1, 1970, the United States government would label me with the number 4 in the draft.

All these coincidences with the number 4 and four base hits (home runs) must mean something, or do they?

A Skeptic's Point of View

Michael Shermer, science writer and founder of the Skeptics Society, makes the following observation:

> We form our beliefs for a variety of subjective, personal, emotional, psychological reasons in the context of environments created by family, friends, colleagues, culture, and society at large; after forming our beliefs we then defend, justify, and rationalize them with a host of intellectual reasons,

cogent arguments, and rational explanations. Beliefs come first, explanations for beliefs follow.[129]

Dr. Shermer goes on to explain that we scan our environment and all forms of media for information. We take note of those things that confirm our beliefs. We easily dismiss data that does not. In other words, as Dr. Shermer says,[130] "[We] are more likely to find significance in coincidences and pick out meaning and patterns where there are none." When we find a pattern that matches our beliefs, there is a neurological response; dopamine is released by neurons in our brain, similar to the effects of cocaine. This gives us pleasure and stimulates us to look for more data that conforms to our beliefs. Contradictory evidence is ignored or refuted: "Still a man hears what he wants to hear and disregards the rest … lie la lie."[131]

I cannot disagree with the skeptics. The significance this book has placed on the numbers 10, 4, 18, and 23 fits the model proposed by Michael Shermer to a tee. (I hope he gets a jolt of dopamine when he reads this.) Just the same, whether or not you believe that the coincidences with numbers presented in this book have any significance, what I do know is that there are basically two kinds of problems or two kinds of memories that interfere with happiness: (1) memories created while doubting your self-worth or memories formed while wondering whether you are good enough, and (2) problems created by acting selfishly or memories formed during the times in which you failed to follow the four bases of the Golden Rule.

---

[129] *The Believing Brain: How We Construct Beliefs and Reinforce Them as Truths* (Times Books, 2011).

[130] Michael Shermer, *How We Believe: Science, Skepticism, and the Search for God* (Macmillan, 2003).

[131] "The Boxer," by Simon and Garfunkel (1970), was number 105 on *Rolling Stone*'s 500 Greatest Songs of All Time (2004) and number 103 on the revised list (2011), averaging at number 104 (10-4, message received).

So how can we go about solving these problems? Einstein tells us, "We cannot solve our problems with the same thinking we used when we created them."

I hope by now you realize that the universal problems of thinking you are not good enough and acts of selfishness cannot be solved by the thinking that created them—they cannot be solved by thinking or demonstrating that you need only be better, smarter, or stronger in some demonstrable way. Instead, I hope you realize that thoughts of not being good enough are distortions of reality—distortions supported by associations made while living in a society whose social and political structures are based primarily on an "instinctually driven brain," a survival-of-the-fittest mentality.

If you choose a different way of thinking by basing your life on a "spiritually driven brain," a "Golden Rule–driven brain" rather than the "instinctually driven brain" that created your problems, then, regardless of what the rest of the world is doing, you can actually solve your problems. With the Golden Rule you will know that you've never had to stand out or win the approval of others to create a wonderful, glorious life filled with a multitude of meaningful memories. In the end, all you really need to do is treat others as though they are good enough too. In doing so, you won't have to wait five hundred years to answer Einstein's most pressing question, "Is the universe friendly?"

Everyone has a story—a story that distorts reality, a story filled with memories of when you did not feel validated, when you did not realize or believe that you were already good enough. It's a story that can weigh you down. But you don't need to "Carry That Weight"[132] any longer. Precisely because you were, already are, and will continue to be good enough, there is something else to believe in. As surely as

---

[132] "Carry That Weight" by the Beatles, from their Abbey Road album, 1969.

you are good enough, you can believe that humankind can "Come Together"[133] and live in peace. But for peace to come about, we will need to listen to the message over and over again—five times a day, according to Muhammad's second pillar of Islam. The message is found in *Abbey Road* and in the works of Dylan, in our math, our mind, and especially in our emotions, and it has been there since the beginning of time. It's the same message delivered by Moses, the Buddha, Muhammad, and the eternal life of Christ. It's the four bases of the Golden Rule:

> First Base: Be aware of and sensitive to how your actions affect the feelings of others.
>
> Second Base: Don't do for others what others can do for themselves.
>
> Third Base: Say no and set limits with those who act selfishly; protect yourself.
>
> Home: Never stop doing bases "1-2-3."[134] Never judge others to be undeserving of your kindness or generosity. By judging others negatively, you will get caught off base.

Seventy-Fourth Book of the Bible

Whether using the King James sixty-six-book Bible or the Catholic seventy-three-book Bible, the book of Numbers accounts for the heritage of Christ. God, the creator, formed a universe with four

---

[133] "Come Together" by the Beatles, from their *Abbey Road* album, 1969.
[134] "1-2-3" is a Len Barry song from 1965.

fundamental forces (gravity, electromagnetism, and strong and weak nuclear forces) driving all known interactions. The language of these four forces is the language of the universe—numbers, the language of science. Consequently, by analyzing the numbers, scientific inquiry brings us closer and closer to the word of God. Furthermore, the fourth book of the Bible, Numbers, preordains that the number 4 (as it did for the life of Christ with the four Gospels) will ultimately let the systematic study of the four fundamental forces write the final chapter, the book after Revelation, the seventy-fourth book of the Bible.

The foreteller of this seventy-fourth book will be inextricably linked to the number 4. The fourth book of the Bible will appear to him after he witnesses the greatest of all heartbreaks, *The Passion of the Christ*. The foreteller's birth will coincide with the product of the first four prime numbers (2 × 3 × 5 × 7), day 210, July 29. He will be from the land of a New World where the number four anchors spiritual beliefs in the fourth world (Hopi tribe) with four directions, four seasons, and four sacred mountains.[135] This land is your land, and it is where all women and all men are created equal. Its people celebrate the 4 × 4 × 44 (0704) day in the year 4 × 444 (1776). At age ten the foreteller will wear that number 4 on his uniform while rounding the four bases of baseball. At eighteen he will be branded by this land's Selective Service System with the number 4. His heart too will be broken by his fourth romantic encounter on the seventy-fourth day of that relationship.

God's words, spoken in silence, will mend his broken heart and in doing so lay the framework to mend the discord found throughout the modern world. He, the foreteller of the seventy-fourth book, will be a scientist, a doctor, an educator with four degrees from four universities. He will obtain clarity while living with his nuclear

---

[135] Mount Blanca, 14,351 feet; Hesperus Mountain, 13,232 feet; San Francisco Peaks, 12,633 feet; and Mount Taylor, 11,306 feet.

family of four by having first a wife and then a daughter and a son. He will draw upon the four greatest deliverers of God's message—Moses, the Buddha, Jesus, and Muhammad—and present their message, His message, clearly, simply, logically, and profoundly in the four bases of the Golden Rule. In doing so, people of all faiths, and those without a faith, will know the word of God, and, with its new revelations, our world will be shifted from its current course toward ultimate destruction and arrive, instead, at the Promised Land.

These four greatest deliverers, these so-called four heavy hitters of history, will connect by numbers to the heavy hitters of this land's national pastime, baseball, and its four bases. The bases will form a diamond, a symbol of the enduring truths to be found in the Buddha's four bases, his Four Noble Truths. Furthermore, Moses's Ten Commandments and the eternal chai, eighteen, found in the life of Jesus, will set apart the greatest hitter of all from his nearest rival by a factor of 10. Thus Ruth's 714 will surpass Foxx by 10×18 home runs. Foxx's 534 will then surpass Ott by twenty-three, one for each year of Muhammad's revelations. Ott's 511 by Jesus's eternal chai, eighteen, will leave Gehrig standing in fourth, the "Iron Horse," a symbol of endurance, honored on July 4, and his number 4 retired, the first number retired in all of baseball, a tribute that points as well (in some kind of kabbalistic way) to the Buddha's enduring Four Noble Truths.

Gehrig will hit a record twenty-three grand slams, twenty-three "four-fours," four base hits driving in four runs as a prefiguration of a new home run king: Aaron, the foreteller's childhood hero, number 44, playing twenty-three years. With each home run touching four golden bases, Gehrig's 493 shines upon the year 1972 ($1972 = 4 \times 493$) and Aaron's 755 shines upon the day 0203 (0203 read right to left is $3020 = 4 \times 755$). Thus February 3, 1972, arrives exactly seventy-four days, or ten weeks and four days, before the heartbreak of the passion (10-4, message received).

Tenth commandment: "Thou shalt not covet thy neighbor's goods." You are free of jealousy, envy, and desire when you are guided by the four bases of the Golden Rule. Thus when you covet your neighbor's goods, it is a clear indication that you have disconnected yourself from your spiritual being and lost your way. Learn from your desires. When you desire something or someone, take this as a sign that it is time to remember the meaning of the Sabbath. It is time to reconnect to your faith, humanitarian ideals, or feelings of love. It's time to make the universe a friendlier place—"A Time for Us"[136] to come "All Together Now."[137] That's my pitch. Knock it out of the park and touch the four bases of the Golden Rule. Then you too will experience life in the Promised Land.

in THE END ...

---

[136] "A Time for Us," also known as the "Love Theme from *Romeo and Juliet*," by Nino Rota, arrangement by Henry Mancini (May 1969).

[137] "All Together Now"—"One, two, three, four, Can I have a little more? Five, six, seven, eight, nine, ten, I love you"—The Beatles (1967). When the big bang happened, according to kabbalah, exactly ten numbers or emanations (the same ten numbers found in "All Together Now") moved the stars, the planets, and everything in between to where they are today. Before the big bang, the entire universe was literally "all together now" in a super-concentrated, infinitesimal point. Unfortunately, during the big bang, bits of energy got damaged, causing humankind to distort reality by thinking that we are not good enough. Thus began our selfish ways—vain attempts to prove that some of us are better, more worthy, or more deserving than others. To restore humankind's ability to realize that we are already good enough (no proof necessary), we perform mitzvahs or good deeds by following the four bases of the Golden Rule.

Appendix

sgnoS seltaeB neddiH 04

Introduction

1. "Come Together"
2. "Across the Universe"
3. "Because"
4. "Something"
5. "Carry That Weight"
6. "Girl"
7. "Boys"
8. "I Will"
9. "Wait"
10. "Birthday"
11. "Money"
12. "The Word"
13. "The End"
14. "Real Love"
15. "Oh! Darling"
16. "I Want You"
17. "In My Life"
18. "Here Comes the Sun"
19. "Let It Be"
20. "Misery"

21. "Golden Slumbers"
22. "Help"
23. "Her Majesty"

Chapter 2

24. "All Together Now"
25. "Get Back"
26. "I'm a Loser"

Chapter 3

27. "Chains"
28. "Here, There and Everywhere"

Chapter 4

29. "Getting Better"
30. "Revolution"

Chapter 6

31. "The Night Before"
32. "The Long and Winding Road"

Chapter 7

33. "Flying"
34. "Yesterday"

Chapter 8

35. "We Can Work It Out"
36. "Bad Boy"

Chapter 10

37. "This Boy"
38. "Drive My Car"
39. "I Should Have Known Better"
40. "Another Girl"

Printed and bound by PG in the USA